The OASIS

ALSO BY PETRU POPESCU

Almost Adam

The Return: A Family Revisits
Their Eastern European Roots

Amazon Beaming

A Memoir of
Love and Survival
in a Concentration
Camp

The OASIS

PETRU POPESCU

www.stmartins.com

Design by Susan Walsh

Library of Congress Cataloging-in-Publication Data

Friedman, Blanka.
    The oasis : a memoir of love and survival in a concentration camp /
[edited by] Petru Popescu.
        p.   cm.
    ISBN 0-312-27869-1
    1. Friedman, Blanka.   2. Friedman, Mirek.   3. Jews—Czech
Republic—Biography.   4. Holocaust, Jewish (1939–1945)—
Czech Republic—Personal narratives.   5. Czech republic—Biography.
I. Popescu, Petru, 1944–   II. Title.

DS135.C973 F754   2001
940.53'18'09224371—dc21

2001031939

First Edition: September 2001

10 9 8 7 6 5 4 3 2 1

Author's Note

This book tells the love story of *Haeftlings* Mirek Friedman (camp number 152345) and Blanka Davidovich (camp number B-25089), who were originally deported to Auschwitz, then were transferred to camp Mühldorf, also known as Dachau 3b, where they met in September 1944.

This book is based on their testimonies, taped by the author.

Part 1

MEETING THE BOY FROM PRAGUE

SEPTEMBER 1944
MÜHLDORF, BAVARIA

Blanka

e were passing bombed cities: heaps of rubble over
which flew red banners inscribed with the words TOTALES
KRIEG, KUERZESTES KRIEG! (Total War Is The Shortest War!)—
the latest Nazi slogan, urging the Germans to make the war so
disastrous that it would end through its sheer destructiveness.

On the gutted streets, I saw the Germans. Mostly older men
and women, pale, bitter, drably dressed. Once, in a ravine, I
saw soldiers shooting another soldier, tied to a post and blind-
folded with a white rag. He was a deserter.

While the sun slipped above or below the horizon, I clung
to the car's grated window and slipped in and out of conscious-
ness. At night, awakened by the cold air, I peered out and saw
dark fields, dark autobahns, car headlights painted blue. In the
daytime, I saw camouflage screens spread over factories and
bridges. Most of those sites had been smashed right through
the camouflage.

Abruptly, the train stopped, its five cars banging their cou-
plings. Some thirty soldiers, all middle-aged but in full combat
gear and with their helmets on, were jumping out of a truck
and lining up before a train station tinted pink by the sunrise.
Pressing my face against the grating, I saw that it looked like
the train stations back home—the same ticket booths, the
same wooden benches facing toward the tracks, the same beds
of daisies and marigolds stretching along the main platform,
dirtied by smoke from the trains. On the upper floor, I saw

bedding draped over the windowsills to be aired. The station-master's family lived on that floor, and the wife was already up, perhaps cooking breakfast for the children before hurrying them off to school.

The iron latches closing the car doors were pulled aside. The doors opened, and a reek of filth blew out toward the Germans on the platform. Orders to disembark. Those of us who lay on the floor struggled to become vertical. Blinking from the day-light, we shuffled down the unloading planks, and I saw *Hauptscharführer* Eberle, the *Kommandant* of Lager Mühldorf, in full uniform, with the soaring tall cap struck with the Reich's eagle and the SS death's-head. He was self-assured and calm. His face was shaved unevenly, with patches of gray stub-ble missed by the razor. Under his arm, he carried a wooden stick.

Beside him stood a civilian in his thirties in a frayed brown suit: Milan Lorentz, the camp's *Schreiber* (head clerk). He held a portfolio of leather, old and worn out, with a broken handle repaired with tape. Behind the Kommandant and the Schreiber fretted two SS *Aufseherinnen*, women supervisors, assigned to handle our transport. The Aufseherinnen, too, were armed with sticks. One—short, red-haired, very young—scanned the cars with narrowed eyes, as if to assess what peril they con-tained.

Outnumbering the soldiers, we filled the platform and fell into rows of five, by rote. From the train's caboose, a *Feldwebel* (sergeant) sauntered onto the platform. He was blinking, too: the arrival had jolted him from sleep. He hurried to Eberle, sloppily clicked his heels, and presented him with a folder. Eberle opened it, glanced at a long sheet of paper with names typed single-spaced. Then he passed the folder to the head clerk, while the Feldwebel swelled his chest and reported:

"*Drei hundert Frauen, aus Auschwitz.*" Three hundred women, from Auschwitz.

Eberle and his aging soldiers gaped at us. Just then, the stationmaster, middle-aged, burly, with his rail cap on, stepped out of the telegraph office and glued himself in place. From behind the station emerged a boy who looked eight or nine— the stationmaster's son. He started heading toward the front of the station, as if drawn by a magnet. And all of them kept gawking at us as if we were Martians. Eberle muttered to himself: *"Die sind Frauen?"* These are women? He was not shocked to see the effect of a death camp on prisoners; he'd seen it before. Most workers in his camp had been transferred here from one of the annihilation factories in Poland. But so far, they had only been men.

Now, what he saw before him did not look like women. None of us seemed to have breasts under our striped jackets. Our bodies were narrow, without any curvaceousness or femininity, and our hair was a thin fuzz that barely covered our skulls. Emaciation caved in our cheeks, wedged our chins, and made our noses and ears protrude. But our eyes stared out, unnervingly human.

As I stood in the front row, right in front of the Kommandant, he addressed me directly: *"Was passiert mit Ihr?"* What happened to you?

I explained, *"Kein Wasser, vier Tage."* No water for four days.

We had received no food either, but the lack of water had been the worst torture.

"You must address Herr Hauptscharführer as Herr Lagerkommandant!" snapped the younger Aufseherin, stepping closer and flexing her stick in her fists.

"No water for four days, Herr Lagerkommandant," I reported.

He seemed unable to understand.

At that time, the work camp of Mühldorf and its subcamps contained only males, about six thousand of them. More than half were Jews from Poland, Hungary, Czechoslovakia, and Holland. Plus six hundred Greeks who had come here almost directly from their homeland, spending just a few days at Auschwitz, that big triage for the Reich's recyclables. The non-Jews were POWs: Russians, Italians, even a handful of English and American pilots who had parachuted to captivity out of their burning planes. A few kilometers outside Mühldorf was the site of an ambitious construction project wrapped in mystery. All that was rumored about it was that it demanded the toil of thousands of prisoners.

I knew nothing yet about Eberle. I was later to learn that he had been an accountant in the RSHA, the Reich's High Security Office. He was drafted at fifty and sent to Poland because occupied Poland needed accountants to reorganize its collapsed currency. In Poland, a partisan grenade thrown into an SS club injured him in one knee, and while convalescing he was sent back to Germany to a school for work-camp administrators. When he finished his training, he was appointed Kommandant of camp Mühldorf, close to his native Munich.

Owing to the demands of that mysterious project, the camp's population had grown in leaps, so Eberle found himself needing a much bigger kitchen, with a far larger cooking force. The growing number of prisoners also required more guards, and all those men needed more laundry and medical care. So Eberle decided that what his camp needed was a female hand. Using the convoluted style of German business correspondence, he wrote to Auschwitz asking for womanpower, fit for work and young, if possible.

He was promised three hundred able-bodied Czech and Hungarian Jewesses, between the ages of fourteen and thirty.

Now he was faced with our human rabble. Even four days of dehydration could not account for how bad we looked.

"*Wie heisst du?*" What's your name? he asked me.

"Blanka Davidovich, Herr Lagerkommandant."

My cousin Margit was standing right behind me. I heard her breathing stop.

In the transport papers, my name was Dora Weiss.

I had never expected to slip and give away my real name, because in Auschwitz we were called not by our names but by the numbers stitched on our uniforms. When I had exchanged identities with the one named Dora Weiss, we had exchanged everything: the blocks we slept in, our uniforms, and our numbers.

I gagged, realizing what I had done. One step behind the Kommandant stood the Schreiber, holding the transport papers, which listed no Blanka Davidovich. Next to the Kommandant was that high-strung Aufseherin. All three had heard me; there was no way I could take my name back. As soon as we reached the camp, the Schreiber would check the list, and the discrepancy would be discovered. The possible consequences were two: I would be returned to Auschwitz and shot, to discourage other cases of switched identity. Or I would be shot here, in Mühldorf.

I looked at the train station, at the stained marigolds, at a roadway curling behind the station house, and started to cry quietly.

The Kommandant could not guess my real reason for crying. This half-dead female wept, he assumed, from hunger and thirst. The little SS supervisor, whose name, I would learn later, was Hulda Braun, moved closer and flexed her fingers, ready for anything that would justify hitting me. But she didn't get her chance.

"You will receive water in camp. Water, food, new uniforms. *Wir sind doch nicht in Afrika, Davidovich. . . .*" We are not in Africa, Davidovich. Eberle tried to be reassuring, but he had called me by my real name. He would remember it, I was as good as sentenced. As for not being in Africa but in civilized Germany, I was in no state to savor the humor of his reassurance.

Needing to justify my tears somehow, I stammered, "*Vielleicht . . . gibt es Wasser hier im Bahnhof?*" Perhaps there is water right here in the station?

I had broken a cardinal rule. Prisoners could not speak to their masters unless spoken to. But what had I to lose?

Eberle glanced at our pitiful assemblage, then over us, at the cattle cars—through the open doors, he saw collapsed shapes who had not managed to get up and out. He suddenly turned crimson. He barked at the Feldwebel who had escorted the train: What kind of *Schweinerei* was this, how could he not give us water for four days? We were work material—was that the way to treat work material? The Feldwebel stammered that he had received water and food for himself and his soldiers only; if the prisoners were in this condition, that was due to someone else's oversight—but Eberle yelled *"Ruhe!"* Quiet! Then he aggressively stuck his chin out and agreed with me: *"Ja. Das Bahnhof muss Wasser haben."* Yes. The station must have water.

I felt the muted throb of the crowd behind me. Water!

Supervisor Hulda Braun looked as if she could swallow her stick.

Eberle was already giving orders. The elderly reservists were to bring water from the station *sofort*, immediately, in the most capacious containers they could find. They rushed into the building, none too pleased about the extra exertion. Dazed, I heard Eberle order a soldier with a motorcycle to drive back to camp and return with more trucks, to transport those prisoners too weak to walk. Then he turned to us and gave us permission to sit on the platform until the trucks arrived.

Then he put his hands behind his back and paced.

Splitting into little huddles, we sat down on the platform. Looking for my cousins (I had no less than four cousins in that transport), I spotted Margit sitting next to an unknown girl who looked at me with a kind of awe. Then I noticed other glances focused on me. I dropped down next to Margit, finding the concrete of the platform warm from the sun, and she gestured furtively with her chin toward the other end of the crowd. Back there, skinny arms rose and pointed toward me, and voices bubbled softly. I had achieved something.

Margit wrapped me in a glance that was afraid to be proud. She became anguished again: "Why did you tell him your real name?"

"I don't know, it just slipped out . . ."

"What if we'll all be punished?" Margit had a galloping and disastrous imagination. "What if they think that all of us have fake names, and start interrogating us?"

Through the last two months, I had played mother hen to my cousins, especially to Margit, so I responded with practiced good sense: "Are you crazy? How many interrogators would they need for all three hundred of us?"

A shadow blocked the sunlight. I glanced up and saw a tow-headed boy. The stationmaster's son.

"Du bist jüdisch, nicht?" he asked me. Meaning: You are Jewish, aren't you?

I nodded. Yes, that was what I was.

He examined me with the curiosity of a scientist encountering a species he had only presumed existed.

The stationmaster's wife flew out of the station house. She wore an apron and was trying to wipe her hands on it, but all she did was wring it in her hands. Passing her husband without giving him a glance—he was still glued to the same spot—she shrieked at the boy: *"Helmuth, geh weg! Die Leute sind so dreckig, und du hast reine Kleider!"* Get away, those people are so filthy, and you have clean clothes on!

The soldiers went through the cars, checking them for corpses. They found a dozen and dragged them out.

I didn't look. Most of us didn't. There was always time later to find out who didn't make it.

I watched Margit, who before the deportation had been a

tall and comely girl with auburn hair. She had always looked and acted older than her age. Her face had lost a little of its strain, and her eyes glittered as we noticed a rusty old tub being brought out of the station by four puffing soldiers. It was filled with cloudy water.

Next to me, Eva Lauber, a Slovak girl whom I had befriended in camp, jumped up. Eva was only five feet, with a freckled nose and full lips that even Auschwitz hadn't managed to shrink. She and some twenty others stampeded toward the tub, almost knocking it over, while the Germans watched wide-eyed. The tub emptied in under two minutes; Eva jumped in and lapped the shrinking puddle at its bottom. A wild crowd started pushing and shoving, and other prisoners yelled for everyone to stop fighting and form a line; if they were giving us water, there would be enough for all. The Germans lifted the tub and hurried back into the station with it.

I stepped toward the station. The door to its basement was open. I peered in and saw the soldiers filling the tub from a rusty tap, probably used for watering the flowers or some vegetable garden, since a garden hose was coiled on the floor.

I entered, descending three mossy brick steps. There were several iron buckets lined up by the wall, firefighters' buckets, painted red. The tub filled up, and the soldiers hauled it out, panting and cursing. I dragged a bucket under the tap, turned the tap on, and listened to the splash of the water in it. I smelled the basement's air—damp, cool, slightly mildewed, yet clean of the reek of latrines or of fumes from crematoria. I turned and saw my four cousins, Margit, Suri, Tsilka, and Manci, watching me from the doorway. Feeling already sentenced, I urged them calmly: "Come down here and drink."

They rushed in. Suri, the oldest, waited for the others to drink first. Then she put her neck under the tap, letting the water run on her nape and shaved head, and groaned with pleasure. Suri was twenty-three, and we had expected her to be the first of us to marry. Her sounds made me think of other pleasures, female pleasures that probably none of us would know. Crush that thought, I commanded myself. I was nineteen, and a virgin. Crush that thought, too. It was as if in a fold of my mind I kept a mallet, and if I had a thought that was sad or just bothersome, I smashed it with that mallet.

The tub was already being brought back, empty again.

"You should let the girls carry it," I advised the elderly soldiers.

"*Maul halten!*" Shut your trap, one of them growled.

But the others understood me and found the idea appealing. I climbed out of the basement and called the nearest girls to help. Within seconds, twenty of them invaded the basement, organizing a human chain, while the soldiers, awash in a sea of striped suits, headed out, elbowing the girls aside, but not too roughly. They seemed afraid to touch us. I climbed out of the basement and found Lorentz the Schreiber in my way, with his folder open.

"Your name's not in here," he said.

"I'm in there as Dora Weiss," I replied, trying to move past him.

"But that's not your name, is it?"

He had very dark eyes, almost black, and a menacing stare. I started to babble, trying to invent a reason for having two names. He cut me off: "Why don't you tell the truth? Did you lie about your name when you joined this transport?"

I looked at him with my most pitiable expression: "I lied before that. I switched barracks to be with some girls I knew. Does that matter now?"

Somebody hurried toward us, boots thudding. It was Hulda Braun.

"You deceived the Reich," she snapped. "We'll send you back. I'm going to talk to Herr Kommandant. . . ."

"I'll talk to Herr Kommandant," said Lorentz, hard. Hulda was stepping on his territory. He tapped his hand on the folder: "This is my responsibility." Maybe he personally did not care

much, but his leverage as a veteran prisoner was more important to him than my fate. He turned to me: "You will not be
issued clothes or a bunk before Herr Kommandant decides
what to do with you." Like a heavy door, slamming shut.

"Go back to the transport," ordered Hulda, and I stepped
wide around her, not to give her stick a chance. "Liar," she
blurted as I passed her.

Squinting in the sunlight, I walked onto the platform and
was hugged by a drenched woman. Drops of water rolled down
her forehead and cheeks. It was Eva Lauber, and I had never
seen her like that. She was glowing.

"I fell in the tub," she said. "This will be a good camp!"

Other women, most of whom I did not know, gave me a
glance or a smile. I had made some friends, and at least one
enemy: Hulda.

I looked around for the Kommandant, ready to throw myself
at his feet and beg not to be punished—which might lead to
my punishment right then and there, but what had I to lose?
Eberle was surrounded by his soldiers. They had turned that
tub upside down, and one of them helped him step up on it.
He straightened his uniform, swelled his chest and blared: "I'm
sure none of you know why you're here . . ." The whole transport, especially those who did not understand much German,
held their breath. A breeze blew in just then, and I, standing
at the back of the crowd, heard only bits of what he was saying:
". . . wonder if you remember . . . history . . . the Great Wall of
China . . . giant defense . . ." The breeze switched directions,
and I heard him again: ". . . our own wall . . . protection of Europe . . . you shall be proud . . ." Proud of what? Was the man
crazy—which might also explain his merciful gift of water?
Eberle was rounding to a close. ". . . All of us together . . . the
organization . . . the best in Germany . . ."

He finished with a wave of the arm that pointed into the
morning mist, probably toward the camp.

I moved through the crowd and found my cousins. Tsilka

was wondering aloud about the Great Wall of China, and . . . an organization? What kind of organization? I shrugged. The Germans were always so fond of creating organizations, who knew what he meant? I pushed my way toward Eberle, but he stepped off his improvised lectern into a motorcycle's sidecar, and the motorcycle gunned away. I had missed my chance.

I dropped onto the platform and stared at the smoke-stained marigolds.

A ghost was hovering over me.

I was not startled or frightened. I often felt the presence of the dead, or heard their voices.

The ghost whispered, "Too few of us do what you just did. Making that request for water, you shamed our persecutor into behaving humanely."

"I did nothing like that," I replied. "The Kommandant just realized that if he didn't give us water now, he'd bring into camp a transport of corpses."

"I'm not saying you were Queen Esther. But had you not asked for water, there would be more of your transport with me now." The teacherly voice continued, above the noises made by the Germans and by our transport: "There's always an individual who speaks out, reminding our tormentors that if God put the Jews on this earth, he did it for a reason, which our enemies, no matter how mighty, cannot undo . . ."

"Thank you, Mr. Tauber. Now please go away. You are dead. I saw the evidence."

And Mr. Tauber, as gentle and self-effacing as ever, fell silent.

Mr. Tauber was my Torah tutor from my home-shtetl, Zhdenev. Zhdenev did not have a *Bas Yakov*, a religious school for girls. But my father, who thought that I had a good head for a girl, hired the boys' *heder* teacher to give me private lessons.

Mr. Tauber was only twenty-eight, but he was thin and sickly, and walked with a stoop. He was paid a modest salary by our *kehilla* (community council), and since he sent most of it to his widowed mother in a neighboring shtetl, the Jews of Zhdenev let him stay rent-free with a different family every week. He stayed with us more often than with others because we put him up in our guest room instead of making him a bed in a hayloft. Compared to other Zhdenevers, we were rich. My father owned the beer distribution for the whole area, we had a big house and land, and my mother always had hired help.

Mr. Tauber was learned in the Babylonian Talmud and the cabala, and had a weakness for me. He taught me riveting chapters from world history instead of the religious routine that my four brothers found so droningly boring. He even discussed politics with me, and there was a lot to discuss in the years 1937, '38, and '39. At Munich, Hitler had prevailed, and Czechoslovakia was to be dismembered: the Sudeten part to Germany, and our part, Subcarpathia, to his ally and subordinate, Hungary. But the Jews of Zhdenev took the news in stride. Subcarpathia had a history of invasions, and in between Crusades (which included the raids of one Ukrainian *hetman*, Bohdan Khmelnytsky, who impaled Jews and Jewesses and threw their children into wells), the Jews managed to beget here in larger numbers than anywhere in the world. Because there was no deeper yearning for life in any other breed than the Jews—so said my teacher, Mr. Tauber. Our history was replete with meaning, and as God's people, we always survived.

"Even the word *Jew*," Mr. Tauber once told me, "is a live word. Listen to how it sounds, Blanka. It is never dull. It is never inert."

So said Mr. Tauber. And I, Blanka Davidovich, was from the country of the Jews, an *echte shtetleche tochter*, a genuine shtetl maiden.

Before the Hungarian invasion, Zhdenev had eight hundred souls, all counted. Six hundred Ukrainians, a hundred and fifty

Jews, a sprinkling of Gypsies, and three dozen Catholic Czechs who had been posted here in the twenties, when the peace of Versailles had granted the area to the newly minted Czech state. Our main street was a segment of the region's north-south highway—we children played on it, dodging peasants' carts, and when we had to clear the road for a motorcar, that was an event. Along this street stood the key institutions: the Czech town hall and police station, the shul and ritual bath and heder, the Czech school, two grocery stores, two taverns. There wasn't a rail line to connect us to Munkács, the one metropolis nearby, thirty thousand strong. If we needed to go shopping in the city, or to seek guidance from the Munkácser Rebbe, a famed spiritual leader (Munkács was a bastion of rabbinical conservatism), we had to walk to Podplazy, a village just up the road, and there we could board a bus to Munkács.

Thus, since isolation is ignorance and ignorance is bliss, I had a very blissful childhood.

When I started my seventh grade at the Czech school, a big event happened in my life: my parents bought me a dowry chest and set it in our guest room. Girls in our parts became wives as early as sixteen, so a few years of gathering expensive multicolored yarn, a traditional dowry article, were in order. Meanwhile, God would steer the appropriate young man down my path. Every morning I awoke at five o'clock, as we all did, because Mother had to prepare my four brothers for the heder, which started at six. Still in my nightshirt, I sneaked into the guest room (unless Mr. Tauber slept there that week) and touched the lacquered lid of my dowry chest, afraid that I might be caught by Mother. A pure young girl like me was not supposed to have marriage on her mind, even if her parents did. Quickly, I stroked my dowry chest, feeling how my palm warmed it up, knowing that the yarn piled silently inside it, like feathers for a future nest.

Then I joined the rest of the family in the kitchen. Father, with his cap on, as pleases the High Being, was saying his morning prayers before leaving for work. Mother, who awoke before all of us, managed to clean here and there while feeding breakfast to seven children. Cleanliness was essential in our house. Ever since I could remember, I mopped and scrubbed, cleaned Shabbat dishes in the stream behind the house (cool in summer, freezing in winter), and brought in water by the pail to have it ready for washing our hands, which we did throughout the day: before the morning and evening prayers, before every meal, and each time after we used the outhouse. God forbid that someone would have the runs. They'd blanch their hands from washing.

I also laundered everything by hand, from my younger siblings' diapers to my menstrual napkins, made of flannel. I took care to wash those when no one was around. Having one's period was treated as if it did not happen—that was the way. Yet I knew when my mother had hers, for on those days instead of handing my father his teacup or his coat, she put them next to him, without direct contact, protecting him from uncleanliness. That, too, she did out of respect for the High Being. At bedtime, she and father always stopped by the mezuzah on the bedroom doorpost, touched it, kissed their fingers, and said the ancient prayer: "*Shaddai, yeshmereinu, umatzileinu mi kol hara.*" God, watch over us, and protect us from all bad. Then they waited for us children to do the same.

In one respect did I plan to be different from my mother. Every few weeks, she ran down the road to Sura Beila Stern, the wife of our shames (the beadle who lit the candles at our shul), to have her head shaved. Sura Beila was our village's ritual barber. Never protesting this additional restriction—our Jewish life was full of them—Mother came back with her kerchief tightly tied round her forehead. But sometimes, as she tousled the locks of her three daughters, I could guess that she missed her hair, and I pledged silently: I'll never marry with my hair shaved—never.

One morning in the spring of '38, I walked to school with Rivka and Manci, my younger sisters, and noticed as we passed the village square that the Czech flag in front of the town hall was still lowered. Usually, it flew up the pole at the first ray of sun. The building's windows were open; we heard crates being clattered inside. Then, a clump of printed pages spilled out of a window. Several doors down, the office of Mr. Carasek, the Czech *notar* appointed from Prague, looked deserted. Usually Carasek's porch crawled with farmers who had slept there half the night so as to be the first to enter the office and register some sale of cattle. Today, no one waited on the porch. Carasek himself stood in the vegetable garden behind his office, arms wrapped around a woman.

Carasek, a bachelor, had a relationship with a local Jewish girl, something very frowned upon in our sanctimonious village. Because of the community's disapproval, no one ever saw them together. But on this morning we saw them—quiet, still, the man cradling the woman to him as if to hide her from an unseen danger. We pressed on to school, and saw Jan Fejtek, our teacher and principal. He stood by the school's flagpole, lowering Zhdenev's other Czech flag.

About fifty boys and girls gathered by the flagpole in less than a minute. Mr. Fejtek stepped toward us, folding the flag. He was always soft-voiced, but today he almost whispered. "There will be no more Czech school as of this morning." We held our breath, expecting some further explanation. There was none. Fejtek's eyes were ringed; his whole person, usually groomed and healthy, gave out an air of defeat. "Go home and tell your parents that they'll be notified of what other school arrangements they can make for you. Thank you for having been good students."

Obediently, we turned on our heels and walked home, past Carasek's garden, empty now, then again past the town hall. Groups of local Ukrainians, mostly men, stood in front of the building, talking in low voices. Their faces, broad and red, signaled a cheap satisfaction. The Ukrainians wanted a state of their own, and saw the Czechs' withdrawal as their chance.

One of them asked loudly, "What are the *Zhids* going to do, without their Czech mayor? They rubbed against his leg like cats."

Christians called Jews *Zhids*; that was a fact of life. "Bad words cannot hurt you," my father had taught us early on, as we grew old enough to go to school, to the city, or to country fairs—in short, into the bigger world.

Believe it or not, the word did not hurt because Father had said so. A procession trampled up main street smelling of incense, led by the Ukrainian priest. He carried a fanciful flag imprinted with crosses, the flag of free Ukraine. They were going to hoist it on the pole instead of the Czech one.

We did not pay much attention—the joy of an unforeseen vacation had dawned on us. My brothers wanted to kick a rag football on the bank of the local river, the Zhdenevka. Rivka, Manci, and I planned to go to the forest and check how early the berries would ripen this year. Let's drop off these silly school satchels. Nearing our gate, we saw Mother hurrying home with her kerchief knotted so tightly that it cut into her forehead. She had been at Sura Beila's again, to have her head shaved.

We followed her into our front yard and found Father, who was never at home on a workday unless he was sick, surrounded by men with their caps on. My father's cousins Yidl and Moishe, who lived a few doors away from us; Kortser Itsik Weiss and Langer Itsik Weiss—Itsik Weiss the short and Itsik Weiss the tall, same last name but not related; and a few other neighbors. Practically our whole *kehilla*, of which Father was the president.

Mother raised her eyebrows (rich and brown, and spared by the razor), and Father glanced briefly at us and announced:

"There's been some trouble, Faiga. Hungarian gangs struck last night in Podplazy and—" He mentioned one other shtetl. "They robbed several homes and killed an old man."

"What are you going to do?" breathed Mother.

She looked above him, to the wooded hills beyond the main street. A few specks of farmhouses hung in the thick green of the woods, but otherwise the landscape was both pristine and disturbing in its isolation.

Father sounded too calm. "We decided to organize some night patrols."

With muttered *git morgens*, the men left. I suddenly connected the lowering of the Czech flags, the strikes of the unseen gangs, and my parents' expressions. Mother said, "Girls, it's good that you're home. We'll start the spring cleaning now." Was cleanliness the reason, or her need to have us under her eye?

"Let the boys go, so they won't be in the way," said my father.

"You think—?"

"Yes."

The boys whooped happily, but Father stepped into the street with them, and I heard him say to our brother Leizer, the eldest: if they should go to the river, they should not lose sight of each other, and at the slightest alarm they should rush home. Leizer listened wide-eyed. Father never urged so much caution.

Mother ordered me to straighten out the guest room—Mr. Tauber was staying with us this week. I quashed a smile. Mr. Tauber collected Jewish folklore and wrote it down in a thick book of which he was very protective; yet just the day before, I had stolen the book from his bag and read from it one whole afternoon. Its most breathtaking section, called "The Sword of Moses," was an ancient manual of magic, a practical cabala that contained advice on making wishes come true, including love wishes.

I had hidden with it in the barn, and read, with my cheeks hot:

How to make someone fall in love with you. The one angel appointed on matters of love is Anael, who is in the likeness of a woman. She holds in one hand a mirror, in the other a comb. If thou wishest to employ Anael, thou must utter: "I conjure thee Anael, inflame so-and-so with my love, and may he (she) not eat or drink, walk or stand, sit or sleep, before he (she) comes to me and fulfills all my desires." Then carve so-and-so's name on a tablet of clay, throw it into a fire so it is consumed with the flames of love, and the two of you shall experience marvelous things. . . .

The marvelous things were not specified. I had blushed, trying to imagine them, but I was too innocent to imagine anything. Recently, with great self-restraint, I had accepted the attention of a boy five years older than me, Boruch, the son of a horse trader. Boruch had promised to teach me how to ride a horse. I did not really like him, but riding sounded exciting, and I was flattered because Boruch was almost an adult. So I had reasons to want to complete my tutorial.

I went into the guest room, needlessly made the bed again, and then plunged into the "Sword of Moses," learning that *to kill an enemy or a rival, including a rival in love,* all I had to do was conjure the spirit Abraksas and follow his easy instructions: "Take mud from the two banks of a river, shape it into a human image, write on it the name of the person, then smash it, saying . . ."

I was thirteen. I sat in a corner of Europe that would soon be destroyed, with a book of spells on my knees, and I read, smiling. I knew that our enemies could not triumph, because our adults, led by Father, would protect us.

. . .

"Girls, look," said a voice from the here-and-now. My cousin Tsilka.

On the road behind the station, there was now a long plume of dust, stirred by trucks speeding over from the camp.

They had arrived.

Hulda Braun and the other Aufseherin selected the ones too weak to walk, and herded them into the trucks, using their sticks. The stronger ones, about 150, were to head for the camp on foot. Hulda put me in the first row of the stronger ones.

TWO

A few minutes later we were marching to camp Mühldorf, guarded by soldiers deployed in two loose lines to the
right and left of our column. They carried their rifles strapped
on their shoulders. Had we had the necessary stamina, we could
have tried to escape. There were too few soldiers, and most of
them, being reservists, were probably poor shots. But where
could we hide? Potato and cabbage fields stretched on both
sides of the road, and farmhouses kept emerging out of the
thinning morning fog. We were not in my forested Subcarpathia, where a human could hide anywhere. A few fir trees
sprouted here and there—insignificant cover.

A truck loaded with prisoners passed us, stirring tall swirls
of dust. Sitting next to the driver, Hulda Braun scanned the
marching rows. I was walking at the left end of my row, so I
was sprayed with dust from my forehead to my wooden clogs.
I marched on, sneezing and coughing.

I kept thinking, How could I give out my real name?

In Auschwitz, I'd seen far less serious infractions punished
with death. At each roll call, a few of us would be disposed of
for as little as a skin rash. So, every morning before roll call,
we pinched our cheeks hard or slapped each other, to look
healthier. Every morning, in scores of women's barracks, the
filthy air rattled with slaps, as if we were clapping for the appearance of a performer—but we would be the performers, and
our audience the SS. Once, two girls smuggled in some beets

grown in the vegetable garden of a subcamp, squeezed out the reddish juice and smeared their cheeks with it. But their ploy was reported by a zealous *Stubedienst* in charge of the barracks' cleanliness, and the smugglers were shot. End of the beet juice makeup.

I had exchanged identities with Dora Weiss in order to leave the *Block* to which I was originally assigned. Before boarding the boxcars, our parents had told us, if we get separated—men to one side, women to the other, or young to one side and old to the other—look for anyone you know, and stay close to them. Relative, friend, village neighbor, it doesn't matter, it will be easier. Just don't remain alone.

The first few weeks, I bunked with a distant cousin, Brana Zoldan, and her sisters Ilona and Regina, in Block 7. Then Brana and her sisters were transferred to a block closer to where they worked, sorting the valuables of newly arrived transports. I remained "alone" in a block with a thousand strangers crammed in a space designed for three hundred. One evening after roll call, I entered the latrine and heard two girls whispering to each other. One I knew from sight; she slept in my block, number 7. The other girl begged her: "My sister sleeps in seven. I want to be with my sister. Will you switch blocks with me?"

The girl from my block hesitated. She was frightened of doing anything against the rules. "What block are you in now?"

"Twenty-nine."

I started. Four of my cousins from Zhdenev slept in Block 29. That seemed miraculous, but it was not. The deportations had netted Jewish communities that were so ancient and closely knit that if you passed the first selection, the one that could send you to heaven, the chances of finding relatives in Auschwitz were high.

"I don't want to move," the frightened girl said.

"What's your name?" I asked the girl who was begging to switch.

"Dora Weiss. I'm from Doulho."

"I'm Blanka Davidovich, from Zhdenev. I'll switch with you."

"Don't do it," the other girl warned us. "You'll be caught and shot."

But I wasn't afraid, because I had learned one secret about this place. For the Germans, our disabilities were visible. But we as individuals were invisible.

Dora and I exchanged our uniforms right there in the latrine, among hundreds of people no longer blushing from the lack of privacy, proof enough that we had become invisible even to ourselves. In Dora's stripes, with her number stitched on my chest, I headed for Block 29, where I found my cousins: Suri, Tsilka, Manci, Margit. At first, they panicked that if I joined them my cheating would be discovered and all five of us would be shot. I argued: "How will they notice? Even our own mothers wouldn't recognize us now!"

My cousins relented. I moved in.

I enjoyed the closeness of kindred blood, and realized the price I'd have to pay for it. Like all other blocks, Block 29 underwent frequent selections, with the prisoners arranged in rows of five. But Block 29's lower angel of death, a *kapo* reassigned here from the kitchen because he stole food too obviously, beat us every morning before the SS arrived, just to bruise us into looking disposable. The block was terrified. When I approached Dora's row to claim my place in it, the other four girls automatically took a step back, and I was left with the most vulnerable spot: right at the front of the row.

I'll use it as a survival strategy, I told myself. See, I'm standing right in front every day because I'm strong and have nothing to hide. No blemishes, no injuries. I am valuable work material. If you're looking for flaws, look behind me.

By sheer luck, I never incurred the wrath of that kapo. But I had worse dangers to confront. Block 29 was often visited by the camp's most famous selectioner, referred to as the Doctor—

because he was a doctor, brunet and handsome like an Italian matinee idol. He had a curious mind, interested in twins, in hunchbacks, in Gypsies. There were thousands of Gypsies here, in a place of their own, a camp within the camp, which no one penetrated except the Doctor. He was Dr. Mengele. When he inspected Block 29 for the first time, wearing his uniform with distinction, hands gloved, boots polished, his entrance was announced by a rowdy gang of kapos shouting at our naked crowd: "*Zwillinge! Wo sind die Zwillinge?*" The twins, where were the twins? They dived into the rows of nude women, pulling out about a dozen, slapping a few of them back to their places, not sure who were twins and who weren't.

Finally, they selected five or six pairs.

"*Keine mehr Zwillinge?*" No more twins? The Doctor asked in a voice that sounded so . . . well fed. Our daily diet was half a liter of ersatz coffee, 350 grams of bread, and one liter of turnip soup. But only half of that ended in our bowls. The rest was stolen by the kapos. The prisoners shrank, which affected the sounds they made. After a week here, my voice had pitched up, becoming jagged and creaky. A normal voice is plump, healthy. Like the Doctor's as he asked: "No more twins?"

The Doctor stepped along and scoped me with calm, pleasant eyes. I froze, although I was not a twin. But I realized that he didn't see me, or any of us; he only perceived the nude specimens on which he would quench his scientific thirst. He was the camp's most feared selectioner. Like a child at play, he changed his mind often, lost interest quickly, and didn't care how many toys he destroyed. Why had he been granted such power? Why, so evil and warped, was he being backed up by history? I couldn't answer those questions. Yet, amazingly, the Doctor rekindled my curiosity to live. I had to see the end of this game, I had to understand it. For if the world had lost all meaning *now*, it could not remain without meaning.

When we arrived in camp, the older inmates gave us an important tip: Don't ever volunteer. You could wind up dead.

But I always volunteered. Work was *life*; even shoveling ashes, I felt better than being alone with my thoughts. After two months in camp, I dragged all my cousins with me to volunteer for a work transport out of Auschwitz. We were told that the work would include construction, maintenance, and cooking. I stepped forward and claimed that I was experienced in all three. I lied that my father was a bricklayer and I had often helped him, and so had my cousins. The SS man doing the selecting widened his eyes. Five bricklayers? Excellent. We were overqualified. He wrote us all down, I as Dora Weiss, of course. The next morning we boarded the train, with Margit whimpering hysterically that she had not touched a brick in her life, and we would be found out (and shot).

After half an hour of listening to the wheels clanging over the rail joints, we realized what we had achieved. We were out of Auschwitz! Out of Auschwitz!

I had done well in my plan to be around for the end of the war.

But now, I had placed my plan in total jeopardy.

A warm burst of sunlight caught me full in the face. I was panting from the strain of the march.

The road hit a muddy stretch. My clogs sank and slipped, twisting my ankles, but I looked at the one walking next to me, Margit, and she smiled. A slight rosiness colored her cheeks. Then her eyes focused, and she said under her breath, in Yiddish, to our whole row: *"Keek, dort ist's."* Hey, there it is.

Everyone knew what *it* was.

The camp.

Margit had exceptionally sharp eyes. I stared ahead and saw only a vague huddle of man-made objects, but I turned and whispered the news to the row behind me. They passed it back, row by row—there it was, our immediate future. The nearest potbellied German paid no attention to us. Hard of hearing? Common in men of his age. As he negotiated the mud puddles, seemingly annoyed that his boots would have to be polished again, we pressed Margit with questions about what she saw.

"*Koimens?*" Suri asked.

One word, the essence—chimney stacks?

"*Yo. Tsvei.*" Two stacks.

Since Margit was easy to scare, her relative calm was encouraging. She told us that the stacks looked old in design and not well maintained. Like the stacks of a kitchen, laundry, or factory.

"*Vus noch?*" What else? Tsilka asked Margit.

"*Toier, turem, elektrische druten.*" Gate, watchtowers, electrified wire.

I sniffed, prepared to choke on the reek of cremated human protein. But there was no stench. Suri voiced my thoughts: "I don't smell ovens."

"One compound is new, I see barracks still without roofs," added Margit.

"Do you see a wall? We're here to help build a wall," I reminded Margit.

"I don't see any kind of construction."

"If they're relying on us to build it, they're really down to the wire," said Manci, usually the most silent and skittish, and we all laughed like parents pleased by the boldness of a bashful child.

"*Halt! Still stehen!*" Our column rippled to a stop.

A convoy of trucks was approaching, driving on a road that crossed ours. Loaded with sacks, they rolled past, raising big swirls of dust.

"What do you see now, Margit?"

"A bunch of people by the camp's gate. I can't tell what they're doing—there's too much dust."

Not willing to inhale the dust, our soldiers shouted us back into a barren field. Our column broke, some women sat on the ground, and the soldiers did not react with kicks and blows. One even volunteered an explanation, which raced around the transport: we'd have to wait here awhile because our camp compound wasn't ready yet. "They're so damn friendly!" said Tsilka between her teeth, angry from fright.

We were all frightened. Something was too good here. Fortunately, Hulda's truck reappeared, and she found us sitting on the ground. She jumped out of the cabin, her stick moving like quicksilver. Hitting at random, she got us all on our feet. "*Fünf, fünf, fünf!*" Five, five, five! she yelled, and we formed rows of five again. That was what she wanted, that we should wait at attention, in neat rows of five.

More trucks passed. I thought that the drivers, German soldiers, were squinting in surprise when they saw us, but I could not be sure because the dust got in my eyes, crackled between my teeth, and made me sneeze. I tried to ignore the pain in my back and neck. I was no longer frightened. Six years had passed since the day when Zhdenev's Czech school had closed, and now being comfortable made me feel endangered, while being miserable brought me comfort.

We finally heard the order: "*Marschieren, marsch!*"

I was in the first row again, with Margit to my right.

The dust floated down, thickening the fog that, despite the sunshine, did not want to burn off. We trooped into the fog, keeping our direction by the traffic ruts dug in the roadway.

"Hey, look!" someone whispered.

On our left, a moving mass of people appeared: a prisoners' column. Stepping onto the main road, they lumbered away with their backs to us, and we immediately strained to examine them through the fog—the way they looked would be our first clue about camp Mühldorf.

"They're carrying shovels," whispered Margit.

Shovels. What a hopeful word. This was a work column, and work was our chance of salvation.

"Are they talking?" I asked, wondering if I heard a buzz of voices.

"They are," confirmed Suri.

Loud talk meant lax discipline. Very encouraging. Maybe Mühldorf was an exceptional camp, with sufficient food, a real infirmary, and easy rules. The thought of being no more, while my cousins would survive, made me gag. I reached inside me for that mallet I used to crush unwanted thoughts and memories. But I could not find it. Suddenly, I plunged back to that time tattooed in my mind, the beginning of my deportation.

On the eve of leaving our home, Mother had helped me wash my hair in the aluminum tub in the kitchen. She had whispered as she helped me comb it: "You know, Blanka, when I was a girl, I had hair even prettier than yours."

"Why don't you let it grow, so I can see it?" I had asked.

"It's no longer pretty. It's gray by now."

"But you're only forty-two."

She smiled as one does to a child. How could she break with a custom at forty-two?

Around us, our house felt inordinately large. It was almost empty. We had lost the business. We had sold the furniture to buy food. Even the chest with my dowry yarn had been sold to a Ukrainian farmer, whose daughter needed a dowry chest urgently—she was three months pregnant.

"You're not ready for marriage anyway," Mother had told me, biting her lips not to cry. All my girlish dreams were woven into that yarn, and also some of her own. What man she and Father would choose for me, my wedding, the arrival of a grandchild . . . But most of the young Jewish men, including my brothers and my official crush Boruch, were already in Hungarian work camps. The rest of the Jews waited every day to be marched away to an unforeseeable future. The Christians

we knew—and they were many in a village as tight as ours—
no longer said hello to us in the street. For years, they had
wished us a good Shabbat on Fridays, they had done business
with us, they had been in our homes and we in theirs. Now
they wouldn't have anything to do with us—unless they could
buy from us cheap, like that farmer who bought my dowry.
Instead, they watched us with cold curiosity. Look what bad
luck befell them. How will they take it? What will they do?

That was particularly devastating when it came from old
friends or childhood playmates. Once, returning from Munkács, I met Olga Mallinich, the daughter of the grocer from
whom we bought all our staples. Olga had a dowry chest just
like mine; countless times, she and I had played together,
looked at each other's yarn, or talked about boys. I met Olga,
her sister Galina, and two other girls I knew from school at
the bus station. They carried packages after shopping in the
city. The bus driver put his head out and yelled the now customary: "Jews, get on last, and wait till everyone else is seated!"
When I got on, there were no more seats. Grabbing one of
those supporting hooks, I saw Olga seated right beside me, and
I said good day. Without a word, Olga turned toward her sister.
They chatted and laughed.

I said good day again, to anyone who would answer.

"Shut up," Olga said. Calmly, as if I'd done something stupid. Something that merited a brief reprimand, but no more.

I would have stepped down, but the bus was already in
motion.

Still, all the way to Zhdenev, I expected that one of my
former schoolmates would turn to me and say something like:
Look, it's not our fault. It's these new laws that restrict our
contact with Jews. We're still the same. You're still the same.

But no one even looked at me. It was as if I did not exist.

I rushed to step off the bus before everyone else, and then
ran home, determined to blast my parents. Why hadn't they
taught me about hate, why? It wasn't made of just words "that

could not hurt me." It was made of twisted laws, betrayal from friends, injustice, silence—did my parents not know that? Why had they not prepared me? Only to realize, when I saw them, smiling, relieved that I'd returned safely to the house that felt mournfully large, that they could not have prepared me for hate. The Jews, so admired for their wits, so famed for their hard-earned toughness, were as dumbly unprepared for hate as anyone. Through their centuries of suffering, they had hoped for the end of hate, for tolerance, for acceptance.

I did not tell them what had happened to me. Just threw my arms around Mother, muttered that I'd dropped in at Munkács's post office but none of my brothers had written from their work camps yet, and then cried. Of all kinds of hate, the worst was silence. The silence of my treacherous friends, and my own silence in response. I was no longer the person I knew. I had disappeared.

Then, on May 20, 1944, I was sitting on a chair, stark naked, in Auschwitz.

I was one of twenty naked women being shorn by three barbers. I had reappeared as a *Haeftling*, a prisoner, in Auschwitz.

There were four SS officers in the room. They walked around and spoke relaxedly, keeping an eye on our progress. Once in a while, another SS walked in and saluted the others: *Gruess Gott*—greet God, a folksy hello instead of the jagged *Heil Hitler*. I noticed a green triangle on my barber's uniform: common criminal. He was middle-aged, rough, smelly. A prisoner with a DDT pump sprayed the shaven women. The door opened, yet another SS came in—Greet God. Seeing the clumps of my hair fall to the floor, I cried so hard that my barber paused with his razor in the air. *"Warum schreist du, du kleine Jüdin?"* Why are you shrieking, you little Jewess? Would you like another outbreak of typhus here, like two years ago? *"Fünfzehn*

Tausend tote Haeftlinge." He threw his arm up in the air to indicate a heap of fifteen thousand corpses.

I thought of Mother. I prayed to wake up in Zhdenev, married and with my head shaved, of course.

"*Hopla! Auf dem Stuhl!*" said the barber.

He pushed me up on the chair so he could take the hair out of my armpits and groin. I stood under a bulb that burned my bare skull. He made me raise my arms and stand with legs spread, telling me with a snicker to be very still, he wouldn't want to nick my anatomy. When he was done, I stepped under a shower that pissed a few drops of cold water on me, then I was handed my striped outfit (no undergarments) and a pair of wooden clogs. They were imbued with an industrial odor that pricked my nasal membranes. They had been deloused with Zyklon B. *Zyklon* means "cyclone" in German, and four kilograms of that cyclone, initially an insecticide, had been found capable of killing a thousand people. The cyclone was used both in the gas chambers and as a detergent.

Then, in a yard filled with shaven androids like me, I found my cousin Brana and her two sisters, Ilona and Regina. We recognized each other by our voices: Cousin Blanka, Brana, Ilona, *wus tist di?* How are you? *Git, ind di?* Well, and you? I swear, we still talked like girls raised in polite society. "I heard that they won't let the old ones live," said Brana.

"I don't believe it; the kapos are saying it to scare us," Ilona countered. We even tried to laugh, making fun of our pitiful appearance. Until we were pushed into another room, made to undress again, and searched in all the crevices of our bodies for hidden jewelry. A woman was punched out of the line. She reeled by a wall, numb and desperate, while in the hand of an SS officer shone a gem of some kind. There was a jabber of voices: one kapo, talking fast, lips turned down in scorn, seemed to argue that the gem had no value. But the German shook his head. The table was covered with a coarse napkin.

The German wiped the gem on the napkin and then slipped it into his pocket.

The kapo pinched his lips in frustration. He wanted the find for himself. Eager to try his luck again, he yelled at the rest of us to step up to the table.

After that day, when we ran into relatives or friends, talk was about life-and-death essentials. How is your block, how are the kapos, do they beat you, did you find a way to organize? (*Organisieren*, this scholarly sounding German word, had a quick shameless meaning here: "to steal.") We did not mention the good times "before." If we did, our feelings would pierce through our numbness, and our numbness was our protection. So, apart from swapping information about the camp, we hardly talked.

Brana, her sisters, and I found places in a top bunk built for four people but crammed with fourteen girls who slept lying on one side. Several days later, Brana and Ilona were selected to sort out the clothes and personal valuables of newly arrived Jews, in a site called Brejinka. We had heard of those sorting sites. The SS who supervised them got rich. The inmates working in them put on weight, and sneaked back to the barracks cigarettes, homemade foods found in the suitcases, and clothes—socks, vests, light sweaters, very prized because we could wear them under our thin uniforms. They also sneaked back Hungarian and Polish paper money. What on earth could one use that money for? Toilet paper.

The first night Brana and Ilona arrived from Brejinka, I was shocked at the expression on their faces. They were frightfully pale, but they also had in their eyes a flat emptiness I had not encountered yet, even here. I questioned them, but received no answer. They climbed into our bunk and sank into sleep. They had not been beaten. I would have noticed bruises or crusted blood.

Exhaustion, I told myself.

The second night Brana and Ilona arrived from Brejinka, they waited for the lights to be turned off in the barracks and for everyone else to fall asleep. Then they woke up their younger sister, Regina, and me. Brana whispered to me that they had brought some food from Brejinka. Moving very carefully for fear of waking up the *Blockaelteste* (a Polish woman imprisoned here in 1940; she had "built Auschwitz" was her boastful announcement to her new tenants), we feasted on a dozen hard-boiled eggs found in a suitcase. I so enjoyed that nourishing protein slipping down my throat that at the end I felt drunk. My first solid meal here. For another week, Brana's and Ilona's kerchiefs would return into our block pulled tightly over their ears, loaded with food which we would savor in the dark.

Then, one night, after I had been sleeping perhaps an hour, Brana shook me by the shoulder. I woke up. Brana was feeling Ilona's face—Ilona's eyes were open, and she seemed to grin. Then I realized that she clenched her teeth to keep them from chattering. She was burning with a high fever. Next to her, Regina, the youngest, slept, and Brana gestured that I shouldn't wake her.

Brana and I monitored Ilona's fever all night. Once, I slipped down onto the floor of naked wood planks and tiptoed to the bunk of the snoring Blockaelteste—she slept by herself and had the use of a little stove on which she cooked her separate meals, burning old rags as fuel. I stole three rags, slipped outside and ran barefoot to a water puddle. In summer, the weather at Auschwitz alternated between blistering sun and chilling rain. We were forbidden to drink from the puddled water, because of the danger of typhus, but I couldn't use the block's only tap; it was too creaky and loud. I dipped the rags in the puddle. Back in the bunk, we took turns applying the rags to Ilona's forehead. The rags dried up from her fever.

Brana and I discussed the crisis. Ilona could not go to work, the minimum we could expect from her was that she would stand through the roll call. Then she would have to spend the day in the bunk. Brana hoped that the Blockaelteste (whom we called *Blockova*, in Czech) would allow Ilona to rest. The day before, the Blockova had approached Brana and cozied up to her: a clear sign that she wanted things from Brejinka. But the Brejinka detail could not leave the barracks with an incomplete number of workers.

"I'll go in Ilona's place," I whispered.

Ilona heard me and gave me that mute grin.

Brana said nothing. There was no place here for thank-yous.

At 5:00 A.M. on the dot, the Blockova awoke without an alarm clock. Brana was already by her bunk, to ask her what she fancied from Brejinka.

My substitution for Ilona went without a hitch. Ilona managed to stand through the roll call. When it was over, the Blockova allowed her to go back to the bunk and even promised to give her some water during the day.

As I helped Ilona climb into the bunk, she unclamped her teeth and whispered to me: "I'm glad you're going. . . . You'll see your parents in Brejinka, and your sisters. . . . I saw them. . . ."

I bit my lips hard. Outside, a kapo was shouting at the Brejinka detail to form a marching column.

"You saw them alive?"

She nodded, with fever in her eyes: "Yes, alive . . ."

I could not speak to Brana on the way to Brejinka. The rule "no talk among prisoners" was strictly enforced. But my wooden clogs, thudding with the marching column, kept pace with my thoughts. Could it be true? It could not. Ilona was delirious. I was convinced of it.

Yet, when we emerged into a wide empty space right by the terminal where the trains disgorged the new transports, my heart pounded so hard, I feared that the Germans might notice its drumming under my filthy uniform.

A train had arrived two hours earlier. Its passengers were not in sight, but their abandoned belongings covered the ground: suitcases, clothes, hats, walking sticks, packages tied up with string, baby carriages, toys, even chairs and radios. Money spilled out of wallets and purses—when its owners had been ordered to drop it on the ground, how many of them had realized that here both money and people were worthless? Cigarette cases, pipes, penknives. Handkerchiefs. And the yarmulkes and black hats of religious men who, upon arrival, had been stripped of their essential trait, their respect for God, expressed through keeping their heads covered.

I had pictured Brejinka as a giant lost-and-found. I had imagined abandoned belongings, but not the feeling they would evoke. The feeling was unbearable.

The suitcases were of every size and color—one was plastered with labels from Europe's most famous hotels. Using hooked sticks, male inmates pulled free suitcase after suitcase, and tore them open with curved knives. Slashing through expensive leather or modest cardboard, they did their own first selection of the goods before bringing them to us.

Suddenly, a woman, almost undressed—she wore stockings and a camisole but no dress or shoes—ran back toward the collecting tables, crying that she had lost her eyeglasses. Blinking myopically, she was stopped by two of the men slashing suitcases. They pushed her toward a mound of eyeglasses— here, take your pick! They laughed while she grabbed several, found one that fit, and nodded a dazed thanks. Then she ran to catch up with a crowd worming its way through a gate beyond which I saw the flat top of a small brick house. German soldiers guarded that gate.

Next to me, Brana said: "You wouldn't believe what kind of things people run back for. They have no idea they'll never use them again."

Her voice contained no feeling, just the fact. *They have no idea they'll never use them again.*

The collecting tables were long, with little partitions affixed upright, so that every type of item could be stored in separate drawers. Wearing distinctive white kerchiefs, fifty females busied themselves at those tables, sorting out the loot. I looked back toward that guarded gate. A brick chimney, square and low, rose from the flat roof of that boxlike house, and several men in clothes black with soot scrambled around on the roof, armed with poles fitted with big brushes. They were chimney sweeps. If Auschwitz had chimneys, how could it not have chimney sweeps? They poked in the chimney with their brushes on poles, and a flame, like a fiery burp, came out of the chimney. The chimney sweeps cheered. Another burst of flame—and a hell of screaming from below, from behind that gate. A whistle cut through the screams, and, grimy and black, another engine pulled its train in. The inmates with hooks yelled at us to sort faster, the next *Zugang* (transport) was already here.

An Aufseherin motioned me toward a pile of religious objects: talliths, zizith, prayer books, tefillin, menorahs, candlesticks. They were to be sorted out by value—many menorahs and candlesticks were made of silver, but the talliths, tefillin, and prayer books had no commercial value and were to be dropped into a big wicker basket by the table. I saw a *shulklapper*'s hammer, a wooden mallet like the one used in Zhdenev by Berl Stern, our shames. He had knocked with it on the doors of Jewish homes to arouse the men for the early morning services. This one was carved, just like Berl's, with Hebrew words: LET US GO UNTO THE HOUSE OF THE LORD.

The Aufseherin snatched it from me, but realized that it was of wood and threw it into the wicker basket. I dug in the pile, felt something square, and pulled out . . . a book.

It was Mr. Tauber's collection of cabalistic lore, "The Sword of Moses," which I had once stolen from him in Zhdenev.

Luckily, the Aufseherin had turned to another table.

I felt like grabbing "The Sword of Moses" and sticking it under my jacket.

But I stopped myself.

I wanted to scream, but I couldn't.

I had become a brainless idiot, standing nude at *Appel* (roll call), using the latrine on cue, slurping dirty water out of a bowl for five without a spoon, fishing for flyspecks of vegetables with my tongue while four other women would wait, keen-eyed, lest I gulp more than my share. The first few times, I threw up. "A *fartzeltete*, huh?" one of the women mocked me. I was a fartzeltete, a spoiled sissy: I would still reject food, even though it could make me survive, and I did not deserve it, I did not deserve to live, because . . . *Don't remember! Don't!*

I tried to escape the memory.

I was in Mühldorf now, in another life. A brand-new life, even though it might last just a few hours more. Or a whole day at most.

I tried to concentrate on the rutted road. On those lucky prisoners I saw ahead of me, through those swirls of fog and dust.

But the memory held me in an unbreakable clasp.

My sister Rivka was twelve, and she could have come with me at that first selection, the one that occurred minutes after the arrival. Rivka wanted to work, so she asked me to take her with me. We could have lied to the selectioner that she was fourteen. But I told Rivka to stay with mother. I thought: I am older and stronger, and Rivka is too frail to work. I will work, and I will bring them some of my food.

I believed I was doing the right thing. Rivka went with my mother and my father and my ten-year-old sister Manci. (She had the same first name as my cousin.) They went to the left, and I, alone, to the right.

How could I do that? How could I not guess? When we arrived and the train's doors opened, a group of older inmates jumped into our cars, laughing like devils at our unkempt and stupefied faces. Using those hooks, they started to pull our suit-cases out from under us. "They'll be given back to you later!" And they laughed and threw the suitcases out of the car; many opened as they hit the ground, spilling clothes, jewels, food. Someone, I don't know who, pushed me out of the car and into a chaos of shouts and of people bumping into each other as if in a grotesque dance. But I did hear, I *did* hear a prisoner, an older man in a striped jacket speaking Yiddish like a Pole, counseling a woman with a baby in her arms. "Give it to me, it's better. Give it to me!" She rolled her eyes, terrified, and wouldn't let go of the baby. The man threw his arms up; he wasn't being understood. "If you don't trust me, then give it to that *altashke* (old woman), and you, walk up to that officer, and then to the right, and you'll live, *fershtaist?*"

The woman stared at him as if catatonic. The inmate was getting hoarse. "Don't you have anyone here to give the baby to, an aunt, a neighbor?" The woman still did not react. And the baby, who should have screamed in that commotion, was totally quiet, and had a face I will never forget: rosy-cheeked, serene, and with a clean forehead. An angel's face. So the man rushed off, looking for another mother to save, and I . . .

I did not realize what was going on, though he had explained it all, right in front of me. Rivka was pulling at my sleeve, and I even thought: she'll tear up my sleeve. As if that had any importance! "Go with Mother!" I urged her with impatience. I was the older sister, and she revered me. Being accepted by me was not only a treat, but a sign of adulthood and emancipation. I saw her shoulders slump as she walked off, and I felt her loneliness. Why did she want so much to stay with me? Had she already guessed, while I hadn't? Did she walk off to her end *knowing?*

I could not bear to imagine her face, her expression, as she turned away from me. But I swear, I never guessed. . . . So I sent her away, like the annoyed older sister who had no time for her whining, I reentrusted her to Mother, denying the obvious, that on this day, on this chaotic platform, among yelling SS men and dogs that barked and looked ready to break their leashes, all parents had lost their power of protecting their young ones. All the skills of negotiation with the tormentors, which the Jews had acquired through centuries of back-and-forth persecution and tolerance, had no currency here. Here and now, lessons as old as the Bible were worthless, because . . . because *this* had been thought out by our captors, not as temporary and partial, but as total, immediate, and final.

I remembered the fever in Ilona's eyes. *You'll see your parents in Brejinka, and your sisters. . . . I saw them. . . . Alive . . .* I had not believed her. Yet, with the insane, voracious need of a heart yearning for what was its own and what had been wrenched from it—I believed her.

But I would never see my parents again, or my sisters.

After what I had done to Rivka, I felt that I had no right to live. Yet I still lived. Why?

I wasn't numb on that morning, in Brejinka. I wept on the things that my hands sorted out, for they were imbued with their owners' presence. Mr. Tauber, who had taught me that among the *sephirot*, the emanations of God, there was one named Binah, divine intelligence; he had smiled, because my given middle name was Binah. I had asked Mr. Tauber what a pure race meant, when news of the Nuremberg laws had reached Zhdenev; he had replied: "How can a human race, the result of continuous sexual mixing, be thought of as pure?" Then he had grown self-conscious for mentioning sex to me, a virgin girl. Mr. Tauber, who had a crush on me, the most discreet and self-effacing crush, he was still here, lingering above me, his touch still imprinted in his book. And he was washed along with the remembrance of Rivka, of Manci, of my mother and father, by a thundering torrent of souls flowing through me, and through my hands.

I dropped something, kicked it under the sorting table, and went down under the table to look for it. Just so I could hide. I bit my dirty hand and took long breaths through my nose. If I wanted to kill myself, all I had to do was run the wire. A kapo or a German would yell after me: *"Halt!"* Then in Polish: *"Stoj!"* Those words were posted on the electrified fences, on warning plates set visibly every hundred meters. I wouldn't stop, and I would get my bullet and be delivered.

But today I had an obligation to survive. Ilona. She was not my sister, but she was Brana's sister, and she was young; she deserved the same chance I had.

From under the sorting table, I heard the orders being yelled at the new transport. *Disembark, leave your belongings, they will be given to you later, form two columns, men to the right, women and children to the left, proceed to the gate.* I heard them distantly but clearly. I could not shut them out, and I realized that I never would. Always, deep down, I would keep hearing them.

God, I prayed, give me the power to control myself.

And He gave me that power. I wiped my face with my sleeves, emerged from under the table, and went back to work.

Our shift ended at nine that evening. We had worked three extra hours and finished sorting out the second transport, too. The tables were empty. Patches of garbage trailed on the ground, scummy little tornadoes stirred by the evening wind.

The SS and kapos were overtired and gave us a minimal checkup. We undressed and dressed again in under two minutes. They knew that many of us were smuggling things in our jackets and headkerchiefs, mostly canned foods and all the cigarettes we could find. But our supervisors' own pockets were bulging, too—theirs with watches and jewels and other high-

priced goods, in flagrant disregard of an edict issued by Heinrich Himmler, which stated: "We have the moral right toward
our people [the Germans] to annihilate this people [the Jews] . . .
but we have no right to take a single fur, a single watch, a
single cigarette. We don't want to be infected by the very germ
we are exterminating." But our guards were already infected.

On the way back to our block, I started to shiver. Had I
caught Ilona's fever? No—I had chills from fear. What if we
did not find Ilona in the block? What if her fever had been
discovered, and she had been sent to the *Revier*, the infirmary,
another place no one returned from?

But when we tramped into the block, we saw her from the
doorway, sitting on a lower bunk. She was pale, her forehead
was clammy, but her eyes were clear. In a voice just a little
stronger, she told us that her fever was gone, and tomorrow
she might be able to go back to work.

The Blockova appeared from nowhere and stood by our little
group, expecting her payment. Brana nodded, and we all huddled in a corner against the wall, where Brana presented her
with the price of Ilona's recovery: an enameled powder compact and a pair of earrings. The Blockova hid the earrings like
a prestidigitator. Now they were in her hand, the next moment
they had vanished I know not where. Maybe she had slipped
them into her mouth, for she did not utter a sound while she
took the other gift, the compact, opened it, and appeared awed
by its quality.

She peered into the little mirror, and my heart started
pounding again. How would she react to seeing her face, which
was ugly and hardened, in total contrast with the delicate
adornment device she was holding?

She stood still, looking at herself; then she did something
that surprised me. She closed her eyes.

Then she hid the compact in her jacket. Still without a
word, she walked away, and we looked at each other, saved.

THREE

$\mathscr{I}$ awoke from the past.

The workers' column was laboring ahead of us, the sun was beginning to stab through the fog again, and next to me, the keen-eyed Margit whispered: "There's something about those women. . . . I don't know. . . . They're so big. . . ."

"They wear heavy clothes from the night shift," ventured Tsilka.

"They're *men*!" Margit whispered.

"What are you talking about?" snapped Tsilka.

I needed a jolt from my memories. Gratefully, I scanned the column ahead. We had not been close to any men, apart from Germans and kapos, since we were deported. Yes, those prisoners trod too heavily and looked too tall and brawny. And not very feminine in the way they rolled their shoulders. Their voices too sounded rugged and low. . . .

"They *are* men," agreed Tsilka, stunned.

"I'm telling you!" Margit's whisper rippled back into the depth of our column.

The men had heard us tramping behind them. Now they were turning, squinting to see us through the fog.

"Look!" said Margit. "That one's walking backwards."

I saw a pink oval shape in the middle of the men's last row: a face. Then I made out a forehead, a nose, the glimmer of the eyes. The man faced forward again, said something to his comrades, and they all started laughing. "Quiet!" shouted a

German, and the men's laughter dropped in volume, but chuckles kept crackling here and there.

The fog was starting to break. Unexpectedly, we stepped into a stretch of sunlight; instantly, the men peered over their shoulders again. I saw their faces clearly—grungy, unkempt, but excited. About what? About us?

The man in the middle of the last row turned toward us again. He wore a beret and a civilian jacket of battered leather, with a stripe down its back—I had noticed the same stripe on the back of Schreiber Lorentz. So he was a prisoner. But he wore civilian clothes, just like Lorentz. The others wore those olive brown fatigues, Russian uniforms with their ranks torn off. The man with the beret came into focus, and it was the fullness of his features that struck me, a face that looked both unstarved and young. He seemed in his early twenties, with light-green eyes, a straight nose, and a night's growth of beard—even his beard was patchy and boyish. Big and broad-shouldered, he seemed so normal that for an instant he felt totally unreal. Dreamlike.

I glanced at the other men. They were skinny—the one in the leather jacket looked the best. But none had that fetid look of Auschwitz, that gaunt hairiness splotched with snot and drool of camp soup.

The young man in the beret called: *"Ahoy!"* Hello. In Czech, in a cheerful tone. He didn't seem to care about the guards. His glance fixed on me, swept away, and then returned to me. It seemed mocking at first. Then I realized that it was just friendly.

"Otkac ste prishli?" Where did you arrive from?

Margit poked me: "He's talking to you!"

I was too stunned to respond. All five of us no longer paid attention to the road. I heard Suri, serious Suri, starting to giggle. The one with the beret focused on me because I marched right behind him. His shovel looked light in the clutch of his hand, which was big and tanned.

"Where are you from?" he repeated, and the friendly flicker in his eyes grew warmer.

Margit poked me again: "He's talking to you! Answer him!"

"Czechoslovakia," I answered.

The flicker turned into a full glow. *"Ja sem s Prahy,"* I'm from Prague, he said cordially, as if we were at a party.

He whistled a few bars of *"Praha je krasna."* Prague is beautiful. I watched him, transfixed. He smiled again. "My name is Cestmir."

"Mirek," others in his row cried out, "Mirek." And they laughed, seeming fond of their friend Mirek, while he cocked his chin at me.

"What's your name?"

"Mine's Suri," said Suri from my right.

"What's *yours?*" he pressed me, ignoring Suri.

"I'm Leib," the man next to him called at Suri.

"I'm Jenda," said another man, toward Margit.

The whole men's row were tossing their names at my cousins.

From nearby there were more shouts of "Quiet!" without much effect. I heard the rumble of an engine: Mirek and his friends quickly faced ahead, and an armed motorcycle with two German soldiers in the saddles and a third behind the machine gun on the sidecar drove along our columns. They vanished ahead, and the men immediately turned toward us again.

Unperturbed, Mirek walked sideways now. "Don't be afraid," he said, grinning at me. "This is a good camp. What did you say your name was?"

"I didn't say my name. What's it to you?"

I didn't want to be rude, just to remove from my face the feel of his eyes, that friendly glow, which I expected to cool off as soon as a direct shaft of sunlight allowed him a better look at me.

Surprised, he raised his eyebrows. I stumbled and lost one of my clogs. I fell back through the row behind me, stuck my foot in that damn clog, and rushed ahead again.

Mirek was waiting for me to resurface. I must have looked scared and confused, a real idiot, and I resented that he was in such good shape. Except that his hands were scratched. I saw on the back of his palms a twisting of scars, some healed, some still healing. Then I saw a red triangle on his jacket— political prisoner. That explained why he looked so good, *politikers* were always spoiled. They ran the offices, they had "jobs under the roof," which were every Haeftling's dream. Jobs away from the rain, the cold, and the selectioners. I was surprised to see a politiker in a working column.

I looked down and saw his boot prints. Deeper than the other men's. He was heavier, stronger. His steps were wider, too.

"*Na shledanou.*" So long, he called at me as if in a final attempt, and then he marched off.

"Did you see his hair?" whispered Tsilka. She had color in her cheeks and walked sticking her chest out.

Yes, I had noticed that under his beret Mirek had rich brown hair.

Our column's front rows were abuzz. "Did you see how they looked at us?" someone gasped. "I think we're the first women here."

"They guessed what we are right away, not like the Germans. . . ."

"Hey! What's that Prague boy doing?"

The Prague boy, easy to spot because of his leather jacket, was slipping into the row in front of him. Another man drifted in his place, and turned and started peeking at us.

"He's letting the others have a look, too," whispered Manci.

"He's not selfish," chuckled Tsilka, as fresh pairs of eyes drifted back to appraise us.

"Wish we looked better," said Manci, and we choked and

wheezed with laughter. We had not laughed for such a long time.

The watchtowers and wire fences of camp Mühldorf became visible, with those HALT! plates warning that the wire was electrified. Drops of condensed fog dripped from the plates and from the wire. Heaps of fresh earth lay outside the fences, giving the impression that the camp enclosure had just been enlarged.

Here was the camp's main gate. The men entered it, and we followed them. Orders were shouted. The men stopped and marched in place, and we, propelled by the rows behind us, almost bumped into them. A soldier ran along the men's rows, counting them. Mirek turned, saw me behind him, and whispered, "Hey, we meet again."

The mist lifted, and the sunlight streamed down. On my right, I could see barracks that looked brand-new. On the left, the barracks were darker, older, and there were at least forty of them. They belonged to the men. The new ones were probably ours. Mirek and his friends were right in front of me. Back on the road, they had seemed unreal, illusory; but now, Mirek leaned closer to examine me, and I cursed the sunlight for exposing me in such detail. I could either look back at him or stare down at my muddy clogs. To hell with it. I looked at him.

I thought that I caught in his eyes just a touch of shock, a tinge of the same disbelieving disgust that the Germans had shown us this morning. I quashed the urge to say something rude to him again, so that he wouldn't pity me. Then I was left staring at him, at his attractive normalcy. He smiled at me. I did not respond. He smiled at me again. I still did not respond.

He said, in that slightly scoffing tone, "We'll have to wait here a bit; there's a little obstruction on the road." I suddenly became frightened and glanced right and left, trying to locate the nearest Germans. "Don't bother," he said, "we're in the coop already. They closed the main gate behind us. They're still making the beds in your rooms," he addressed all of us, and the other men laughed. "You know how good this camp is? It's a *pensionat*," he said mockingly, a bed-and-breakfast. "You want to hear the latest news from the front?"

"Mirek can tell you that," confirmed the one named Leib.

The other men laughed again, as if eager to hear a joke, while a few stood on tiptoe, staring rapidly right and left, to make sure that there were no Germans nearby. Mirek stepped almost inside our row, lowered his face toward us, and grinned conspiratorially.

"The news is great," he said. "Better than next week, much better than in two weeks, and infinitely better than in a month!" His friends stifled their laughter, while we listened with mouths open, too stunned to get the joke right away. Mirek continued: "As for the final victory, I heard two SS talking yesterday, when we went out defusing unexploded bombs. . . ." He smirked. "Lousy bombs. You'd think the Americans would send us their best stuff, but thirty percent of them don't explode. The poor SS have to run out all the time to defuse them, otherwise what'll happen to the innocent population?"

The men laughed. The ones in the row behind them laughed, too, peering at the women's column. Mirek went on, whispering not because he might be overheard, but for effect, "So one SS says: I have it from a high source, we're certainly going to lose the war. Wonderful, says the other, but *when?*"

I could not laugh. None of us laughed. Too afraid to believe that there was any truth to that kind of joke.

"You don't like Mirek's jokes?" Leib whispered to Suri.

Mirek studied Suri's face, then mine. "They're still a little shy," he said. "Don't worry, you'll be all right here, all you have to do is build a great big wall." He too stood on tiptoe and looked above the men's column, somewhere ahead. A German soldier ran along the men's column, counting the rows.

"Any time now," Mirek said. "Listen, girls. When you go in your gate, look straight ahead. Your barracks are right against the forest. Like a summer camp. All right?"

Someone shouted a command, and the men started regrouping. Mirek grabbed his shovel, which he had dropped by his feet.

The men's column hurtled forward. We marched to the right and passed through our compound's gate, whose frame of wood was brand-new. The electrified wire ran behind our barracks. A few hundred meters beyond it, straight and symmetrical, stood a pine forest. A bird soared from a high branch, crossing the sun.

"Is this Mirek's summer camp?" asked Tsilka ironically.

"It's not so bad," said Manci. "It looks clean."

It did look clean. The barracks' walls had a reddish hue, like the logs piled in Zhdenev's lumberyard, in which my father had owned a share. That color from home warmed my heart, and I thought giddily, Hey, I met a boy from Prague. Fancy meeting a boy from Prague here. Maybe it's a good sign.

I turned toward the men's side and winced. A few meters inside the men's wire, a man hanged from a crude gallows: a platform with two wood posts and a cross-beam. Two soldiers had just stepped up on the platform and were untying the hanged man's noose. The body fell stiffly onto the platform, and the soldiers threw him into a cart.

Look straight ahead, Mirek had said.

I faced forward. My cousins were still appraising the barracks.

I looked back again. The soldiers had gathered the noose and were wheeling the cart away, and the gallows looked very unmenacing now, like the goalposts of a soccer field.

There was a bustle of men by the older barracks, and I

strained my eyes to spot Mirek, but couldn't find him. He had wanted us to miss that scene, to shield us from our new home's first blow of reality, and had succeeded. Except for me. I had not been spared. But I had glimpsed Mirek's attempt to be kind.

I'll probably never meet him again, I mused. Then I touched Margit's arm, and when she looked at me, I managed to smile. She did not know why I smiled, but she smiled back.

Part 2

THE GOOD CAMP

*T*he soup of camp Mühldorf smelled good.

Given our state of starvation, the Kommandant had ordered that we should be fed right after showering and getting new clothes—a few hours before the regular dinnertime. The showers poured real water, cold and plentiful, but due to my undecided status, I was not allowed to shower. I waited outside the *Kleiderkammer*, the office that distributed the clothes, which adjoined the showers, until the girls started to emerge from it. They had been issued a mix of striped fatigues and captured Russian uniforms that did not smell of Cyclone B— they had been laundered, though poorly. Many were stained and still wet. Margit stepped out of the Kleiderkammer in a Russian uniform two sizes too big, which actually made her look better, fuller. "What do you think of this?" she chirped, and held under my nose . . . a chip of soap.

It looked rich and yellow like butter. It was industrial soap, yet I inhaled its scent as if it were the finest perfume, and thought, God, let all this not be the beginning of some cruel trick.

Each girl got a little piece of soap. Not knowing how long it would have to last them, they had used it sparingly, but even so, what a difference it had made. Wherever I looked, faces were bright, puckered with little rashes from scrubbing.

Then the cleaned-up transport was ordered into a big, still-unfinished barrack. The two Aufseherinnen stood by the door, supervising two male inmates who handed each girl her own soup bowl and spoon out of a big straw basket. The bowls were old and dented, but they had been washed. The spoons were plain and bent, but they, too, had been washed. One inmate who handed out bowls was about fourteen, tall and lanky, with thin arms; he had three inches of curly hair on his head, and looked at the girls with shy curiosity. The innocence of his face, the delicate fuzz on his upper lip reminded me so much of my brother Mechel that I tottered as I stepped toward him to get my bowl. Hulda noticed, and shouted me out of the line. No bowl or spoon for me until my fate was decided. "Hurry up, Mayer!" she snapped at the boy, because he had paused, wondering why I was excluded. Mayer quickly got back to work.

I was allowed to enter the barrack with the other girls. We sat on the bare floor. The two men walked among us with a big cauldron from which they sloppily ladled out the soup; I could tell by the way it poured that it had consistency.

Then an SS man entered the room, accompanied by Lorentz and another prisoner, bald, older, in striped fatigues. We all jumped to attention, but the SS man lazily gestured for us to sit and then introduced himself: *Untersturmführer* Rühl, Kommandant Eberle's deputy. Where did we come from? Lorentz whispered in his ear, and Ruehl nodded. Aha, Auschwitz. He'd served there himself, for two years. "*Ein sehr nettes Lager,*" a very neat camp, he commented. Now, we had been brought here to help in something vital for the quick conclusion of the war. Even though we were prisoners, we should consider ourselves witnesses to history, as our camp would engage in a construction on a scale never before achieved by man. Deputy Rühl had thick features, small eyes, and an uneducated manner of talking, but the casual way he addressed us was so unusual that the girls, sitting with their bowls (he had given them permission to keep eating), were mesmerized.

But, Rühl concluded, that didn't mean we were here on a

picnic. Had any of us noticed the gallows on the men's side? I could hear the change in the girls' breathing. That was for escape attempts, or—Rühl stared meaningfully at the girls—contacts between male and female inmates, which were strictly forbidden outside work situations. He raised a hand as if to preempt protests. I know *was schlangelt*, what wriggles inside each of you girls. You can't wait to check out the fellows on the other side of the wire. He laughed, pleased with his own astuteness. It's human nature—but not here, and not before we win the war, am I not right? After shower, soap, and soup, the girls, terrified that this feast might end, bleated: *Jaaa*, Herr Deputy Kommandant was absolutely right.

Halfway through his speech, the door opened, and who else walked in but the boy from Prague.

At first I did not recognize him, even though he wore the same clothes, minus his beret. He lugged a big toolbox with his left hand, while his right hand balanced a ladder on his shoulder. The difference was in his expression—he seemed as if he had forgotten how to smile. Stepping through our seated crowd, he crankily planted his ladder on the floor, right next to Rühl, forcing him to step aside. The room was lit by two naked bulbs hanging at the end of loose cords, but under the ceiling, dug into the beams, I saw electrical sockets that were still empty. Mirek climbed into the dusk of the unlit ceiling and screwed in a big bulb. Brightness flashed on, so cheerful that the girls let out a big *Aaahh!*

"See, you'll have it good here," Rühl concluded. "Just stay out of trouble." He exchanged a word with Lorentz, then marched out, and Hulda trotted out after him.

Even after the SS man had left, the girls still chewed fast, afraid that their food might be taken away from them. Some ate with their eyes on Mirek, watching him like a circus performer. He screwed in another big bulb: more light, more *aaaahhs*. Margit collected in her bowl a few spoonfuls of soup from each of my cousins, and brought it over to me, with a spoon. The soup was thick, made of crushed potatoes and strips of fat and tough meat. It was coarse, nutritious, bad, and exquisite all at once. Dipping into it, I remembered the feeling of eating with a spoon instead of with my mouth or with my fingers.

Margit darted her eyes at the light-producing acrobat. "That *Prazhan* (Praguer) is funny." I nodded, yes he was funny, and cut the thick potato mush with the spoon. I had not seen so much potato in a bowl since I was deported.

"He's a *politiker*," Margit said. "I wonder what they got him for."

I shrugged: Politiker or not, he was a prisoner like everyone else.

Hulda peered in and saw that the transport had finished eating. "All outside in the yard!" she commanded. The girls snapped to their feet, each nursing her personal bowl, and Margit picked up hers. I got up, too, and wanted to follow her, but Lorentz said: "You stay here, Davidovich." My body obeyed the command quicker than my mind.

Lorentz and the bald older man strode toward me. My heart started pounding; my breath grew quick and harsh. The older man was pudgy and stared out of dirty glasses whose broken bridge had been tied together with wire. The girls were still filing out; I spotted Tsilka and Suri and Manci streaking through the crowd after Margit. By the door, all four paused to peer back at me. Was I going to receive my sentence? Then they were sucked into the stream of exiting women.

Hulda walked up to Lorentz: "What are we going to do with her?"

"I don't know. Herr Kommandant left for Munich without giving me any instructions. Oh," he said, as if he had just remembered, "the other women should be issued blankets. Would you go tell the Kleiderkammer?"

Hulda pinched her lips before walking out again. Lorentz

glanced at Mirek. Mirek had gotten the last bulb in and was coming down his ladder.

"I don't have a decision about you yet," said Lorentz slowly, and looked at Mirek again. "But your case is serious. Explain to her why, Herr *Unterschreiber*," he told the man with broken glasses.

The Unterschreiber (subclerk) wore a criminal's green triangle. He issued a string of words, which I strained to understand, for they sounded very official: "Apart from breaking the safety regulations in Auschwitz, you are guilty of identity fraud toward the Reichsbahn." The Reichsbahn was the German National Railroad, a huge ministry employing close to one million people. "You were booked as a passenger, as passenger Dora Weiss. You cannot travel on the German Railroad as someone else . . ."

I opened my mouth. I would have laughed, but I could barely breathe. Was this man crazy?

Mirek folded his ladder and leaned it against the wall. He picked up his toolbox and walked over. "What's going on?" he asked in confident German. Pretty jovial now, he pointed at me. "Why is she still in her zebra suit?"

"I was just explaining," replied the subclerk. "She came here under someone else's name."

I was facing men who had power in this camp, but they were still prisoners. That emboldened me to speak: "I didn't know we came here as passengers. I thought we were Reich property."

"No, no," hastened the myopic bureaucrat. "Your ticket was issued as a passenger, at the third-class fare, which the Reich paid for you to travel on the German Railroad. The Railroad has a contract with the state to transport every passenger on a *Sonderzug* (special train) at the cost of four pfennig per kilometer of track. The Railroad is responsible for the condition and identity of the passengers, so it cannot default on its contract, and transport someone other than Dora Weiss."

Was I dreaming, having my fate debated in terms of the German railroad code?

I thought: the Reichsbahn had already defaulted on its contract. If it was responsible for the condition of its passengers, what about those girls who had died? Weren't they covered by the contract? What if I said that out loud? Would it make any difference? Lorentz looked at Mirek again, and that struck me as odd. Mirek asked practically, "Before you decide what to do with her, can you assign her to me? I need someone to help me turn on the lights in the barracks."

"Of course," Lorentz agreed quickly. "Take her back to the office when you're done."

Mirek nodded.

But the one with the broken glasses uttered a phlegmy protest: "Herr Schreiber . . . Herr Kommandant wouldn't allow anyone with undecided status to work on something sensitive . . ."

"What's sensitive, screwing in bulbs?" laughed Lorentz.

Hulda walked back in and headed for our group. Instantly, Mirek stopped grinning and acted tired and moody again. "I don't care. I need someone to help me right now. Are you coming?" He suddenly swung that toolbox toward me. I caught it, and grimaced. It was very heavy.

Sly little conniver, I thought to myself. He changed his act any time the Germans were around.

Lorentz turned to Hulda: "Are they giving out the blankets?" Hulda nodded. "Right. Then you can start assigning the bunks."

Hulda pinched her lips again. "Right," she muttered, and lashed her stick at the wall, just to vent. Mirek grabbed the ladder and hauled it on his shoulder; without one look back, he stepped out of the barrack.

I had no choice but to follow, gritting my teeth from the weight of the toolbox. But Mirek and Lorentz had managed to keep Hulda out of the room while my situation was being discussed—and maybe that meant something. These men might help me, out of pure pity, of course, for I had nothing to bribe them with. . . . A tiny fibril of hope fought for space inside my chest.

The barracks were long rectangular boxes, with double bunks set perpendicular to the long walls, twelve on either side. There was an aisle down the middle, and three bare bulbs hung right above it, at regular intervals. An extra bunk was set against the back wall, next to a cement stove with a tin stovepipe. No doubt, the extra bunk would be occupied by the Blockova, since this would be the room's warmest spot.

We were in Barrack 2. Mirek was up on the ladder, which he had ordered me to hold steady, and I passed him the bulbs, which he screwed into their fittings. This was the last bulb. I reached for the switch and flicked it on. The bulbs glowed faultlessly.

Mirek came down and folded the ladder. I grabbed the box, and we exited past a tight group of girls who, now that the barrack was ready for habitation, started to file in. Fifty girls to a barrack. The sticks supervising their entrance belonged to Hulda and to an older Aufseherin, Gudrun. Mirek had already advised me not to be afraid of Gudrun, who was senior to Hulda, and slow and reasonable. Hulda was bad, though. She had only joined the SS two months before, and felt that she had missed the fun. This was important survival information, and I absorbed it greedily.

The girls had been issued blankets. Gray, coarse, ugly—yet *real* blankets. None of us had blankets in Auschwitz.

I followed Mirek the light-giver into Barrack 3, and he closed the door after us. I positioned the ladder and secured the box on the sixth step, so I could easily take out the bulbs and hand them to him. He went up, making the steps moan under his weight.

We would be alone for a few minutes. I cleared my throat: "That man they hanged, did he try to escape?"

Mirek had indeed tried to spare us that scene, because he hesitated now, then grunted, forcing a bulb into a misshapen fitting. "Yeah. A Greek boy. He wasn't so smart: he took off from the work site when a guard fell asleep. But there's a mobile SS unit in Mühldorf village. Rühl called them, and they chased him." He chuckled glumly. "With dogs and motorcycles, it still took them two days to catch him."

"Did he know he had no chance?"

"You never know your chances till you try."

He tightened the bulb, came down, and faced me in that narrow space between the bunks. He was sweating, but his sweat smelled good compared to the body reeks I had gotten used to.

"That old clown the subclerk is harmless," he whispered. "He worked for the railroad and was involved in some embezzlement. Lorentz is tough, but I can work on him." I stopped breathing. Was he offering to work on Lorentz *on my behalf?* "The bastard is Rühl. We had some hail two weeks ago, a lot of boys slipped and broke an ankle or a leg . . ." He gestured me to the switch. I stepped and turned the bulb on, and shaded my eyes from its brilliance. "Guess what Rühl said? That would've never happened in Auschwitz. We would've spread some nice ashes on the footpaths, and no one would have slipped."

Nice ashes. Nice human ashes. But I was too elated to care about Rühl's callousness—these men might help me! I walked back to Mirek. "What do you eat?" I blurted. I had wanted to ask him that since I had first seen him.

"I go out with the Germans after the air raids, to defuse the unexploded bombs or to fix the downed wires. So I eat what they eat." I pictured fat German sausages, nicely browned piles of roasted cabbage, and I swallowed even though I had just gulped that soup.

"I was in Auschwitz, too," he added. "I was sentenced in Dresden Prison and sent to Auschwitz, but then I was put in a transport of technicians to go to Warsaw and help clean up the ghetto."

"The ghetto?"

"There was an armed uprising in the Warsaw ghetto. The Germans put it down."

"An uprising . . . by Jews?"

He nodded.

I remembered my task and moved the ladder. Mirek went up to fit in the last bulb. I had never heard of an uprising by Jews against Germans, not anywhere.

I asked hoarsely, "When was that?"

"In April '43."

I flipped the switch on again. All three bulbs glowed nicely. I left them on and opened the door for the girls to come in.

Barrack 4.

Silently, I sorted out my thoughts. This was the first time I had heard of Jews taking weapons in their hands and using them. Was Mirek telling the truth? It seemed impossible to believe.

I asked him if he had been shipped back to Auschwitz after cleaning the ghetto. He said no, he had been held in Warsaw's Pawiak Prison, then sent to Dachau—"for the second time," he inserted casually—then here. I asked why he was arrested, and he replied that he had fought in the Czech *podzemny* (underground). I did not know that the Czechs had an underground, but I started to feel resentful—because I did not believe him. He had really survived that many camps and prisons? Meanwhile, his feet, in sturdy work boots with thick soles and leather pull-straps on the sides, kept moving up and down past me. Each time he stepped down again, we shared the narrow space for a few seconds; then I moved the ladder.

"So, you are Czech?" I asked.

"Yes."

"*Czech* Czech?"

He laughed. "How many kinds are there?" His eyes had regained that warmth that I found so hard to take while he talked to me on the road, walking backwards. "Yes I'm Czech, completely. Cestmir Vencera, but they all call me Mirek. *Elektrotechniker* by profession." I opened my mouth to introduce myself, but he grinned. "I know your name now. Your real name."

"Who told you?"

"The Schreiber." He grabbed both the ladder and the toolbox, as if signaling compassion for my plight. When had he talked to the Schreiber about me, and why?

The curled-up blazing wires inside the bulbs reflected directly on Mirek's eyes, making the green of his irises a soft heather. I gave up trying to avoid them. I felt too weak, too starved for a little compassion, and on top of that, he looked so pleasant—strong without being hard, and emanating a lack of fear whose secret I couldn't pierce. Even if you're not Jewish, Mr. Mirek Underground, you cannot feel entirely safe here, you cannot be above making a fatal mistake. But I had no time to ask the secret of his fearlessness. We were done, and I heard the voices of the fretting girls outside.

The older Aufseherin, Gudrun, opened the door. A throng of girls holding their rolled-up blankets trooped in, and a voice hissed in my ear: "Is the *shidach* over?"

I spun around and faced someone I knew and never liked: Ida Blumenreich, the daughter of a pharmacist from Munkács, who had done a year of medical school in Prague, found it too challenging, returned to Munkács, and started a kind of political salon—her parents had money and satisfied her every whim. She made herself the local hostess for the meetings of the *Ha-Shomer Ha-tzair*, the "Young Guard," a Socialist Zionist organization that sent activists to our boondocks to recruit people for emigration to Palestine. Young men suntanned from driving tractors on some *moshav* in Galilee—with a rifle slung on a peg behind the driver's seat—plowing for a Jewish nation that was slow in returning to Israel, even though every Pesach we toasted, "Next year in Jerusalem." Those activists so completely outshone our stooped and pale yeshiva students that we shtetl girls flocked to Munkács to check out the Ha-Shomer at Ida's lemonade socials. They wore trousers and sweaters, never suits and ties, and however much they washed their hands, dirt from the Holy Land stayed under their fingernails. We didn't care.

The one who cared was the Munkácser Rebbe, the region's spiritual leader. Afraid that he might lose his flock to the Ha-Shomer, he thundered against them in the temple. Were those true Jews, who regarded the Arabs as fellow workers and went to the beach on Saturday instead of davening in shul? Was a Jewish Palestine even conceivable before the arrival of the Messiah? Here was the Jewish country, right where we were, living in awe of the High Being! As long as we honored the Torah and the Shabbat, God would shield us *against anyone*. (How wrong he was, he and most rabbis in the area—anxious to keep their congregations, they advised us to stay right in the path of the hurricane.) Meanwhile, we girls flocked to Ida's. A gramophone played at her gatherings, tangos and foxtrots shook the floor of the Blumenreichs' drawing room, and rumor had it that Ida, who was tall, big-boned, and bold, had flings with those boys, because her talk was now as radical as theirs. . . .

Ida was still tall and big-boned, and had managed to retain some of her weight even in Auschwitz. She looked at Mirek, then at me, and smirked.

On to Barrack 6.

Barrack 6 was the last one. The seventh, under construction, was still missing its roof.

Mirek placed the ladder under the first empty socket. "Get up there," he said suddenly. He kept rubbing his eyes. He had told me that after the end of his night shift he had slept only one hour before being called to help finish the women's compound.

He wanted me to screw in these bulbs. I slipped off my wooden clogs and climbed up barefoot. Right under the roof, I faced an air vent.

"What do you see?" he asked me.

Peering through the air vent, I saw the wire fence separating the women's compound from the men's. I saw the access road into the camp, the watchtower rising by the main gate, and the gallows.

Mirek's hand touched mine as he passed me a bulb. I started, and almost dropped it.

"Easy," he said.

I screwed in the bulb and stepped down. He didn't move aside. "After the evening roll call, come to that wire fence," he said. "About two hundred meters from the gallows, there is a patch of tall grass. Crawl across it, to the fence. I'll wait for you on the other side."

The roof of my mouth got so dry that I licked at it desperately. "Why?"

"We'll talk about how to keep you here. I know what everyone wants in this camp." There was a boastful ring in his voice.

I was ready to cling to a straw, but that boastfulness immediately raised my defenses. Wait just a minute. I was a dumb *shtetl meidlech* when I was deported, but that was a lifetime ago. I survived Auschwitz. I stood eye to eye with the Doctor. You seem nice, you well-fed little partisan, but are you trying to sell me cheap hope?

I whispered sarcastically, "Thanks for offering to use your influence, but maybe the Kommandant already phoned Auschwitz and hasn't told the Schreiber. . . . I may be sent under escort to the train station tomorrow—"

"What day is this?" he cut me off.

What day? I had lost count.

"Friday," he said impatiently. "Eberle is in Munich with his wife, and won't return till Monday morning. Until then, no one is going to send you anywhere. You think it's so easy to send back *one* prisoner? They can't give you a special train."

That sounded credible.

"After the evening roll call, you'll be free to go out in the yard. Just walk to that last barrack; then start toward the fence. I'll be there. I can't promise anything, but if you tell me your whole story, I'll get an idea about what can be done."

"But Rühl said contacts with males are strictly forbidden."

"What contacts? I'll be on my side and you on yours."

I'd gone through the cycle of fright, hope, and renewed fright so fast that I arrived at hope again, exhausted and breathless.

"All right." I nodded, my cheeks flushed.

He stood in front of me, smiling. "When we get out of here, I'll take you to Gudrun, and she'll take you to the showers. Don't be afraid, they're really showers."

"How do you know Gudrun will do that?"

"Trust me." He started up the ladder. "Blanka, right? If you're afraid, you don't have to come."

udrun escorted me to the shower building, holding her stick under one arm and a folded set of fatigues under the other. She had given me a piece of soap. I clutched it as if it were the evidence that I would survive this.

Still, when I stepped into the shower room, I was shaking. To control myself, I clenched my teeth and held my arms tightly to my sides. Behind me was the stick of the Aufseherin, and the Aufseherin herself, who had a furrowed face and seemed slightly cross-eyed.

The room was entirely empty. I looked at the shower stalls, long partitions of plywood, unpainted, mapped with big splatters of wetness. The showerheads were of the familiar shape: a pipe curled downward, affixed with a flat sprinkler face, round like a clock's. "*Kannst schon duschen,*" you can start washing, urged Gudrun, not understanding why I was hesitating. She *was* cross-eyed, though not repulsively. "Make clean after," she added, reducing speech to a few obvious words, so as not to strain my non-Aryan's comprehension. Little did she know that I had taken German in the Czech school, and besides, German and Yiddish are really twin languages. Even their differences are regularized and predictable, consisting mostly of mutations of the vowels: *shein* in Yiddish, instead of *schoen*, *ois* instead of *aus*. Over time and during the Jews' eastward wandering, Yiddish was enriched with many Hebrew and Slavic words whose meaning eluded non-Jews, but still, our mother tongue was formed here, in this land that was now destroying us.

Gudrun dropped my new fatigues on the floor. "Report to Barrack Six after you wash." She dropped on the fatigues a towel that had been laundered so often, its ends were shredded. A rag. But a clean rag, my very own. Then she left me alone, unsupervised, in the women's shower room.

Report to Barrack 6? What else could that mean but that I would sleep here tonight?

I undressed, walked to the closest shower, looked up at that clocklike face, and still wondered if it might sprinkle death instead of water. Then I grabbed the hot and cold faucets. As if struggling with a pair of steel hands, I turned them on. A cool rain hit me. I closed my eyes.

I remained like that for a few instants. The water did not get warmer, but soon I felt that it was just the right temperature. Maybe my body was hot—from that gulped food that had activated my circulation, from talking to Mirek, from hope.

I started to soap my body.

The caress of the water made me think of home. I almost heard our little river, the Zhdenevka, as it flowed between shores rich with wild grass. A narrow arm of the river entered the pool of our ritual bath, the *mikva*, where I first washed in a regular bathtub, instead of the one we used at home, which was a simple wooden cask.

Water, cleanness. The past.

Our shames's wife, Sura Beila Stern, had a soft spot for me because she missed her children, now grown. I liked her, too, and called her my second grandmother. After I turned thirteen, Sura Beila told me that I could take baths at the mikva. Not in the ritual pool, but in one of the tubs, which were made of copper and sat on turned-out feet somewhat amphibian in shape. I took a bath there every week, usually on Thursday. In a shtetl, a hot bath that you didn't have to boil water for was a luxury.

Not being married, I never dunked in the ritual pool: I had as yet no need to purify myself for a husband after the two weeks of menstrual uncleanliness. (Not one, but *two*. The first week covered the period itself. Then, for another week, impurity lingered in a woman's body because, with the expulsion of an unfertilized egg, something had died in that woman—an unbegotten child, a potential of life. Even the death of an unfertilized egg was unclean, as all death is, and had to be mourned seven days, like a real human being.)

The mikva's brick building, small, square, with narrow windows always obscured by curtains of cotton, so that the children passing in the street would not glimpse the bathers inside, sat practically astraddle our little river. Its pool had two openings, one for the river water to flow in, another to flow out. Under the raised sides on which the wives sat after dunking were the heaters that warmed up the river's flow. The wives first took a bath in one of the copper tubs; then they descended the tiled steps into the pool and dunked, making sure, as was prescribed, that the water completely covered their heads. Sura Beila, our fertility priestess, watched from the top step, and when a female's face got completely immersed in that steamy water, Sura Beila raised her arms, smiled, and murmured approvingly: kosher, kosher . . .

The uncleanliness had been purified. The wife was touchable again, kissable and beddable. She was awaited with desire at home, for not to have something means to value it fully, and for two weeks wife and husband had not touched, let alone had sex. The master bedroom, if the couple had any social standing, contained not one but two beds—in order to maintain purity. We children never wondered in which bed we had been conceived. We were not curious. There was little prurience in a way of life that was so devoted to marriage.

After dunking, the women sat on the steps and on the pool's

raised sides, drying themselves off and chatting. Although they talked only of day-to-day matters, there was a strong sensualism in the scene, in the preparation for another two weeks of fruitfulness—witness how many shtetl families had throngs of kids. Once in a while, I saw a just-married bride, not pregnant yet. Dark-haired, as were most girls in our parts, round-faced, naive—that naivete was part of the propriety expected of a young wife. But I could see through it the glow of her new experience. The young bride bathed hastily and went home quickly instead of lingering by the pool.

Thus, contrary to what one might believe of rural, religion-bound Jews, sex was alive and well in Zhdenev. The women coming to the mikva were always in between giving birth and becoming pregnant again. Our mikva had a lot to do with keeping marriages going. In fact, the mikva was so important to Jewish life that Jews could not live in a place without one. They could live even without a shul, and were allowed to sell a shul to finance the building of a mikva. But without a mikva, Jewish marriage, and thus life, was impossible. And its water had to come only from a natural spring or river.

As for the way my parents behaved during the two weeks of ripeness, there was no way to guess what was happening in their bedroom. They were utterly silent and discreet. But during the weeks of abstinence, there was a gentleness between them that bonded them as much as sleeping together. My father was more attentive about mother's health, and he helped more with her chores. And while they could not even hold hands—on "clean" evenings they often sat hand in hand at the kitchen table or on the porch—I was often surprised by a look they exchanged, which was not the look of raging passion, but the peaceful signaling, "I miss you."

But if the day was a clean day, they made love to each other in one of the two parental beds. And they begat. Chaim Ye-huda, my father, and Faiga, my mother, begat three sons, Leizer, Naphtulah (nicknamed Pepo), and Henju. Then me,

Chaia Binah, the eldest daughter (Blanka was my official name on my Czech birth certificate), then another son, Mechel, and two more girls, Rivka and Manci. In all of Subcarpathia, thousands of Jewish children were begotten the same way, in one of the two beds.

"It's a good deed, a mitzvah, to be married," Sura Beila taught me.

"And it's a mitzvah to have sex on Shabbat," the mikva women chuckled to me, when I was old enough for the yarn to start piling up in my dowry chest.

But when I turned eighteen, Sura Beila suddenly banned me from the place.

"Starting next week, you bathe at home again," she ruled. "You come back here when you are a wife."

I accepted, recognizing in that decision that I was a step closer to womanhood. I walked out with my hair still wet, with my towel in a bag held under my arm, and took a mature look at the place. It was an unassuming building. The fence around it was sagging, the yard before it was overgrown, the bricks in the walls had chipped. But humble as it was, *it*, not the shul, was the core of our shtetl. The shul was the spiritual heart. But the mikva was the regulator of our most important desires: uniting with other humans.

SIX

*S*oftness of the shtetl, like a ripe womb. Soft hope. Soft power.

Forgiveness . . .

One day, if I survived, I might forgive God.

But would I forgive myself?

I had lost my sense of time. I had dreamed awake.

I had a vague sensation of physical pain, though no part of me ached just now. It was a pain that started in my womb, a womb that might never be impregnated. I no longer felt the passage of time; I no longer cared about being punished. Standing under the shower, I touched my thinned womb and wanted desperately to be aroused, to be filled. I had never known desire, other than as that magic haze lifting from the mikva's pool.

But I was ripe in my soul. I had been ripe in my soul a long time.

I turned off the taps and stepped out of the shower. Running the water for so long, I had made a big puddle on the floor. I picked up the coarse towel that Gudrun had left for me, dried myself, savoring the feel of a clean cloth on clean skin, then got down on my knees and started wiping the floor. The towel grew soaked in seconds. I wrung it out into the shower drain, and as I started mopping again, I noticed my toes, my feet. They looked pink, as if I had shed a skin.

Maybe you'll tell me your whole story, Mirek had said.

What a normal request! I pictured meeting him in ordinary circumstances, through friends, or at a party. Chatting with him with the total freedom of choosing what to mention, what not to mention. The wonderful freedom of not being known by a stranger, especially a stranger I might like. The right to my own secrets.

But I realized that I had no secrets.

Even though that Prague boy knew nothing about me, my extreme situation made it such that he could see through me and probably had already. I had lost my kin, my place in the world, my past. Mirek had secrets. He was not slated to die. He had the secrets of his unknown future.

I unfolded my new fatigues, a Russian infantry jacket and pants. Clean, dry, lumpy from not being pressed. I pulled them on, quickly, for I was late for a *randke*, as we called a date in Yiddish. I opened my mouth and declared to the walls: *Haint bai nacht, Ich randkeve mich mit . . . Cestmir.* Today at nightfall, I'm meeting Cestmir. And I waited for the silence to break. But it did not.

I felt that I was finally utterly and truly deranged.

Cestmir.

Could he at least not have such a *goyische* name? *Cest-mir.* "Peaceful purity," in Czech. Czechs loved compound names like Cestmir, Jaromir, Vladimir. Let's settle for Mirek—it's less full of incense and the ringing of church bells. There were Jewish boys called Mirek. No. No, this was all wrong. Chaia Binah Davidovich, shtetl maiden, what the hell did you say you were going to do? Sneak away to the wire, to meet the *camp electrician?* Thank God for that wire, it'll hold back your insanity.

I stepped into my clogs, still muddy and smelly from my feet, which I had not washed for days before this shower. Still Auschwitz-imprinted, which brought back reality. I would meet Mirek for no reason but to help my situation, and he would gain nothing by it. Besides, he'd never be interested. Had I forgotten what I looked like?

There was a closed window by the door. The overhead light and the night behind the glass pane turned it into a mirror. Not a very clear one, but still . . .

I looked in that makeshift mirror.

I saw a stranger.

In Auschwitz, I had never looked at my reflection in anything, not even in the water puddling between the barracks. I was too afraid to find out what I was turning into. I glanced at my clean hands—their palms were thinned, scratched, and callused (despite all the housework, I had never had calluses in Zhdenev), and my nails were short and cracked, yet I recognized them as my hands. But, when I looked at my face . . . What did they do to my face?

My eyebrows and eyelashes were intact. They alone I recognized. But *my eyes*, what was wrong with them? What was that distrust, that fear, settled inside them, grown hard, like an opaque matte? I smiled at myself. My eyes remain fixed and dim. I leaned into the glass and peered into the depth of my irises, with a mute plea, Come back, you, the one I remember! I was always slender, but I was lively, with light brown hair sweeping a lean forehead, with fresh cheeks, with a nicely drawn mouth . . . Where was that girl? They had killed her, and substituted this stony-faced convict. I had never mourned for my parents or my sisters, so how could I mourn for myself? I just stared, tearlessly.

Ironically, the Russian military jacket, too big, made me look more female. The jacket's breast pockets added size to my breasts. The trousers widened my hips. My gender was a little more obvious. Otherwise, I looked awful.

I rubbed two fingers on my cake of soap and brushed my teeth with my fingertips, scouring as hard as I could. Then I rinsed my mouth.

The entrance door opened, and Margit ran inside, uttering a stream of talk. "I looked for you everywhere come the roll call is in five minutes that Aufseherin bitch separated us I'm in Barrack Five Suri is in One Tzilka in Three but we'll find girls to switch with—" She drew a breath. "And you?"

"I was told I'm in Six."

"This camp's not like the others. You'll see." She reopened the door.

We stepped out, and there was a loud crack, like that of a big gun. And then more cracks. Margit pushed herself against me. Not like the others? Death and brutality, loud and hard-hitting, were here. In the yard, the women from our transport stood frozen, facing the wire fence. In the men's compound, a light beam flooded about a dozen men cornered by a tall kapo cracking a bullwhip. The men, dark-haired, with burning eyes, stood massed together as if pledged to suffer the whip together. The kapo, standing over six feet, athletic, with a face so red that it looked like a balloon ready to burst, flogged their legs below their knees. Then he turned toward the fence and toward us.

He was carbuncled all over his face, and had a mouth like a red bivalved shell, which shouted at us, in accented German. "Get back, you won't learn nothing from these men—nothing, nix! They don't know about your parents or brothers, they are Greeks! You speak Greek?" he yelled at the closest stunned woman, who happened to be my cousin Manci.

Hypnotized, she answered plaintively: No, of course not.

"I am Maurice," he clamored, as if his name were a title. "I'm here to keep things in order. Men with men, women with women!" He cracked the whip at the wire, making it utter a long hum. "Everyone, *weitermachen!*" Back to your chores!

The Greek men's eyes devoured Maurice. They retreated into the dark, moving together like a multilegged creature. The red-faced kapo followed them. The light beam was turned off.

In the sudden silence, Manci breathed, "They crawled up to

the fence to look at us . . . couldn't guess what language they were speaking. . . . It was like nothing from our parts."

A minute passed, or perhaps more. Then Gudrun climbed the steps to the nearest barrack, stood tall on the top step, and yelled. Roll call. We would have one and a half hours of free time before lights out. Dismissed.

SEVEN

*N*ow the transport was clustered by their barracks' stoops. Those with enough energy walked around looking for relatives or friends, and my cousins rushed to find other girls to exchange barracks with. I paced back and forth, getting a little farther from the barracks each time, noticing how perfectly my fatigues blended into the night. The sky was overcast, another stroke of luck.

I stepped past the last barracks. I could see the main gate.

Suddenly, I faced that patch of tall grass indicated by Mirek.

A few hundred yards ahead was another watchtower. But its light was aimed outward, toward the road. Probably to provide orientation for late-arriving trucks.

I dived into the grass. It was almost waist-high and smelled like the grass at home.

I started crawling. The wire was somewhere ahead, but I couldn't see it; I was blinded by the grass. My heart beat fast from the crawl—just from the crawl, I told myself. Was this like anything I'd done before? I was meeting a stranger, defying camp regulations, and wondering whether I looked less repellent in my new fatigues and after showering.

I bumped hard into the fence. Dizzy, I stood up, passed my fingers over the crown of my head, and found it sticky with blood. I had cut myself on the spiky mesh of the wire. I spat on my fingers and applied that natural ointment to the cut;

then I wiped my forehead with my sleeve. Keeping an eye out the entire time, I saw only motionless darkness on the other side of the fence.

Mirek had said: Right after the roll call.

He was late.

If I turned left, I saw the end of our compound, marked by the electrified wire, the gallows, and the German guards' quarters, a low building with lit windows. In the distance, I saw a vague reflection of lights on low clouds. Probably Mühldorf. That Greek man, what did he think as the noose choked him, what did he remember? His sunny Greece? Or was his mind dull with fear? I stared at the guards' quarters and made out silhouettes moving across the windows, soldiers who had finished their shifts. I stared at the big watchtower—soldiers loomed in the lookout at its top. I stared at what I could see of this enemy land and screamed silently: You have taken my face from me, my face, my face! You have taken the freshness of my eyes, the beauty of my hair and my flesh, and the purity of my thoughts! You have taken my parents and my sisters and ground them into atoms of smoke! You have put your vile breath on my world, even my sky you have taken away, even the God that was mine you have tried to make into a Haeftling. But *that* you have not managed, and He has not abandoned me. He is here, under my feet, in this earth, suffering with me and with all of us! You have desecrated all humans by showing your face to the world, proud in its crass bestiality. But . . . You have not conquered my soul.

You have not conquered my soul.

It will be mine to the end. And if I don't make it, I still *know* that from this earth, which never belongs to just one race or nation, will rise a revulsion of your crimes that will crush your weapons, flatten your bunkers and forts, and defeat you and humiliate you. Even if you revive, you will be distrusted, you will be known, and your injustice will be branded on your great-grandchildren, like a curse. The curse of the innocent dead. You will not escape, and you will have no peace. So says my soul.

My knees gave in. I crumpled down by the wire fence.

Oh, how good it was to let out hate, hate born from being hated. My hate will nurse and inspire me. And if I am to feel love again, I shall do so only through my choice. I will not be bought with one cake of soap, one clean set of clothes, one less beating. If I survive, I will exact the price that I deserve, for everything that I suffered.

I leaned my body against the fence. Though I had often thought of running the electrified wire (480 volts of power: boils the blood in the veins and cremates the brain in the skull), I was glad that this wire was free of deadly power. I was alive, and it was not over. I would find my army. It would not be of Jews only. It would be of every good breed that God put on earth. It would be of the nations.

I cried. Terrified that I might be heard, I grabbed the collar of my jacket with my teeth and bit into it.

I saw someone moving through the tall grass on the other side of the wire. He was slinking through it much more skilfully than I had. He inched above it just once, to indicate his position to me, and I recognized his hair and the gleam of his eyes. Then he burrowed again and reappeared so close his eyes fitted two openings in the wire, and his mouth another opening.

"Hey," he whispered.

The lower part of his face emanated a subtle glow. He had shaved.

EIGHT

I could not stop crying. I had cried in the shower. It had not been enough. I was streaming, quietly, for all those weeks and months of not mourning.

I guessed from the changing outline of Mirek's lips that he was preparing to ask, What happened? Then he was silent. He gave me time to gather myself. "It's good," he muttered. "Crying eases the heart. Long time?"

I nodded. Yes, I was crying again after a long time.

"You the only one left?"

He did not have to ask more. I replied, thick with tears, "I don't know. . . . My brothers were sent to work camps in Hungary. . . . Maybe they're still alive. . . ."

"You," he whispered, "*you* are alive. That's the main thing."

I found his words hard, almost sacrilegious. And yet, they sounded right. What else was there to say? If I decided to live, then I was the one who mattered.

Mirek seemed nervous. He cast glances over his shoulder, toward the Germans' compound, then toward the men's barracks.

"Follow me," he said. He pointed to the camp's outer boundary, the electrified fence, and then sank in the grass. I started crawling on my side, trying to follow his rustling sounds. He was always ahead of me; he was an ace at crawling.

The grass opened—on either side of the fence there was a strip of dirt, like a bare little island crossed by the wire. Around it, the grass was waist-high and dark, but inside it there was some visibility, maybe reflected from the nearest tower. As I reached it, panting, with grass stuck to my face, Mirek was already hunkering down on his side. "Here we'll be safe," he whispered.

Right. The other wire, the deadly one, almost leaned over us.

"I'm sorry I'm late," he said almost socially, "but I took care of Lorentz. He's going to write a Dora Weiss among the girls who died on the train, and add a Blanka Davidovich to the transport list. Rühl is asking a little more, but I'll get him what he wants." He looked up, appraising the dark skies. "The Americans might bomb tonight, that would be good for you. After an air raid, whole walls fall, the houses are open, you can take anything. Rühl wants a big expensive radio."

So, a radio was Rühl's fee for my staying in this camp.

I was curious to know what I was worth. "What does Lorentz want?"

"A Swiss watch. Or a good Walther pistol. Nothing. Easy to find."

"A *pistol?*"

Were the rules here utterly different? Was this another time, another war?

But Mirek explained logically, "He'll hide it so no one can find it, he knows every hole in this camp. When we get liberated, the prisoners will tear to pieces anyone who was a kapo, or even a Schreiber. Lorentz doesn't plan to die."

I remembered the Schreiber's hard eyes and felt that wrath deep inside me, in my womb. "Doesn't he deserve to die?"

"Don't you deserve to live? He's going to help you." He paused. "I shouldn't have told you that. . . ."

"It's all right."

"Do I scare you?"

"A little . . ."

"Everyone who comes from Auschwitz is dead scared. Doesn't trust anyone or anything."

I cleared my voice. "I trust you. . . . What do you usually do with those things, sell them?"

His lips tightened. "I'm not a black marketeer. I go into buildings to defuse bombs, that's why I'm out of the camp all the time. Munich gets three, four air raids a week. Mühldorf is beginning to get the same treatment." He looked offended and handsome. "If it wasn't for the bombs, the SS would strip the houses themselves. But they stay two hundred yards behind me; they don't want to get hurt."

"You work with the SS?"

"They run everything. And if I want to be able to help a friend, I have to give them the best stuff, you understand?"

I suddenly felt that he was very alone, forced to make all his decisions by himself, to weigh all the risks by himself.

I rushed to reassure him. "Of course I understand, I worked in a sorting center, in Auschwitz . . . We took things from the dead. . . ." I tried to laugh and managed an awkward cluck. "Why don't you leave those bombs undefused? If they blow up later, who cares?"

"They'll blow up and kill civilians."

"So? They're Germans." It was them or us, wasn't that clear?

But Mirek exhaled tiredly, then let himself slouch to the ground, as if lacking the energy to deal with that issue. "I don't want to do that. That's what *they* do, Blanka. They're the ones who kill civilians, women, babies. That's why they'll lose the war." I waited, frozen, and he peered at me with curiosity: "You know what's happening." I had no idea what he was talking about. "The Americans landed in France on June sixth."

I heard what Mirek said.

Inside my chest, I felt the squeeze of fear. I had seen

Germany from the train, I had seen its disarray, but also its defiance, its mad shrieks for Total War. They'd never let anyone invade them; Mirek was telling me good lies. Boldly elaborate ones—in a Normandy landing, the Allies had used thousands of ships supported by thousands of planes. The *Luftwaffe* could throw into the battle only a few hundred planes. In a day or two, the Allies would be in Paris—which was why that brute Maurice was exploding. France was being liberated, and Maurice was stuck here, on the wrong side of the war. If the Greeks didn't tear him up, the Frenchmen would. There were Frenchmen here, Mirek informed me, POWs. And Russian and Italian POWs. A sprinkling of Czech and German politikers. And thousands of Dutch, Hungarian, and Greek Jews.

Good lies were the best that a stronger prisoner could offer, to alleviate the suffering of a weaker one. They were what one needed to hear: There are no *Selektions* here. I'm sure your family survived. The Russians just beat the life out of the Germans at a place called Stalingrad. The radio for deputy Rühl, the pistol for Schreiber Lorentz, were they also good lies?

I wanted so badly to trust him. Staring at him, I suddenly lost myself in his eyes. I struggled to pull myself away. I could have drowned in his eyes.

"If you don't believe me," he said, "go back to the barracks now. You'll still find Gudrun there. Ask her about me, ask her who runs the camp's bomb squad. She'll tell you it's me—it's no secret. She won't hit you if you ask her. Go." He moved as if to plunge back into the grass, and I jumped and clutched the wire.

"Mirek . . ."

He stopped.

"I want to believe you," I said.

"Then believe me, Blanka."

"All right."

When he said my name, I'd felt a tingle. I had a name, I had stopped being a number.

But I was shaking. I had seen another side of him; he could be hot-tempered. But I excused him; he was nervous to be here with me. Or scared of what lay ahead, the next air raid.

Humbly, I asked him if he was frightened when he defused bombs.

"Oh, no," he said, "that's nothing. You just cut two wires. I learned that in Prague, when I was studying at the Electrotechnical Institute. In Warsaw after the ghetto uprising, *there* I was scared. I led a search team, and they lowered us with ropes into the ghetto sewer, to look for weapons and gold. Always, they think the Jews have gold," he snickered sarcastically. "But I did find gold. Coins, jewelry, unexploded grenades, and bodies . . . swimming in . . . you know. When we were pulled back up, guess who waited for us, to see what we found? An SS *Obersturmführer* sent by . . ." He paused for effect. "Eichmann himself."

I had no idea who Eichmann was. But he sounded like someone important, and I didn't want to reveal my ignorance. To keep from drowning in Mirek's eyes again, I inspected his chin and noticed that it was adorned with a little cleft.

"Oh, I forgot," he said. He scooped inside a pocket and produced two dark, round objects. I couldn't tell what they were. He grabbed the base of the wire right where it seemed planted firmly in the earth, and yanked it up. A hole gaped instantly. Before I could react, he put his hand through the hole and passed one of them to me. I took it with a tremor. It felt soft like a live creature.

It was a ripe plum. He motioned with his chin—*eat it.*

I put it in my mouth. My teeth broke its skin, and my mouth filled with sugary juice. I almost swallowed the pit, but I managed to catch it with my tongue. Politely, I spat it into my palm instead of the grass. Like a child, I expected him to give me the other plum, but he put it in his mouth and chewed it quickly.

"You like fruit?"

"Yes."

"There's a satellite camp, Mittergars, where they grow the produce for all the camp kitchens around here." He spat the pit over his shoulder. "There's this Polish Jew in my barrack, Jacek. He brings the produce to your camp with a cart. I'll tell him to bring you some fruit."

"Thanks."

"You want a dress from Munich? Last time, I saw all these fashion stores with broken windows, with fully dressed mannequins lying in the street."

This had to be a lie. "Who would ever let me wear a dress here?"

"The Germans—you'll see. They have plenty of clothes from dead civilians, but they're running low on camp fatigues. They're short of everything, and they do things so stupidly— look at this shoddy work." He pointed at the hole in the wire and sucked in his lips scornfully. "Look at how poorly they designed your compound." I relished each time that he abused the mighty Germans. "They should've separated it from the men's by *two* wire fences, with a road in between. Like this, everyone's going to stick their nose through the fence to chat with the women. I don't care what Rühl says—it's human nature."

He rubbed his eyes, then lay on his back on that gravelly plot. "Want to lie down, too? It's easier to talk."

Now, how about that? Lie next to him, like in a bed? The fence suddenly seemed like a very frail barrier. That hole in the wire was open, and he was so strong. . . .

I was still clutching that wet pit. I put it on the ground and lay down next to him. Nothing between us but the wire. I waited for him to talk.

He said reflectively: "They'll let you grow your hair here. You'll be really pretty, with your hair grown."

What? I found my voice. "Thank you."

"I mean it. You looked good before, didn't you?"

My God. I heard a flirtatious inflection in my voice. "I've

been told so. . . ." Then I coughed and asked importantly, "Why did you join the underground?"

"Someone had to. Don't ask too many questions; you'll grow old too quickly."

That was a Czech saying. I ignored it. "How did they capture you?"

"Two idiots in my unit knifed a German officer. They were caught, and they talked."

"Were you beaten?"

He shrugged silently. I could feel his shrug through the wire. He leaned his shoulder right into it. But I didn't want him to slip away. "Do you help a lot of people?"

"When the SS let me. They usually do. I defuse the bombs, I repair all their things, from heaters to telephones . . ."

I did not hear the camp's noises anymore. A few feet of grass, this man's voice, and I felt so far from the war.

I relaxed my body, clean for once, and breathed the night air.

"Now I must tell you something," he said seriously.

I bolted up. This was it, he'd either admit that he couldn't help me, or name his price. Nothing came free in a camp, I'd learned that much. I expected him to shoot his hand through the wire and grab me, I was almost certain of it because—because he could probably tell how inexperienced I was as a woman. If he was allowed out of the camp, he probably saw plenty of women. But a beginner like me, even pitiful-looking, could be a thrill—

"You'll find out who's dangerous here and who's not. You're a smart girl. But there's one man . . ." He sat up too and shook his head. "One man who's so evil, he kills with his own hands. He ran over a Russian with his motorcycle. He crushed him to death because he complained about mixing cement without gloves. . . . But the worst is, you never know what to expect from him. He's fine, quiet, and then . . . he kills. Stay away from him. He's the Kommandant."

"The Kommandant?"

Our savior? I wondered, reliving the feeling of standing before him this morning, asking for water. He had given us water, he had sent trucks to pick up the weaker girls.

I told Mirek about how decently Eberle had behaved. He shook his head.

"He's evil, then he throws you a crumb. This morning, he started with a crumb. You'll see."

"But then . . . he'll still send me away . . ."

"Oh, no. You don't count enough, and I told you: Lorentz is writing your own name in the ledger. When Eberle comes back on Monday, you're already here as yourself. So remember that I helped you. One day, if you see me in trouble, you'll help me, too."

All right. I felt a little more settled. The Kommandant might be a beast, but I had a made a friend, a skillful, experienced one.

I asked Mirek what the Kommandant had meant by the Great Wall of China. Mirek laughed silently and somewhat scornfully. "You girls must be very important, if he started with that. Lie down, I'll tell you."

He explained that just now, as the Allies were fighting their way through France, Germany possessed only one fortification on its French border: the West Wall, sarcastically referred to as the Great Wall of China—although Eberle had called it that with a straight face. The West Wall was a long spread of minefields, bunkers, and antiaircraft flak towers completed back in 1939. The construction company in charge was Organization Todt, OT for short (I remembered Eberle gabbing about some organization). In the thirties, OT had provided work for millions of unemployed Germans by building the autobahns. Then it had become the army's invaluable auxiliary by building just about everything: roads into Russia, bridges over the Volga, bunkers, railroads, airfields. And camps.

Now, with their conquests in jeopardy, the Germans were

falling back on the West Wall. They planned to add to it thousands of new bunkers, requiring millions of tons of cement and reinforced concrete. But there was not enough rock to grind and mix into cement, to build so many new bunkers. Before the Americans' landing, the Germans had even dredged the sea bottom off the coast of France, mining tons of maritime gravel. It lay now in heaps in American-occupied territory. There was not enough rock, not enough cement to hold the Allies back. And not enough workers.

I still did not believe Mirek, but I was spellbound. "Where do you get all this information?"

"You'll grow old too quickly," he reminded me.

Then he returned to his main topic: my future in this camp.

"The chief OT engineer for our camp is Alfred Losch. He's the one you should try to get close to. On Monday, go to the office and tell Gudrun that the camp is dirty, and you want to start a cleaning team. If you show that kind of initiative, she'll put you in command. Start with Losch's offices—he's got two, one in camp, one by the construction site, and they're a mess." He smiled, inspired. "Try to catch a rat"—I shrank, repelled— "or if you want, I'll get Jacek to bring you one in a box when he brings the produce tomorrow. You go to Gudrun with the box under your jacket and offer to clean the OT offices; then you go to Losch's office, and make sure he's there when you let the rat loose. And that's it, it's done."

First the West Wall, and now releasing a rodent in the OT engineer's office. Somehow, I was still taking this in. I even smiled. "Where did you learn this trick, also in the underground?"

"It can work. The main thing is to take the initiative."

"What if your engineer beats me or reports me to the Kommandant?"

"He's an old fart, with glasses this thick—" He balled up his hands into fists to show the thickness of Losch's glasses. "He won't even see the rat unless you scream and point to it."

"Mirek . . ."

I was bewitched by this dreamer who wanted me to infiltrate the office of the camp's chief engineer by means of a rat.

"Mirek, this morning . . . You didn't want me to see that hanged man. . . . Why?"

"You looked so scared. That's when I decided to help you."

"You decided to help me, and now you want to put me in danger again?"

"No. No, no," he insisted hurriedly. "It's all in your interest. Number one, if you work for the OT, you'll get the best food, and you'll have very little to do. Losch has a hole of a bedroom and two offices four meters by three—you think they're that hard to clean? Number two, you'll never get the lash. And three, you'll help me. Who knows what information you'll get hold of?"

"Information about what?"

He peered past me, toward the women's barracks. "They're going to call lights-out in a few minutes. Listen carefully. Eight kilometers from here, the OT built a foundation hole so big, half this camp can fit in it. It's covered by an iron roof three meters thick, with a layer of dirt on top sprouting grass. That kind of roof can withstand any bomb. It's obviously an underground factory—but for what weapon? Maybe you can find out."

"I?"

I laughed. I covered my mouth with my palm, but I laughed the same way I had cried before, with a long-stored need. Mirek waited. He raised his eyebrows, glanced up at the starry sky, breathed patiently—all right, let her have a little fun here . . .

I stopped laughing. "Why would you trust me?"

"It's up to you. . . . There will be an air raid tonight, and I'll have to go out. If I don't return, don't worry. They won't send you back, they need everyone here, because . . . there's no West Wall really. The bunkers have no guns, the roads to supply them have been bombed, it's all a fake. We are the human wall," he declared, "you and I, the other girls, the men, and these German farts who would bring the white flag out tomorrow if it wasn't for animals like Eberle. We are the wall. . . ."

He seemed so lonely, and so accustomed to it. Waiting for the air raid, hoping to return in one piece. Dreaming to pry into what last-minute weapon the Germans were building in that hole . . . And trying to acquire an unlikely and scared partner, me . . .

"How old are you?" he asked.

"I just turned nineteen."

"Jesus holera," he swore like a true Czech. "These bastards . . . You should be dancing with a boy somewhere."

"Stop it." That vision of me, so simplified but so desirable, put a knot in my throat. I stared at the scars on his hands. "How'd you get those?"

"Cutting the wires in the bombs. I had gloves, but they were stolen. I'll get another pair out of one of those broken shops."

"All right . . ." I felt that I was embarking on an act of great courage. "Send that rat over. I'm not going to catch one with my hands."

His face lit up. "Good. If this works out, I have another favor to ask."

"What favor?"

"I'll tell you then."

"All right."

What could it be?

An explanation sprang up in my mind: he would ask me to carry a message to some other girl. He'd had his chance to check out a few, as we went from barrack to barrack, turning on the lights. So he didn't want anything from me, except to help him in his mission. I felt relieved. Or actually . . . I did not know what I felt. . . .

There was a muffled thud, and another. In the distance, an invisible city flashed spotlights at the sky. Mirek grinned. "Air raid. You're in luck."

"I—? Oh. Yes."

I saw a man running, not crawling, toward us. "Mirek! Mirek!" he called in a strangled voice, because he was trying to shout under his breath.

"That's Jacek," Mirek said. He grabbed the open wire and pulled it down, anchoring it in the dirt. I blinked—the hole had disappeared.

"If I don't see you again, good luck."

He rushed toward that other silhouette. Jacek looked tall, stooped and thin, and he didn't move very fast. Mirek passed him, and Jacek followed. They walked across the lights from the men's barracks—Jacek bent like a big question mark, Mirek strong and vertical. They rounded a barrack's corner and vanished.

I looked at the empty spot where he had lain down seconds before, while the German guns went off, and bombs started dropping on that unseen city. The bombs were quieter than the flak guns, but I could feel their explosions. The clobbered earth carried them over in long unsettling shudders. For the first time that day, I was not worrying about me, but about someone else. A stupid thought crossed my mind: If Mirek didn't come back . . . would I have to catch that rat myself?

But there would be no need for a rat. He had told me that they would not send me back.

I felt a rush of fresh tears. You were a good lie that won't last, Mirek Underground! I couldn't even savor you properly. But unexpectedly, I felt the presence of something familiar in the folds of my mind. That mallet that I used to crush unwanted thoughts. I grabbed it and held it at the ready. You start haunting me, Mirek, I'll crush you without pity.

I slipped back toward the barracks. Just as I left the tall grass behind me, I bumped chest to chest into someone. A woman.

I stepped back, only to realize from her expression that if she had not seen me sneak toward the fence, she had certainly seen me return from that direction. She asked in a mocking voice, "Ready for bed? I'm in six, too. You and I are sharing a bunk."

It was that brat who threw dancing parties in Munkács, Ida Blumenreich.

NINE

*M*y upper bunk was almost under one of the bulbs Mirek and I had fitted in together.

For a few seconds, I enjoyed the rough comforts of my new bed: the wood planks, which were hard but smelled new and unsoiled; the scratchy blanket, which I pulled over my face; and the forgotten freedom of sleeping without rubbing against other bodies, in a space all my own.

Then I slept, packing the fatigue of the last four nights into a few hours, and woke up in the dead of night, when the second wave of bombers hit Mülhdorf. Thoughts crackled in my head—Mirek, the Allied landing, the West Wall, the mysterious construction, the rat. Mirek, the unexploded bombs, my fate if Mirek would not return. Mirek . . .

I remembered how easily he had pulled that wire open.

But he hadn't even tried to take my hand through the wire. I found that peculiar now—after all, why would he take any risks if he did not like me a little, well, maybe a tiny little, but still . . . Then I had a new thought. Maybe Mirek was only interested in the information I might gather if I started working for the chief engineer.

I hated that thought. To get rid of it, I imagined the feel of Mirek's hand. He had a muscular palm, I was sure. But it was elastic and pleasant, not battered like a peasant's. He did not do field work, his tools were sophisticated, he was an electrician.

I felt the warmth of his hand on mine. The bombs were falling, and I clung to his hand, praying that they would all explode, that he would have nothing to defuse tonight. Then I became scared. What was I doing to myself?

In my mind, I released his palm.

But he did not let go of mine! With my other hand, I felt those trails of scratches on the back of his hand, and tried to stroke them. Then, remembering the kind of person I was, I mustered some scorn: "Hey, let go of me. D'you think I'm one of those easy Prague girls?"

He smiled, and let go of me.

Slowly, my fantasy subsided. I shivered under the coarse blanket.

I no longer heard the thudding of bombs or felt the rippling of the earth rocking the barrack. The air raid was over. Maybe he was dead, after telling me that I'd look pretty again with my hair grown, that I could help him, that I was alive.

You *are alive. That's the main thing.* He had said it with near fierceness.

I whispered those words, under the coarse blanket, which my breath had warmed, until I fell asleep again.

Part 3

THE HUMAN WALL

e awoke to boots thudding from barrack to barrack, fists drumming on the barrack doors; then Gudrun slipped her head in and gave us ten minutes to be out in the yard. We poured out and formed rows of five, bleary-eyed against a sunrise that smelled of smoke. Two trucks idled outside the women's compound, and an officer blared through a loudspeaker, asking for fifty volunteers to go into Mühldorf with him and clear the rubble left by the air raid. I didn't even know when I stepped forward and lined up. Then I remembered Mirek, the talk by the wire, the rat he would send me with Jacek—all of which seemed entirely dreamlike now.

I stared around for my cousins, fearful that today we would be separated for the first time. There were other Germans in the compound, squinting under a wide pall of smoke that swallowed the dawn, shouting for volunteers for other duties. I knew what that smoke meant, I remembered the antiaircraft guns pounding all through the night. Mühldorf had been hit badly. Mirek sprang up in my mind again, this time not as the confident man outlining the Allies' victory, but as a terrified animal burrowing through dust and rubble. Through the night, he had been there. He might still be there—as a charred corpse.

I saw Tsilka. She, too, had volunteered and was now winding through the crowd toward me. Mayer and another young man ran among us with kettles of coffee and two baskets of bread.

Standing up and choking from the hurry, we ate a lavish breakfast of two slices of bread each, dark and heavy and smeared with a thin layer of margarine. We washed it down with hot bitter chicory coffee and held out our cups for more. They were refilled immediately, which made me cringe—that seemed like a confirmation of the severity of the bombing, and of the desperate scurrying and burrowing of the humans caught underneath it.

Tsilka dunked her bread in her coffee. "They want to fatten us up, then kill us." I gritted my teeth and craned my neck in all directions to spot Margit, Suri, or Manci. I only saw Suri standing before an older man with a purple triangle on his stripes, who seemed to be interviewing her. Two steps from them, Hulda was talking to a tall girl who looked older than me and answered Hulda in such resounding good German that I knew on the spot: she would be appointed our Lageraelteste.

"*Gut*, Herta," Hulda concluded, and handed the one named Herta the sign of power—a stick.

Ida Blumenreich had volunteered, too. Left behind the wire, Suri was following that older prisoner in an unknown direction. Maybe she'll get a safe, easy job, I prayed. Hulda jumped onto the step of the lead truck and waved her stick at us. There were two soldiers with rifles in each truck. They did not bother to lower the backs of the platforms; we climbed over the sides, falling over each other as the trucks instantly hurled under the front gate and out. Tsilka and I grabbed on to the roof of the cab. The smoke of farms smoldering on both sides of the road blew into our faces, pricking our nostrils and making us cough.

The road was filled with orderly marching columns of men in stripes. The disaster had not interrupted the clockwork toil of the camp. I recognized those darkly handsome Greek Jews, sprayed with mud by the passage of trucks. Motorcycles loaded with armed soldiers veered off into the muddy fields, trying to overtake the slower traffic. Then I started to recognize the place where we had disembarked and stood before Kommandant Eberle—now we were approaching it from the opposite direction. I saw from its rear the little café whose customers had gaped at our arrival. It looked as if a giant fist had flattened it to the ground. The train station was no more: All that remained was the black rectangle of the foundation loaded with shattered walls and smoking woodwork. Bodies, at least a dozen, lay by the ruin, covered with blankets or overcoats pulled over their chests and faces. Legs in pajama pants stuck out of those bundles. Next to the platform, a train lay derailed, spilling big wooden crates that had been flung out of flatbed cars and felled open by the impact. The crates had burned on the ground. I glimpsed an airplane wing whose aluminum had melted and dripped onto the grass. Soldiers, helmeted police, and prisoners in stripes swarmed by the bombed train, trying to sort out the wreckage.

Our driver turned back into the town, zigzagging to avoid whole blocks still in flames. Mühldorf was—had been—a charming medieval little town with ornate old churches and merchants' and tradesmen's houses. Gothic parapets shored up a river (the Inn River, I was to learn later, flowing east toward Braunau, another charming old town, which was the Führer's birthplace). Heads of baroque angels, ripped off by the bombs, cracked under the wheels of our truck.

Finally, our destination became visible. It was a hospital, built in neo-Gothic style to blend in with the rest of the town. One wing of the hospital had been hit, and the main entrance was blocked by a collapsed upper floor. Soldiers were trying to break a hole in the surrounding wall, to gain access to the other floors, from which came screams that mixed with the blare of fire sirens. There were patients inside those floors, pinned to their beds by the collapsed roofs. We were almost by the wall when a charge of dynamite went off with a big roar. We were ordered off the truck and on the double to that smoking hole, to clear it of rubble so that ambulances could be driven inside.

I was the first to stand by the smoking hole, lifting clumps of bricks and passing them to another girl, who passed them to another, on and on. Tsilka was lost near the end of the clearing line. I heard an almost regular booming and wondered if Mirek was nearby, defusing bombs. I didn't even know what defusing a bomb meant. To prevent it from exploding? To blow it up safely? I kept picturing Mirek being hurled up in the air, in pieces, his severed hands still clutching some cluster of wires. Through the enlarging breach in the wall, I saw nurses carrying loaded stretchers out of the hospital, laying the bodies on the ground and rushing back in for more. I didn't know how I would have felt had the victims been women or children, but they were men, soldiers in bloodied shredded uniforms, bombed in their hospital beds. I passed on the bricks and fought to keep myself alert, but a delicious sense that justice was done fogged up my brain. I was feeling justice—and my body was relaxing from a dread that I had carried with me for months, every hour, every minute, nonstop. Until now. Pain, illness, torture, death, had been our lot, ours only. Now they were the lot of the enemy, too. Then the face of that towheaded boy, the son of the stationmaster, passed before my eyes. He might have been one of the bodies lying next to the charred station. But I could not feel pity.

I bent down to pick up my next load of bricks. Hulda stepped around me, and I saw that she was shaking. Her hair had escaped from under her cap in sweaty wisps that stuck to her freckled forehead. "*Arbeitest, du kleine Lügnerin?*" You're working, you little liar? She swung her stick, aiming for my face. I ducked, but she caught me with a lash on my back. Our officer paced over just then, but wily Hulda had an excuse ready: "She's blocking the way, this idiot!" A horse-drawn ambulance painted with a big red cross jolted into the hospital yard—one pitiful ambulance, Germany's answer to this disaster. Swallowing my tears, I picked up more bricks. While you hit me, you bitch, a few of your soldiers died, and that's not even enough justice! I'm not satisfied, I want more! The

ambulance driver jumped out, opened his arms impotently—
the hospital yard was inundated with bodies, which should he
pick up? A chaplain in military uniform walked among the
dying, making absolving signs of the cross, wholesale, powerless. A civilian limped out of the hospital yard guiding by
the arm a woman whose face was gray from fallen plaster. She
stared blindly through her dirty mask, in shock. Justice. For the
first time since my deportation I sang in my mind: I'm alive
again! I'm alive! Justice!

We were yelled at to regroup, then marched around the hospital to clear the rubble at another makeshift entrance. Men
in brown uniforms appeared, wearing armbands marked OT—
the first men from the Organization Todt that I'd ever seen.
They looked like army officers and carried pistols: the only
difference was their uniforms' color, an ugly, fecal brown.
Grim, they stopped to let us pass. I heard one say: "Kreis Mühldorf ist ganz zerstört, Herr Bürgermeister." The Mühldorf district
is totally destroyed, Mr. Mayor. The mayor, in SS uniform
adorned with silver leaves, had turned up his collar against the
cold wind. He nodded, nose in his collar.

My hands were bleeding now, my thick uniform was soaked
in sweat. We had not had water since we had left the camp. I
turned with a load in my hands and found the line behind me
at a standstill. The sweat stung my eyes. I dropped my load,
stepped down the immobilized line, and found Tsilka arguing
with another girl and looking ready to burst into tears.

"Blanka!" she exclaimed, happy to see help coming.

Begging the girls ahead of her, she had moved up from the
back of the line, so she could work closer to me, until she encountered some dunce who wouldn't let her move up. She
looked at me with hope. Working at the head of the line had
silted my throat with dust, so when I spoke to the other girl I
growled, "Why don't you let her pass? She wants to work next
to me—isn't it all the same where she works?" The other girl
did not move, just watched me with hostility, and behind

Tsilka the rest of the line waited, with their arms hanging tiredly, for the conflict to be resolved. I realized that she would not move, and turned to Tsilka, trying to soften my voice but growling at her, too. "Couldn't you stay where you were?" I saw Hulda rushing over, happy to use her stick. "You're making this harder for everyone!" I said to Tsilka. (I had never spoken to her in such a tone.) Tsilka rushed back, and Hulda chased me with lashes to the start of the line, shrieking: *"Weitermachen!"* Go on! I worked on, beaten but alive. Justice.

A column of prisoners in stripes trooped into the hospital yard. One, with a yellow star but also wearing a faded red cross (he was a prisoner paramedic), bumped into me and cursed me in Hungarian. Then he stopped, startled that I was a female. I passed back a load of rubble, wiped my nose with my bleeding hand, and straightened up, panting. The man stood there, gaping at me.

"What are you doing here?" I asked him, in Hungarian.

"We're giving blood," he said, turning and staring down the line of girls.

"Blood for transfusions?"

"Uh-huh."

"For the German soldiers?"

"Uh-huh."

He was either insane or a liar. "What camp are you from?"

"Ampfing. Ten kilometers from here." His voice gained some of that mellowness a man uses when addressing a woman, no matter where or in what circumstances. "Where are you girls from?"

"Mühldorf," I said as if we had always been there.

"They brought you in from Belsen? From Dachau?" Inspecting me with avid eyes, he did not wait for the answer. *"Istenem,"* God, he intoned, "are they sending women to Ampfing, too?"

"I don't know—"

"I'm Pista," he said with haste, as if his name would establish a vital link. He looked the girls up and down, and they straightened themselves and returned his look. He was not danger; he was confirmation that we were alive and recognizable as women. Then Pista ran after the men he was escorting.

"Did he say the Germans are using Jewish blood for transfusions?" asked the girl working behind me. Her name was Mila; she was Lithuanian, and we had met in the truck.

"I think he was lying. Maybe he was trying to impress me."

"Definitely," opined Mila. "They would never do that."

"Come get water!" Gudrun called from the bombed street. And we turned and pushed each other toward a truck loaded with aluminum pails.

He could not be alive anymore, I kept thinking.

I tried to pray, but I could not utter one word of prayer. But I told myself that thoughts themselves were prayers, and everything here reminded me of Mirek, so almost all the time I was praying for him, too.

After we were given water, we were ordered to sit on the ground, and another truck brought us soup. After we ate the soup, we were driven to the other end of town, where a coal factory was burning, threatening to spread the fire to the nearest urban blocks. We helped clear a road of splintered concrete, so that fire trucks could drive up to fight the blaze. Families fleeing burning homes dragged past us, their belongings piled on barrows, on carts, even on children's tricycles. A boy in a kind of scout uniform with a swastika armband screamed at us: "*Ihr Schweine, ihr dreckige Schweine!*" You filthy pigs! Disheveled, dirty, crying from exhaustion and fright, he tried to lift a slab of concrete and throw it at us. The soldiers held him back until he was pulled away by his family. But his scream had ignited the refugees' anger; our officer grabbed his bullhorn and yelled that the prisoners (we) were here to help put out the fire; then he ordered us to keep our eyes on our work and not provoke anyone. As I kept my eyes on the broken concrete streaked with blood from my fingers, I choked from not being able to yell back: Are we the ones who started this war? Did we bring it home to Germany? Finally, a dozen old men from the *Volksturm*, the local civic guards, appeared and started to hurry the homeless along.

We had cleared the road, but our trucks were not here, so our officer marched us into a deserted street. The burned shell of a milk van was parked by a caved-in sidewalk. The sun beat down hard on us; we asked and received permission to sit wherever we could find shade. I climbed behind the van's combusted steering wheel, sat on the front seat's rusted springs, but could not even lean back. My back stung as if Hulda had flogged me with nettles.

Tsilka sneaked into the seat beside me. She had found some rags and wrapped her bleeding hands in them.

"Are you angry at me, Blanka?"

"No. I just need to gather my thoughts."

"We have to stay together. Otherwise, how are we going to survive this?"

I snapped. "I didn't say we shouldn't stay together! I just wanted to gather my thoughts!"

She jumped out.

I heard a church bell clanging four times, and I calculated that Mirek might have been in this flaming hell for sixteen hours.

A truck roared into our street, braked, and several men jumped out of it. All in OT uniforms except for two: a young SS and a civilian with a firefighter's helmet on. The SS man and one OT called our officer over, and they studied a map while the man with the firefighter helmet walked over to us, carrying a coil of wire. He put down the coil and took off his helmet. His face was crusted with dust, smoke, and sweat glued together, but his eyes were young, alert. He scanned the crowd, saw me through the dirty windshield of the van, smiled, and combed his hand through his matted hair.

I jumped out of the van, feeling that I was carried out not by my body, but by Mirek. I landed on the cracked pavement, and he stepped closer, glanced at my bloodied hands, and said, "I found some gloves last night. They're in the truck. You want them?"

He waited. I cleared my throat. "Don't you need them?"

"I do, but when I open a bomb, it's better that I feel around with my bare fingers to find the right wires."

"How many bombs did you defuse?" I savored the feeling that we were talking as if we had been separated for only a few minutes.

"None here yet, we just got here." My heart sank, then started to pound. "We were in Munich all night, the radio station was hit. . . ."

So. Last night's encounter by the wire had been real, and the way I felt now was the price for that reality. I mumbled that I'd been hearing blasts all morning. Burning gasoline barrels, he explained, then turned amiably toward the older Aufseherin, who was walking over slowly. "*Wie geht's*, Gudrun?" How are things?

"I'm all right," said Gudrun, looking wasted. "This one," she pointed at me, "worked really well, and hard."

"Tell Rühl that she would be good at running the tea detail," suggested Mirek, turning and inspecting me as if he'd noticed me just then. "The OT engineers want the tea kitchen set up right by the *Stelle*." The Stelle was the camp's construction site. "You need a sprightly kid like her to race back and forth up there, and put speed into the other ones."

"Good idea. I'll talk to Rühl," said Gudrun after a moment of thought.

"What's the situation in Mühldorf?" Mirek asked.

"A mess. The damn bastards."

He appraised with a professional air the smoke writhing above the coal factory and then turned back to Gudrun. "With your permission, I'll give this girl a pair of gloves. She'll need her hands in good shape to handle the tea."

Gudrun shrugged. The gloves were fine with her.

All three of us looked away toward the end of the street—a second truck appeared. I tensed up, but Hulda was not in the truck.

Mirek walked off toward his own truck, picking up his coil of wire on the way, and Gudrun said to me, "That boy likes you."

I held my breath, fearing that the slightest reaction on my part could upset my prospects of working in the tea kitchen. In a camp, any kitchen was a safe haven, yet just now I could not enjoy that thought. Mirek still had to defuse those unexploded bombs. I had seen the "justice," and it could kill him. The energy generated by his arrival left my body. I sat on the charred step of the van and watched, powerless. Ida Blumenreich leered at me, and for the first time I felt that had I been a kapo, or the camp Aelteste, I could use the stick on her.

The men wearing those dirty brown OT uniforms were standing by the trucks, talking. As Mirek approached them, they turned toward him vivaciously, as if to say, Ah, here is our man. Mirek threw the wire in the truck, then pulled out a clipboard and appeared to review some data. He jotted something on his clipboard and kept writing while the OT men and the SS lit cigarettes and talked, staring grimly at the smoke-loaded sky. Mirek rummaged inside his truck's cab, then walked back toward me still holding the clipboard and a pair of gloves. I noticed how many of the girls were staring at him. He stopped by the van, examined it as if it were part of his job, made more notes on his clipboard.

I breathed, "Mirek . . . I hope you're being careful. . . ."

"Mm-hmm . . ." He looked at me over the clipboard: "You slept all right last night?"

That sounded so strange that I started to giggle, and choked.

He watched me. He couldn't allow himself to touch me, but he whispered, "You look rested. Where are your cousins?" When had I revealed that the four scared hens clustering by me constantly were my cousins? Maybe yesterday while he joked with us by the camp gate? I could not remember. My mind was numb. He would head off in a few moments, toward the bombs waiting for him in the devastated town.

I said plaintively: "That Aufseherin bitch separated us—"

"That's good, you'll get different jobs, maybe one in the Kleiderkammer (the effects room), one in the *Wäscherei* (the laundry), one in the kitchen or the infirmary . . . You'll have someone in every place that counts. You plan to stick to each other even after the liberation, like Siamese twins?" He whispered, "I'm going to crumple this"—he tore the paper he had been jotting on, balled it up in his fingers—"and slip it into a glove. Read it only when you're back in camp. If a guard or a kapo sees you with it, swallow it." Suddenly the paper had vanished, and he handed me the gloves—big and gray, of frayed, scratched leather. I pulled them on. At least two sizes too large for me, but given the swollen state of my hands, they fit well. At the bottom of the right glove's middle finger, I felt the gob of paper.

"See you in camp." As social as that.

I watched his broad back as he walked off, throwing a greeting to a girl here and there, trying to make his lingering by me seem insignificant, all part of his friendly routine. Ida stepped forward to catch his attention, and he nodded to her. The SS man shouted unnecessarily loudly: "*Vencera! Los!*"

"*Gleich da,*" be right there, Mirek Vencera shouted back.

Climbing in the truck, he looked briefly in my direction; then he and the truck turned the corner. I felt that everything inside me was racing after him, wanting just to be with him, to be protected by his broad shoulders and smiling eyes, and maybe . . . maybe my skinny ugly self could protect him, too. I was crazy, wasn't I?

As we gathered to climb into our truck, I stayed back. We would soon join up with the other truck, I reckoned, and if Hulda was in it, she might notice my gloves and rush to tear them off my hands. I had to save Mirek's message. I quickly peeled off that glove, turned its middle finger inside out, and seized the paper. Reaching under my uniform, I pretended to scratch and stuck the paper in the safest place I could think of, my underpants—they wouldn't search us bodily after this detail, they had no reason. I put the glove back on and climbed into the truck. I pushed my way toward Tsilka, then wrapped my arms around her. "I'm sorry about how I behaved . . . I was just frightened . . ."

A sob swelled inside Tsilka's chest. "I wasn't f-frightened. I just . . . wanted to be close to you. . . ." A tear rolled down her cheek. "I thought we were not just cousins, but also friends. . . ."

I squeezed her tighter. "We are friends. . . . Please forgive me."

Ida popped up behind us and said in her sneering manner, "Blanka's so happy that her *moiker* (loverboy) gave her his gloves! Ask her for anything, Tsilka—now is the time."

"He's not my moiker, and here, you can have the gloves." I peeled them off and handed them to Ida. Both Ida and Tsilka gawked, each with a different expression. Tsilka's said: Are you crazy? Ida's said: Gladly, you fool—and she snatched the gloves. "You think that boy might be Jewish?" Ida asked, off-hand.

"Absolutely not," I said quickly. "He doesn't wear a star," I added, puzzled by the strength of my own reaction.

Ida was pulling the gloves on, flexing her fingers to adjust them. "You made them dirty inside," she pouted. Then she admired her hands and beamed like a selfish child.

I did not care. What counted was Mirek's message. Now I had to find a safe place to read it.

ELEVEN

When the fifty of us returned to camp, all the barracks were already dark. Our officer took a quick head count while crisscrossing our rows with a flashlight and then ordered us to slip inside.

I remained last, stepped in and closed the door, and listened to the other girls, groping for their bunks with groans of exhaustion. As quietly as I could, I paced over to the stove. There were matches and several candles on a shelf behind it, in case of a power outage caused by an air raid.

I waited, wondering why I had responded so forcefully to Ida when she had questioned whether Mirek might be Jewish. I had blurted that denial—Why? That made no sense. But . . . he's *not* Jewish, I told myself. He was too bold around the Germans, and too able to talk to them as if they were human. I remembered how he had addressed Gudrun, all of a sudden making her seem like a tired old woman, harmless, an obeyer of orders, almost an innocent. Yet . . . there were Jews who had slipped through the net by using *goyische papiren*, gentile papers, there were Jews who lived in big towns, who had consorted with the goyim from childhood, looking the same, behaving indistinguishably. I shrank at the thought. To be a Jew who who did not live like one was worse than to be a Christian— that was what I was brought up to feel about the *umreligiezer* Jews, the *asimilirten*, that they were doubly undesirable because they had betrayed themselves. But . . . the warm smile of the

man who was, rather inexplicably, helping me find safety here
pushed that thought aside. Jewish, not Jewish—it did not matter. He was helping me.

I decided that I had listened long enough to the other girls'
snoring. I groped for the carton box behind the stove and lit
a match. No one stirred from their sleep. I spread out Mirek's
message, but the match burned my fingers and went out. I
pressed the paper flat and lit another match. Mirek's note was
no larger than four by four centimeters, written in a minuscule
and disciplined hand, in Czech:

20 *cigarety koupit jeden kousek chleba* (20 cigarettes buy one
lump of bread).

50 *cigarety* = *lepsy misto praci* (a better workplace).

40 = *jeden den v Revieru* (a day in the infirmary).

30 = *jeden den v bloku* (a day of rest in the barrack)

The second match died, and I lit another one.

20 = *boty* (shoes; leather, not wooden clogs)

15 = *rukavice* (a pair of gloves)

Vidis jak vsechnou je dobre? (You see how everything is
turning out all right?)

The match burned my fingers again. I lit yet another one,
turned the paper on the other side, and found it blank. Was
this Mirek's secret message, the one that warranted swallowing
in case a guard caught me reading it?

I groped my way to my bunk, confused and disappointed. I
climbed past the lower bunk, in which Ida snored heavily, and
lay in the upper one, aware of why I was disappointed. I had
expected instructions for another rendezvous by the wire fence.
Or anything personal about Mirek. Anything explaining his

behavior toward me. Yet Mirek had wasted his note on a list of commodities which I could not acquire anyway. Maybe there was a black market in the camp, but he wasn't telling me how to find the currency for it, the cigarettes—and I had nothing to barter to obtain cigarettes, except my food. I lay in my bunk, clinging to that final cheerful line. *See how things are turning out all right?*

In spite of having worked an eighteen-hour day, I was so wound up that I felt like jumping down and pacing. Again, the thought of Mirek came back to me. All right, he was different from the Ukrainians in my shtetl, and maybe he was no Christian at all, maybe he was a *bezviznany*, an unaffiliated agnostic. A dropout from the folds of Czech Catholicism, heavy with the smell of incense and crowded with saints led in procession by that particular Jesus figure, the infant of Prague, bedecked in brocades and with cheeks plump and red like ripe apples. Even in our shtetl, I had glimpsed that figure. I always felt threatened by Christian imagery, but now it blended with Mirek's face—I knew nothing about him, yet felt that while he was not my kind, he was safe, to be trusted completely . . . God, what was happening to me? I could *not* be in love with him. . . .

I had hardly ever seen men naked—a few times, I had glimpsed boys bathing in our local river, the Zhdenevka. And, of course, the nakedness of my brothers when they were little was no mystery to me. But I had never seen adult men naked, Jews or non-Jews. I couldn't help hearing of the racy affairs that two Jewish sisters in our village had had with two handsome Czech officials; one was Carasek, the *notar*, the other our own school principal, Fejtek. I had even overheard one of the sisters, Shari, Carasek's sweetheart, joking to another woman, "When they're up, they all look the same"—meaning penises, circumcised or not. What else could Shari have meant, judging by the flushed and deeply interested look on the other woman's face? Shari was divorced, therefore "free," and the other sister,

Esti, younger and very pretty, had simply fallen in love. Both were attractive—Shari ran the counter in Arendatzki's tavern, and everyone believed that her presence explained the success of his business. Their widowed father had remarried, then he divorced his second wife, an almost unheard-of event in Zhdenev; that, in some eyes, excused the two beauties—at any rate, they were not shunned or barred from our wooden shul, where they went regularly and prayed devotedly. Shari especially knew her prayers better than I, the daughter of the *gabbai*, the elder of the shul—

As if a crack had opened in my head, I imagined Mirek himself. Naked. Naked and coarse in a masculine, feral-looking way. His pagan genitals, which I could not picture too clearly, were like him, paganly beautiful, an evil purified through belonging to him.

I panicked. What gave me the right to think of him, naked and virile, as if he were my husband? Ordinarily, in my mind, Jews and Christians did not even belong in the same sentence. I tried not to toss in the hard bunk, for my back still hurt, but otherwise I felt amazed and excited. Chaia Binah, Chaia Binah, you're not thinking of death this minute, you don't feel doomed, you are almost hopeful. To whom do you owe all that?

To God, I declared righteously and safely.

But then, God had purposely created Mirek.

Then I had an illumination: If Mirek wanted to make me fall in love with him, he could do it more easily than he imagined. I had lost everything that I loved, and yet, frail and alone, I had started to live again. I could not be more vulnerable. And that was why I clung to his not being Jewish. I needed a rampart, a protection, anything that could hold me back.

See you, he had said.

Maybe I would see him again tomorrow. . . .

Aware that I was not making it easier for myself (yet I was, because he was such a relief from fright and death), I fantasized about a future encounter. Tell me who you really are, Mirek.

I was the one who did all the talking, while he smiled in a way that made words unnecessary. And if you cannot tell me the truth because your life or the lives of your comrades would be at risk, then . . . let's just look at each other. That's all I want. (My eyelids were getting heavy.) A few . . . weeks— months?—of seeing you, and in you the proof that God is with us, and He has a plan.

TWELVE

Mirek

*S*he looked at me, as I stepped into the truck, with a stare that bore into me. Like the stare of a lost child. Outsized fear fitted onto a tiny face. Or the begging in the eyes of a wounded animal. I once saw a doe with bullets in her, still alive after a hunt. That incredible yearning for life, still shining under the thickening glaze of death.

She won't survive. None of those girls will.

She almost did not survive that stupid name switch.

Funny that we met because of such a trivial thing. I'm on my third name since I joined the podzemny. And Jews are said to change their names just like that, whenever they need to. Custom of a wandering people. Treated as wandering even after they settled and bred a thousand years in one place. In Prague they lived for over a thousand years. South of Prague, there is a village where Jews came even earlier, as Roman citizens— Rome had not fallen yet! Mrs. Pendek, history class.

You've got a good head for history, Karel, but you're even better in science. What would you like to become?

My first given name was Karel. Charles, like the Charles Bridge in Prague.

I'd like to become an electrical engineer.

I don't think your father will allow you to pursue that.

I nodded. Mrs. Pendek knew my father. And I thought to myself: I will be what I want to be.

I'm in the truck now, bounding over Mühldorf's rubble.

Next to me, my young SS escort, Ostrander, rereads a letter written in a graceful hand, a female's hand. *Meine suesse grosse Liebe* (my sweet great love), I peek at the top line over his arm. He grits his teeth. He already told me what the letter says. The woman's husband came back from Russia with both arms missing, his face scorched from a flamethrower's tongue of fire, and with shrapnel in his lungs. She decided to break it off with Ostrander and stand by her invalid husband. Ostrander is too young to have received many letters like this. He doesn't even know how it will hit him tonight, when he lies down in bed and feels alone and abandoned.

I know. Everyone in the podzemny, everyone but me, clings to the ghost of a woman, alive or dead, sometimes a woman they never touched—she is there, in the folds of the brain and the twitches of the groin. The groin throbs at the strangest moments. It does it even under enemy fire. I'm down here! I'm *you*! If you die, I die.

How could I take it, being alone for so long?

I close my eyes and hear the creaking of the ropes that lowered us into the Warsaw ghetto's sewers. Corner of Gesia and Nalewki streets. Right under what used to be the Jewish Combat Organization. Before the war these were busy streets. Every day, the sewers under the buildings moved tons of human dirt. In war, the dirt became a stronghold. In that stronghold, dying men who hadn't seen the sun for weeks smeared their names with dirt on the walls. I remember a few: Adam Bendler. Leon Wasserman. Kaminsky, Isak—some wrote their last names first, like in school. I believe that those were their real names. Even if they had underground aliases; if you sign before dying, why not sign as yourself? Some also smeared pledges of victory or of revenge. I saw them. Months later. Long after the ghetto fell. When that mysterious Obersturmführer rumored to report directly to Eichmann started to send us down, to fish gold out of shit.

The Jews always have gold, he said.

We found some.

More often, we found weapons and decomposing bodies.

I felt like smearing my own name next to those corpses, but which name? Karel Elias, Mirek Vencera? I just felt like marking that I had witnessed what other humans did. No one would have found my name any more than theirs. I did not do it. I was not dying, and those fighters' names were their only memorials to themselves.

I went up and turned over the gold and weapons to Eichmann's man personally; those were my orders. He sat at a plain desk, clean of everything except what loot we laid before him, and he dirtied his hands with it, holding up to the light this or that filthy gold piece or jewel. On the wall behind him there was a picture of Eichmann, before the war, wearing a colonial helmet, in a landscape of arid hills. Palestine. Eichmann was said to be very fond of that picture; bestowing it upon a subordinate was a sign of appreciation. The Obersturmführer turned the ghetto's booty in his hands, growling softly at the scavenger standing at attention before him. "You're not Jewish at all, Vencera, not one bit? You seem quite familiar with Jewish things."

"You do, too, Herr Obersturmführer."

He looked at me with cold surprise, then wagged his finger: *"Du hast humor, du Verbrecher."* You're funny, you criminal.

"Sie auch—you, too, Herr Obersturmführer." My heart pounded so wildly, I feared that he could glimpse it beating inside my filthy jacket.

"You're pretty bold, Vencera." He was curious to see what I would say in reply.

"Not as bold as the ones rotting down there," I said. "I'm sorry for you that they were such paupers. . . ."

I thought I had signed my death warrant. But he just kicked me out of the office. I stood outside with my back to the padded door, breathing hard, my collar black with sweat, facing the surprised eyes of an armed guard. Adam Bendler, Leon Wasserman, this was my meager attempt to honor you.

How does she feel, now that she's free to use her name? When we talked, I saw how she was coming alive, how that need for hope was unfolding inside her soul. *What can I do, what is the right thing to do about her hope?*

At 1:00 P.M. last night, the building of the Munich radio station looked like a torched anthill. The fire was out already, but everyone, civilians and soldiers, feared delayed explosions. So they took a few steps inside, then panicked and rushed out again, while several phones, spared by the fire, rang with a frenzy. Someone finally picked up a phone and clicked his heels. It was the Propaganda Ministerium, in Berlin! They wanted the station to broadcast right now, under the next tide of bombs if there was a second raid, that Munich was alive and holding! That Munich was giving it back to them (with words). Around us, streets were aflame, people with their pajamas on fire jumped out of their bedroom windows to their deaths. I got out of the truck and almost stepped on a man's body, still twitching, with a hair net on. His hair was crackling with little flames. Maybe German brilliantine is flammable.

I didn't expect radio announcer Kempner to be so cool under fire. I broke into the basement, which was brightly lit by the auxiliary generator, and found him there, wading in two feet of water from a broken pipe. The shortwave radios were in their boxes but had fallen off their racks and were floating on the rising water. All by himself, Kempner tried to turn upright racks that even I could hardly move. SS Ostrander was far behind me and would never dare approach the basement. The all-clear had not sounded yet, but Berlin wanted to know what was going on, to the minute—even down here one phone rang insistently. I saw the radio I myself had built, copying the design of a captured American No. 19—it was floating on that gushing water. The capacitor had given out in a week, and I had to build a new one. I used leftover wire. Metal, clips, plugs I could pinch anywhere. Keeping that radio alive was like nursing a premature infant in an incubator.

So I jumped to rescue it like it was my baby drowning, and Kempner said, "You tell me what they're building in camp Mühldorf, and after we have it leveled I'll get you a new Mk-111 instead of that piece of junk. A brand-new Mk-111 from Moscow, but American-made. Sent to Russia on Lend Lease."

I breathed, then shoved my radio onto a dry desktop.

I told him that I hadn't found out what they were building in Mühldorf, but when I did, I'd wait to make contact with the Czech podzemny first, to report my finds. He smiled with thin pale lips. What podzemny? The intelligence networks "in the pie" (we called Germany "the pie") had been incorporated, with Moscow in charge of ground operations south. We were all allies, *da*? Moscow says—

I cut him off—What did London say? If I gave Moscow the information, in order to level camp Mühldorf and a dozen others around it just to make sure they hadn't missed anything, Moscow would have to ask London to supply the air strike, *nyet*? If Kempner brought in his London contact, and we all had a conference together, I could establish whether the cause was best served by giving Kempner the information. For what if Kempner was a double spy? I had been *verhaftet*, detained, for almost two years, dragged through eight camps and prisons; I could have been killed any day. But Kempner sat calmly in the radio station, before the microphone, with coffee (not chicory) in his china cup, waiting for the red light to come on, to plead to the advancing Russians, in Russian: *Dorogye Russkie bratya*, dear Russian brothers, Germany is preparing a super-weapon, and if you remember '41 and '42, you should overthrow Stalin rather than enrage Hitler even more.

He interrupted me. They had gotten me out of Auschwitz, hadn't they?

I turned red. The Czech podzemny—and not Moscow—got me out of Auschwitz! That was still before you infiltrated our every last unit.

He smiled—that was exactly his point.

The all-clear sounded just then.

We heard boots crashing down the stairs. The door opened slowly, mired by the water, and Colonel Henck, the station's Kommandant, waded in. Seeing Kempner, he almost burst into tears. His chief announcer was here, rescuing the precious equipment! Up into the studio quick! Vencera, up on the roof to reset the antenna. The Russian-language section, the English, the French—all the sections down to the Bulgarians must be activated immediately, to tell the world that Munich was *intact!* *"Zu befehl, Herr Oberst."* At your service, Colonel, said Kempner in his sparkling German, and we all trampled out, I clutching my radio box to my chest. I could have been asked what I was carrying, but given the commotion, no one asked anything. I squeezed my baby with wires to my chest. Was this all I had in the war?

It's that girl, no doubt. Bringing up such thoughts in me.

I never counted on a woman's help after I left Prague. Keeping one's cover was hard enough.

The antenna was back in use, and Kempner went on the air in his soaked pants and shoes. Everyone went on the air, sending out a Babel of propaganda. Meanwhile, the local news came onto the reanimated switchboard: so many city blocks destroyed and counting, so many dead and injured and counting, the *kreises* (counties) all around Munich in flames, bodies floating in the rivers, polluting the water supply . . .

After an hour of broadcasting, Henck ordered a break; some brandy and wine were brought in. Henck toasted his irreplaceable staff, starting with Kempner, the Volga-born German who, though raised in the Slavic wastelands, was so loyal to the Reich! Glass in hand, Kempner wormed over to me and whispered: "We'll get you out of the camp before we hit it, don't worry. You're too useful."

I saw in his eyes numbers, as if on a screen: 3,000 prisoners in Mühldorf—3,300 hundred, adding the women. Leveled. Two thousand men in Waldlager. Leveled. Four hundred only in Mittergars, but growing fast. Hoffman, the Mittergars Kommandant, would soon call me in to wire the extended electrified fence. Four hundred only in Thalheim, but growing. Thousands more in the other subcamps—every village around Munich had some wire pen clamped to it. How many thousands? Fifty perhaps? Leveled.

"There are American pilots in Mittergars," I said. "And Russian soldiers, in all the camps. Russians, your people. And women."

He smiled with his pale lips. "What's the difference? They're being killed anyway, you gave us that information yourself— two months of work, then declared unfit, *piff*, back on the train. To the ashcan. Fresh transports in, two months, *piff*... The Jews, forget them, they're gone already. The others... Shall we think of people already condemned, instead of how to win the war?"

"They're not condemned as long as they're still alive. The Red Army is in East Prussia . . ."

"But Patton's bogged down in the Ardennes, and the Germans are designing new weapons. London's cratered with V2s." Kempner's eyes glittered from the brandy. "The next V2 might be built in Mühldorf. Should we take that chance? You took an oath to the podzemny."

"I never betrayed my oath."

"Then don't betray it this time. That train bombed near Mühldorf carried crates of plane parts. It's probably an assembly line for a new plane. You tell us when it becomes operational, we pull you out, then . . . *piff!*"

"What kind of medal would you get for that, Captain Kemp-ner?"

I took him by surprise. His white face colored slightly, and he passed his pale tongue over his lips, giving them shine. "I would be advanced to major. Maybe even smuggled back to Moscow and put in charge of war propaganda . . ."

I thought, Or maybe sent to America as a pre-peace nego-tiator. The winners were meeting frantically, to plan the shar-ing of the spoils. The losers were just a few yards away, but they could not hear us, someone had put on a nerve-soothing *Lieder* record. Kempner's calm made me feel like throttling him. There were weapons around; I could grab one, shoot him, shoot them all. I had good odds of fleeing uncaptured—chaos still reigned on the lower floors, and I knew the building like no one else, I knew the city . . . Just rip off this stupid red triangle, and I could look and act like a German civilian.

But how far would I get? How long could I stay hidden? And if I were arrested again . . . The cellar of the Munich Gestapo flashed in front of me. The chains dangling from the ceiling, the handcuffs with spikes on the inside, the ammonium baths, the "boot" . . . Kempner knew about all that. So he was con-fident that he would get what he wanted from me.

He lowered his voice and said, smiling toward Colonel Henck, who was slurping red wine, "You know, we had some-one else like you, who started to question our instructions. But this is '44, not '42. We can correct any situation. Now even the SS doubt that they will win the war. The smarter ones are looking for new friends, you understand? Even the Gestapo are looking for new friends, you understand?"

I breathed deeply. "Is there nothing we can do to save the prisoners?"

"No. Let's say that they're soldiers. Soldiers die in battle."

"What would London say? America?"

"America won't know. London won't care. And I'll recom-mend you for a promotion and the Red Star."

Colonel Henck was drunk. He beckoned me invitingly toward the table with the brandy and the wine. I said under my breath, "This is an astounding night: I can drink with the Germans and plot the death of my campmates with the Russians."

Kempner missed it. "Come in the hallway," he said.

I followed him out. "Mirek, I already reported to Moscow that we have to bomb Mühldorf, and London agreed and is awaiting the signal. You're one of our best fighters, but you're a one-man unit. That's a very small unit. We made you important. We gave you your mission. Don't play with your life— you did well so far."

I hit him in the jaw, and he flew into the wall, arms flailing. He leapt back and stood blinking, aware that he could not call for help. I spoke in his face, spitting on it, "You're a bastard and a murderer."

Even now, he found the nerve to smile back. "You have to be everything, to do what I'm doing." He wiped a trickle of blood from the corner of his mouth. "What exactly do you want?"

"To meet the London man."

"With London under V2s, d'you think he'll be sympathetic? Anyway, that's impossible."

"Then get your information from the Gestapo."

I went in and called Ostrander; then I started down the stairs. Ostrander followed me, but I heard him pause. He had bumped into Kempner, holding his swelling jaw. I heard Kempner mumble, "I slipped . . . my shoes are still wet . . ."

"Put some ice on that," Ostrander advised, then hurried to catch up with me.

I had stashed my radio box behind the elevators. I picked it up and walked past the sentries with it under my arm. In a minute we were outside, and back in the truck.

· · ·

There is a Gothic stone bridge in Prague probably more famous than all other bridges in Christendom. It bears my initial given name, Karel. Karluv Most—Charles Bridge. King Karel of Bohemia built it in the fifteenth century and decorated it with statues. Saint Nepomuk, Saint Luitgarda, Saints Cyril and Methody. Thirty saints in all. There's more religious history concentrated in this granite spine of Prague than in the Vatican's stately Saint Peter. Until a hundred years ago, the citizens of Prague would not cross this bridge without doffing their caps to the statues, thirty times, even in a pouring rain.

There is also among them a crucified Jesus of bronze, pinned on his cross by three large pegs—one for each open palm, one for the two feet sadistically stacked on top of each other. Above and around the thorned forehead, there is a crown of gilded letters in Hebrew. Five words, surrounding the Nazarene's famed agony. *Kadosh, kadosh, kadosh*, holy, holy, holy, *Adonai Tz'vuot*, Lord of the Hosts.

A great curiosity, that Jesus with Hebrew writing. That shtetl girl surely doesn't know about it. In front of it, I had received my current and third podzemny name, from two comrades who met me on the bridge and identified themselves by password. My new name would be Mirek Vencera. The older of the two, Frantisek Vencera, was about my father's age and would be my new podzemny father. I would keep the same podzemny *babicka*, grandmother, as my mailbox. I was to be moved out of Prague, to Vienna. They already had a full cover for me in Vienna, electrician at the State Opera, a member of a local boxing club, and so forth. But I had to leave immediately, otherwise I'd be captured.

This departure would conclude a whole year of narrowly missed arrests, and constant dread of house raids and identity checks. When the SS boss of occupied Bohemia, Heydrich (known as *der Henker*, the hangman), had been killed by a Czech commando trained in London and parachuted into the

Czech countryside, London had taken no responsibility for the killing, and the SS had unleashed their fury on us. It was open season on the podzemny as it had been on the Jews and the Communists. Our only hope of survival was to keep moving and changing identities.

I turned and looked at the Vltava River, at Prague's spires, gilded by a quiet sunset, and knew that this would be harder for me than leaving home. Memories of my years in Prague rose in my mouth, bittersweet, starting with the dry bread I munched on as I walked to Prague, following an eastbound railroad track. Straining to leap over two crossties at a time and missing—my legs were not fully grown yet. I was thirteen. Thinking of my father, who worked for the railroad for over twenty years, walking along the tracks and banging them with a big hammer, to check that the joint bars and spikes and tie plates were all in place, that the track bed had not shifted, causing dangers of derailment—a good lesson for later, when I joined the podzemny. I knew how to mess up a track, how to derail a train. It's so easy, it's a wonder it doesn't happen every day, naturally.

I want you to be more than I am, Father had told me when I finished seventh grade. More than a railroad man. I want you to be a tailor.

The next day, our class took a field trip to a salt mine. I cried during the field trip and claimed it was from the mine's salty air stinging my eyes. I did not want to be a tailor. I could not obey Father's plans for my life. I would have to leave home. I had two brothers and three sisters. I would leave them all behind; I would walk to Prague if I had to, to a trade school. I wanted to be an electrician. I had the school's address, torn out for me from a newspaper by Mrs. Pendek, who thought I was gifted in science.

I walked sauntering from crosstie to crosstie for three days, and finally entered Prague. I knew that the school was downtown and kept stopping passersby and asking directions. By four that afternoon, I made it, and collapsed on the school's front steps.

I woke up later that evening in a short, hard, typical boarding school bed, and heard in the next room an indistinct male voice sounding as if it was praying—the cadence of the words was familiar, a vague smell of candles was familiar, too. Then a man with a beard came into the dormitory, empty at that time (the boys were at dinner), and told me that the school took in orphans, which was what I had told him I was before passing out. But I had to tell him my faith. This was a Jewish school. I looked him in the eyes and said that I was not of any faith. He noted in a book: *bezviznany*, nonbeliever. That allowed me to register, but I had to pay for the tuition, which would have been free had I declared myself a Jewish orphan. I replied that I had an uncle in Prague, and he would pay. Mr. Bobasch, the school principal, narrowed his eyes as if hearing a made-up story, but told me that I could stay if I was honest and showed aptitude. If I changed my mind and needed religious guidance, that could be arranged, too. "Now go to sleep, breakfast is at five-thirty in the morning."

I slept.

I had not lied about that uncle, but he did not help with the tuition. I wrote home, and my father paid for the first year. At the end of that year I was already making money from house calls—Mr. Bobasch, the bearded principal, even let me rewire his house. Then I moved out of the school and rented a one-room apartment. Rushing to my jobs on foot and then on a bicycle I bought secondhand, I got to know Prague like the back of my hand. I spoke in a singsong accent, like a real, indistinguishable Prazhan. I crossed Charles Bridge countless times and got to know every statue on it. The bridge was a favorite meeting place for lovers—they exchanged their pledges here and sealed them with long kisses. I had no time for kisses. Just a night with a paid woman now and then. I worked around the clock, saving for tuition at Prague's Technical College.

I allowed myself one amusement, the movies. Almost every afternoon, I walked out of the Electrotechnical Institute and went straight to see Charlie Chaplin, Errol Flynn, Douglas Fairbanks, Wallace Beery. I saw Hedy Lamarr when she was still an obscure actress named Hedy Kieslerova. She made her name in a Czech film called *Ecstasy*, in which she had a nude scene, swimming in a lake and then running on the shore till she bumped stark naked into the man who would become her lover. That was the film's peak, the one that justified the ads: THE SCREEN'S HOTTEST STORY OF CARNAL PASSION.

I'm crawling now under a half-destroyed Mühldorf home, hunting a bomb that the inhabitants say they saw falling, piercing down through two floors, leaving big holes in the ceilings and floor panels, and then vanishing—probably buried under the foundation. Flashlight clenched in my teeth, I'm crawling after that bomb alone, but I'm thinking of Hedy Lamarr in *Ecstasy*, then of that skinny Jewish girl with doe eyes. I wonder if she saw *Ecstasy*. Even shtetl girls must have been crazy about Hedy Lamarr, and probably sneaked away from home to the nearest town to see her. Hedy was married then to a gun manufacturer, Fritz Mandl, who tried to buy up all the prints of the film, so no one could see his wife naked.

But I saw her, three times. After the third showing, with my bladder bursting, I went to the theater's men's room, which was smoky and smelled of disinfectant, and found it packed with boys who, just like me, had watched the movie over and over. Several had huddled against a urinal, and I heard one ask another to piss in sync with him, in a cross pattern. If we piss in a cross pattern, he said, a kike dies. His accent was not singsong; it was flat, working-class. I'd heard that jeer before and never reacted to it, never lost control. This time I lost control. I threw myself at the huddle, slamming a nose into the tiled wall, bashing a head against another. When they turned, I went at them with my fists. They regrouped and fought back. The police came. They asked me what happened. I wouldn't talk.

I spent the night in a cell in Prague's Pankrac prison, not knowing that, come the war, I would see that cell again, and many others. In the cell, there were three Communists who had returned from the Spanish Civil War by crossing the border without passports. Their passports had been confiscated in an internment camp in France. One was missing a leg. Cut off right under the groin. They were discussing Hitler's demands on Czechoslovakia. I was not a Communist, not even a sympathizer. But I told them that if they knew of an anti-Nazi organization, I would join. They grilled me with questions— they were afraid of police stool pigeons. But finally they led me to the podzemny.

In May '43, I went to Vienna, and I was captured. Strangely, in a way I am thankful. Before my arrest, I was nothing but an amateur. Only after my arrest did I start to understand true danger, true comradeship. I learned that the front line shifts all the time, not just where everyone can see it, on the ground. It shifts insidiously, traitorously, inside people.

My flashlight suddenly encounters a cylindrical shape. The unexploded bomb. Large, gray. Lying still. Its cone-shaped nose ripped through some wallpaper, which remained stuck to it in little colorful bits, giving it an uncanny festive look.

I stop crawling. I try to catch my breath before dealing with the bomb.

Ostrander is outside, safe, perhaps looking again at that letter. He once showed me a picture of the unfaithful wife: handsome, standing on a snowy slope in a ski outfit, gleefully raising her ski poles. Tonight, he told me that he is very sad, but he admires her dutifulness. A true German woman. Nothing touches me about his story—not him, not the woman, not her unfortunate husband. But when I think of that Jewish girl, of her eyes that looked at me as if trying to become part of me, I feel like hiding the bomb by shoveling earth over it with my hands, then crawling back out and telling Ostrander, There was no bomb there. We would get back in the truck and return to camp. The unsuspecting inhabitants would return to their home and start fixing it, leaving that deadly guest undisturbed, until one day, for no reason, it would go off. As Kempner said, *piff!*

Could I do that?

I think of Blanka's hands. Horribly scratched, repellent almost. Her cheeks were red and sweaty, but right under that brush of hair her skin was marble-white, and laced with sapphire veins. Her real self, forced inside a grotesque camouflage. And the way she walked, even in those—What is it about some women that makes them step as if they floated above the ground? Of course, she can't weigh more than a hundred pounds.

Let's say she's a soldier. . . . Soldiers die in battle. . . .

That cold, self-assured bastard.

I could do something else. Once we finish tonight's assignment, we return to camp, only us three—me, Ostrander, and our driver. Relieved that the danger is over, Ostrander dozes off as soon as we head back. I could swipe his gun, shoot him and the driver, and I'd be alone with a truck and a gun, only a night's drive from the Swiss border.

It's the sight of the bomb that tells me, You can't do it, you can't quit. What about Jacek? And my new trainee, Joska? And the Greeks—the other night they could have killed Maurice, and Eberle would have strung them from the watchtowers, like steaks. Other people I did favors for, and they returned the favors. Even that dull old jailer Gudrun—when I asked her to close an eye, she always did. When I asked her to put someone in a good place, she always agreed. There is a network of needs

and obligations forcing me into not breaking out, into staying,
as if within a badly adjusted family—but nonetheless, a family.
That's how you win a war, from within; that's the only way.
Maybe I'll see her again. She's got two months. At the most.
I don't crawl back. I crawl forward. Toward the bomb.

THIRTEEN

Blanka

*T*hree days after clearing the rubble in Mühldorf, at half past seven on a cold morning, I walked alone to the construction site, escorted by an armed soldier.

On the way, one of those big military bikes passed me. Gudrun sat in the sidecar, head lolling tiredly onto her chest. She had still not recovered from the rubble-clearing.

The road left the forest and followed the edge of the construction. I saw the lid covering the main site, like an enormous turtle shell. Men finished layering dirt on that lid, and planting grass and fully grown trees on it to make it undetectable from the air. Powerful reflections of lights shone from underneath. Next to the turtle shell, in a wide-open pit, not covered, not camouflaged in any way, I heard a deafening noise of breaking and crunching. That was the cement quarry, swarming with men in stripes loosening and breaking rock slabs. Other men in stripes loaded them in mining wagons and rolled them on a narrow gauge track to the mouth of the quarry's only machine, a tall tower of steel topped with a chute that looked like an open beak.

"There," said the soldier escorting me. He pointed, and I heard the pride in his voice. "The bird!"

The camp's most notorious tool looked, indeed, like a bird, and was filled inside with grinders with big steel teeth. It insatiably swallowed rocks, digested them, and then excreted them as cement powder, which was gathered in sacks and carried away on the backs of more men in stripes. As we passed, a man emptying a wagon into that beak slipped and rolled down with his rocks. Others grabbed him by his striped jacket and pulled him back—otherwise the powder pouring from the bird's steel craw would have turned red.

We passed a cube of cardboard sitting right on the lip of the quarry—with a small door, a flat roof topped by a radio antenna and connected to a power pole by a thick bundle of electrical wires. Then we arrived at the tea kitchen, set in an old flour mill with its machinery removed. I was in an excited mood because things were really falling into place. Suri worked now in the effects room, Tsilka and Margit had landed in the laundry, and Manci in the best place, the main kitchen. Of course, the absolute best job in terms of easiness—who else could have pulled it off but Ida Blumenreich? She oversaw the cleaning of the barracks, meaning that after two sweeps with the broom, she could slip back into bed and go to sleep, while others scrubbed in her place.

No matter. I was determined to work.

We had to brew the tea in big thirty-gallon vats, using leaves that came in counted packages. The Kommandant himself would drink our tea along with the men laboring in the cement quarry and the Stelle proper—he was here every day, supervising the work, so we could not relax about the quality or be unpunctual. At 10:00 A.M. and 3:00 P.M., carrying big jugs, my whole tea detail would descend into the quarry first, to quench the thirst of the men laboring there. Then we would do the same in the Stelle, where the workers were not prisoners but civilians, trained builders and draftsmen, who had signed on with OT, the camp's contractor, for a salary. I also had to deliver two separate tea thermoses, in the morning and in the afternoon, to the camp's chief engineer, Dr. Alfred Losch, whose office I had just passed. Also to bring Losch his lunch at noon, when the lunch trucks arrived to feed everyone in the area.

I stepped inside the mill, which was built of old bricks, and squinted from the darkness. The lights were out, and the narrow industrial windows were bleary with filth. Mirek was here, ghostly at the top of a tall ladder, wrestling with an electrical panel—otherwise, the only glow came from the fires being lit under the brewing vats by Mayer and by an older, sullen prisoner called Ivan. I had asked for Mayer to be one of my fire-stokers, Gudrun had approved him, and Mayer had brought a mate. Gudrun lay on a stack of teabags, happy to steal a minute of rest; as I stepped in, she stirred and called out to Mirek, Why were the lights still not working? He mumbled that the mill was on the same circuit as the office of Engineer Losch, who had probably turned on his heaters, his radio, his tele-typewriter, his desk lamps, and his air filter all at once.

Finding Mirek here made my heart beat fast, but I knew I would be calmer and more ladylike this time. That is, if we got a chance to exchange a few words. I inspected the dank, depressing place. Tomorrow, I'll get those windows to sparkle, I told myself, all zeal and responsibility.

Under the cobwebbed ceiling, the bulbs flickered on, then off, and Mirek cursed. "I'll go over to Losch's office and dis-connect some of his stuff."

Then, I couldn't believe it, Gudrun said: "Why don't you take the girl with you and show her the site?"

Mirek came down the ladder. I felt safe enough to sneak him a smile, but he did not respond. He just went to the door and held it open for me. Grumpy this morning, aren't we? I thought, still full of cheer. I passed him very close, but he looked down stubbornly and then followed me out. Still not very concerned (amazing what a few days of safety and a job of some importance can do to a human), I closed the door and waited for him to catch up.

He took off his cap and offered it to me. "Put it on. The Kommandant can see us from the pit."

I understood. With the cap on, I would look like a man.

Not very flattered—was he aware of how my breasts had shrunk?—I took the cap and inhaled its smell. It stank of sweat and dirt soaked into fabric long unwashed. In broad daylight, Mirek looked unkempt and thinner, and he had not shaved. God knows where they had dragged him the last few days; besides, he probably didn't expect to see me. I excused him and then asked conversationally, "Is anything the matter?"

"Yes." He looked me straight in the eyes. "I thought only of you, for the last three days."

My heart stopped; then it surged back, beating furiously, and all my senses seemed heightened, so as not to miss an iota of what he would say next. He bit his lips. Interpreting that as shyness, I gave him my most encouraging smile, then pulled that filthy cap over my stiffening brush of hair—three days only, and my hair had recovered some energy.

"We could become too . . . important for each other," he said heavily, "and that wouldn't be good. I didn't want to come here this morning. But I had to, because my trainee Joska is sick."

I made a leap—"Do you have someone on the outside?"

"A woman?"

My voice was thin like a fledgling's peep. "Yes."

"No, I don't." He sounded truthful.

My voice gained a little strength: "Is someone waiting for you back in Prague?"

"No. Let's walk, otherwise we'll attract attention." He started away, then waited for me. "You don't have to roll your shoulders, walk normally." Unconsciously, I had tried to imitate a man's walk.

At least he's honest, I told myself. It took me a few minutes to realize what he was really saying. He was saying good-bye. Then I felt sick. But I fiercely ordered my stomach to not bother me and said with a tinge of flirtation, "Maybe I thought about you, too. Maybe I didn't mind. Maybe that made me feel better."

"It's not that simple. If we go on like this . . ." He kicked a stone, seemed not to know what to do with his powerful hands—he balled them into fists, stuck them in his pockets. "Let's just say it's not a good thing because you don't know what could happen to me, I have missions, I don't . . . really belong to myself . . ." He avoided my eyes and his tone had changed; it was angry. "I could die . . ."

"We could all die," I said, trying to sound appeasing.

Mirek spun around. He looked at me avidly, as if wanting to engrave me in his memory; then he shivered. I lost my composure. I had not seen him disoriented or frightened, not even in that ruined burning town. And now . . .

"Mirek, what's the matter? You're scaring me."

"Blanka . . . This is still a camp. . . . You know?"

I shrugged. How could I forget that? "But you said that the Allies are coming, and we would be liberated."

"Yes, and that's true, but . . . Blanka . . ."

I savored the way he said my name, each time he did it. He looked into the pit. A voice inside warned me, Don't look down there. But, of course I looked, because Mirek was looking.

On the bottom of the quarry, I saw Kommandant Eberle facing several prisoners standing at attention before him. Eberle's arm moved, and his fist rammed a prisoner in the face. A jet of blood gushed out and fell at the prisoner's feet, dark and twisting like a live creature. Eberle struck the man again, again, again, until the man collapsed and lay still. Then he took one step aside and struck the next prisoner. I started to shake. I looked ahead at that little cube of cardboard: Losch's office. I noticed its tiny windows, the radio antenna, and a round porthole with a spidery helix in it, turning slowly (the air filter). A pair of garbage cans were affixed to its rear wall. What an ingenious, self-sufficient, portable office. The Germans were so devilishly clever, how could they lose the war?

Steady, *meidlech*. You met a kind man, and because he is kind, he doesn't want to lie to you. You knew what lay hidden behind the face of the good camp; you learned it the first day, when you saw that corpse being carted off from the gallows. So brace yourself. Soon, in a few minutes, Mirek won't be around anymore to block out the camp's sights with his healthy body, and that's normal. The worst of life we endure alone— that had been my experience so far. Is this different? No. Is Mirek at fault for wanting to protect himself? No.

At the cube's door, I turned and faced Mirek. He looked at me the way other men or boys had looked at me before I was deported, and not being interested in them, I had learned to discern the meaning of that look. A look of uncertainty, a kind of scared awe. The most powerful man, as he shed his indifference toward a woman, stared like that: avid and lost, realizing that in a particular way, before a particular person, his strength and experience, his trusted defenses, were no longer enough. If he wanted me at all, he had to let himself slide over that edge and submit to my power.

Despite my inexperience, I had that power now, and I knew it. I was exerting it from my underfed but slightly stronger body, from my skin, cleaner now and pink from the faster coursing of my blood—even from my body's hairs, which were growing back now, silly and hopeful. I had that power, and he was responding to it.

God, let it be, let it be.

For just that instant, I felt no fear, no fear at all.

He watched me as if I had hypnotized him and then said, low, from within his gut, "I got you this job, it's one of the best in the camp, but now that you have it, I cannot worry about you every minute, all right? You've got to steel yourself against what you'll see. All right? You can pass on this job. You want to pass? Someone else will fill it in no time."

"No," I said quietly. "You got it for me, I'll take it. Thank you, Mirek."

He shrugged, and I found his modesty touching—he'd done his best.

I was terrified of the next question I had to ask, but I needed to ask it. "Are you really leaving the camp?"

"Yes."

"Are you leaving for good?"

"No. No, no," he said with growing strength. "But I don't know for how long, and I don't want anything to happen to you. . . ."

Oh, God. What could happen to me, except for losing my life? The turmoil on Mirek's face was exaggerated—poor sweet man who thought that I had not been at death's door. He looked so sincerely worried, I could not help but savor this proof (perhaps the only proof I would ever get) that I could interest him.

"I'll handle the job, Mirek," I said. I felt sad and painfully proud. "I'll handle this camp, even if you have to go. You don't know where I've been."

He nodded, then strode jerkily toward the little cube. He threw the door open too hard, without his usual mastery over his strength.

I choked from a disgusting stench of cigarettes. The portable office was in the dark, just like the kitchen. Someone inside yelled in a high-pitched voice, a yell of impatient relief.

"Good morning, Herr Engineer," Mirek addressed that person. "Just as I thought, both heaters on again, the air filter, the lamps, the teletypewriter, too . . . You need your own private generator, Herr Engineer. . . ."

A lit cigarette flew past my nose and landed with a fizzle in a glass bowl filled with water. It plopped among the corpses of two dozen other cigarettes, on which our camp's chief engineer Alfred Losch had puffed only four or five times, maniacally and greedily, before discarding them.

Mirek, with the authority of the older prisoner, had ordered me to sweep the floor. I raised my head from where I was sweeping and calculated the trajectory of the cigarette. With a little practice, I could spring my fingers into their flying path, and catch them before they landed in that disgusting makeshift ashtray.

Mirek had introduced us: Chief Engineer Losch—Haeftling Davidovich. Chief Engineer Losch had bowed formally, like a German of the old school, searching for me through the fattest lenses I had ever seen. Behind the glass, his face looked tiny, as if a shrunken Losch contained within the full-size one peered out at me through peepholes.

Meanwhile, Mirek tinkered with the fuse box at the back of the office. The desk lamps (very high-voltage ones) flicked on and off every few minutes, and the teletypewriter clicked alive, then died again. Losch talked on the phone—on a separate circuit—calling offices in Berlin, addressing aides and secretaries with *Guten Tag*, and their bosses with either Guten Tag or Heil Hitler. Having shut away my memories, I'd given my unburdened mind a green light to retain trivia. I filed away every word and name out of Losch's mouth. Herr Engineer Dorsch, at the OT *Zentrale* in Berlin, Guten Tag. Herr Polenski, at the firm of Polenski and Zollner, Guten Tag. Herr Minister Speer, Heil Hitler. *Fräulein Reitsch, wie geht's dir, Suesse?* How are you, sweetie? That Fräulein was the only female in the bunch, and had no title, but her secretary elicited a very zealous Heil Hitler. *Kommst du zu meine Yause, Schatz?* are you coming to my party, honey? Was she Losch's girlfriend? I tried to imagine Losch, with his triple-breadth glasses, in the embrace of someone he could barely see, even with powerful lights on.

The not even half-smoked cigarettes flew and plopped, flew and plopped into that dirty water, until I picked up the bowl and stepped outside with it, to empty it and clean it. I inhaled fresh air, and lifted the bowl to slop out its contents.

"Don't!" Mirek snapped, turning around from the open fuse

box. He took the bowl from my hands, carefully poured out the water, then scooped out the butts and lined them by the cube's back wall, under the midday sun.

"They'll be dry in a few hours. From two butts you can make one whole cigarette." He spaced the butts so they wouldn't stick together. "Remember the note I wrote you? Losch wastes sixty cigarettes a day—he's trying to cut back. You'll be a cigarette millionairess—the men here smoke the soles of their shoes. The camp has a canteen, run by a politiker from Luxembourg, Otto. He trades in cigarettes, and he likes young girls. If he strokes your arm, let him; he's harmless."

To myself, I intoned a song of confirmation. He likes me, and not just a little. *I know it, I feel it.*

We reentered the office. Losch was up, groping around on his cluttered desk. He fished an Agfa camera, mumbled that he was going to the Stelle, and left.

I asked how he was taking pictures if he saw so poorly.

"He asks other people to do it for him." Mirek refilled the bowl with tap water from a tiny sink with a postcard-size mirror. With mathematical precision, he set it back where it had stood before. "Gotta be right, or he'll miss it with his next cigarette and start a fire."

"He should be watched."

"He starts screaming if anyone comes near his mess. You want to see your name in the camp book?"

I jumped. The magic had dissolved.

Mirek pulled a ledger with black covers from a loaded book rack. He opened it, thumbed through the last pages. "Here you are." *He likes me, he's doing this to reassure me. I'll force myself to look.* He showed me the list of our transport. Under *D*, typed in a space cleaned with correction fluid: Dawidowitch, Blanka. *Alt*: 20 (I was actually 19), *Relig*: Mos. (Mosaic, meaning Jewish), *Rasse*: Sem (semitic), *Staats-angehoer*: Ung (nationality Hungarian). I laughed—having been deported by the Hungarians made me Hungarian! *Arbeitsfaehig* (fitness for work): T.

Mirek's thumbnail drummed on the *T*: "This is the key word, *tauglich*, fit. You want to stay *T*. If they change your *T* to a *U*, you're in trouble. But if Losch doesn't mind having you in here, you can keep checking that you're still a T."

I gaped. I could monitor my own odds of survival! Mirek closed the book, planted it back on the shelf.

"Other things you need to know. Losch is OT. If I'm not here anymore, you want the protection of as many OT as possible. And if you're a smart girl, you can learn everything about this camp. Just look around."

I shivered with fear just like in the shower. But I did look around.

The walls were so crammed with thumbtacked diagrams, invoices, blueprints of the construction site and black-and-white photos of its stages of completion, I wondered how Losch found anything. The only orderly display was a kind of memorial: the portrait of a shortish balding bureaucrat in a suit and tie, with an uptight smile. DR. FRITZ TODT, 1891–1942. Surrounded by photos of his achievements—autobahns, bridges thrown over the Meuse and Marne and Don and Volga; roads and airfields thrust into the wilds of Russia; models of bunkers, forts, pillboxes; designs of future concentration camps. And a quote: IF AN INDUSTRIAL PLANT DOESN'T FUNCTION PROPERLY, YOU CALL IN AN ENGINEER TO OVERHAUL THE PLANT. TODAY, IT IS UP TO US TO OVERHAUL THE PLANT OF HUMAN SOCIETY.—DR. FRITZ TODT.

Mirek took my arm. I leaned against him without shame, craving his strength, as he explained, "Todt employs three million workers, drawn from thirty-four nationalities."

He pointed to a map. The Todt Organization's network started in Berlin and spread over all of Germany and Europe. Lines specifying allocations of materiel and prisoners connected task groups and planning teams, construction offices, security troops, medical facilities, even a calendar of forthcoming inspections from the Red Cross. Germany's key cities were all secondary octopuses, with tentacles to hundreds of dots, too many to be explained individually. They were numbered and named in a bulky legend. All camps. I found Dachau. Like a supply duct, Dachau regularly pumped prisoner packages of a few thousand each (their transfers were marked on the map) into medium-size camps like Mühldorf. But even the medium camps sprouted camps of their own. Mühldorf trailed a herd: Thalheim, Zinecker, Ampfing (I remembered those Jews who gave blood for transfusions; they came from Ampfing), Mittergars, Waldlager, Mettenheim . . . and more, all with peaceful names of innocent towns and villages.

I uttered a strangled sound. So this was the present. And the future.

Mirek breathed next to me. "Don't get scared." He added, as if reading my thoughts, "That's why it isn't the time for . . ."

He did not say *love.* He just stroked my arm.

If he would at least keep stroking my arm. But Mirek pushed me onto a chair. He rifled behind books and ledgers, and pulled out a bottle. I shook my head, but he opened it and held it under my nostrils. A stink of strong schnapps made me feel better. I told him it was probably that reek of cigarettes.

"Can you walk?"

I nodded.

"Then go back to the kitchen and make some tea. Losch's thermoses are there, fill them both, and bring them back here. We'll have tea."

"But what about—?"

"He won't be back for at least an hour. This is the time when he inspects the construction and takes pictures."

He disconnected the heaters, then unplugged the teletypewriter and the air filter. The desk lamps came on, shining harshly. "Now you'll have light in the kitchen too."

The phone rang. Neither of us answered it. It stopped.

I was out the door already.

FOURTEEN

*T*ea. Tea with sugar.

Real tea with real sugar.

Mayer helped me make tea in a household-size kettle that he found lying dirty and stained on the floor. He washed it with boiling water, shined it with ashes from the fire, and then washed it again, all in less than two minutes. Then, anxiously standing by me, he asked how long he could work here, *for me*. I guessed instantly that he lived in dread of ending up in the quarry, feeding the bird and facing Eberle's fists. "He beats the slower ones, and there are always slower ones," he whispered. The sullen Ivan, a Russian POW, slinked up to us, assured me that he'd never let a fire go out, and waited with the same fearful expectation. I said I'd keep them both for as long as I had this job—while thinking: Mirek likes me. I just have to find a way to make him come back here.

Gudrun still slept, her face so relaxed that she looked ten years younger.

I filled the two thermoses, then, past the quarry (Don't look down!), I raced back to Losch's cube. His (my) cigarette butts warmed in the sun. The little cube was shaking: Mirek was pacing inside. I opened the door and raised the two thermoses. He took one, uncapped it, blew on the fogged-up rim, and took a sip. He passed the thermos to me, and I drank from the same spot. He sat on a box of files, making it cave under him, and I took Losch's chair.

"Losch is trying to bring some bigwigs to a meeting here in camp," he said.

I asked what for. If you hang around here, you might find out, he replied.

"And tell you?" I asked rather coquettishly, sipping after him again.

He looked out the window toward the Stelle and nodded. Why not? That's how you win a war from the inside.

We were both red in the face and sweating, and passing the thermos. Mirek examined my hands. Why was I not wearing the gloves he'd given me? I replied that I had given them to one of my cousins. (In fact, Ida put them on, every day, for her two sweeps of the broom.) He shrugged and sipped more tea. I took the thermos from him and swigged a big mouthful, felt the sweat on my forehead, and looked for a towel by Losch's minuscule sink. There was a towel, but it was stained yellow, as if Losch had smoked through it. I used my sleeve. Mirek told me that Otto at the canteen had cans of lanolin, for the Germans only, but Otto owed Mirek a few favors, so I should drop by at the canteen after the evening roll call. It would be closed, but if I went around the back and knocked, Otto would open for me and give me a can. Just mention Mirek's name. By the way, Rosh Hashanah was coming. Next Saturday I shouldn't fast or anything, I was looking a little better already.

I said, "Jews don't fast on Rosh Hashanah. And how would you know when Rosh Hashanah is?"

"I don't. Other men in my compound told me."

So he was not. But I had already discovered that it didn't matter enough to really matter.

Still, I was careful with my words as I asked, "Do you . . . hold anything against Jews?"

"Would I have helped you if I did?"

"Why not? I'm a woman."

"I don't hold things against anyone. I was in trade school with a lot of Jews. They're no different from anyone else."

I had my own ideas about that, but I let it pass. "Have you ever been in love?" *Now, this was really crossing the line.*

"I don't think so," he said, straight away.

In that case, how could he be sure about his feelings for me? But . . . I felt pretty clear about *my* feelings, realizing fully by now that I had not been in love with Boruch, not at all, not even for one afternoon. Boruch, with his magical horses, had never swept me off the ground and put me back down with his gaze alone.

"All right." He rose and put away the thermos. "I'm going to be here," he touched a spot on the octopus map. "Mittergars, a new camp. I have to do some wiring. I'll try to keep in touch." He surveyed the office. The lamps shone brightly on the appalling clutter. "Tell Losch not to use the heaters, not before he gets his own generator. If he's cold, bring him some hot tea."

"All right." I got up and stepped around the desk. I will do this without losing my head. I moved toward Mirek while he, not expecting my boldness, watched with bulging eyes. I slipped my arms under his and hugged him.

"Thank you for helping me."

He closed his arms around me, but not tightly, and stood in my embrace, uncertain. My face came to his shoulder, my lips were level with his neck, with the dip of his clavicle, all sweaty, and I kissed his neck, quickly, lips shut, like a schoolgirl. He pressed me to him, not quite to full contact, but I felt his body—thinner than it looked. A supple body that reminded me of Mechel, my younger brother. But Mechel was frail, while Mirek was all muscle.

"Blanka . . ."

"Yes?"

Whatever he says, I'll use it to get a kiss. Even if he kisses me hard, I'll let him, because he'll be doing it, not me.

"Today at lunch, you'll eat from the officer's lunch truck. You'll get real good bread, a lot of it. Finish it *here*. Don't take it back to camp."

Now, how do you turn that into a kiss?

"And start gathering those butts, don't be squeamish. You were rather spoiled at home, weren't you?" Not conducive to a kiss at all. He gently opened my arms. "Let's get out of here before Losch comes back."

He turned to the door. Deflated, I followed. What else could I do?

On the doorstep, he said, "I'll see you. If it's in a few weeks, you'll be really pretty by that time."

Then he stepped out, and I felt like screaming: Oh, no. No, you can't play with me like this, Mirek Underground. Vanishing again, like after we met by the wire, like on that dead street. You're always vanishing. I rushed outside. He had vanished.

"They need a few more hours to dry."

I jumped. He was crouching by the wall, feeling those cigarette butts.

"Don't forget about them, they're priceless." He stood up, handed me that filthy cap again. He did remember to protect me, I could not fault him for that.

I stuck it on my head angrily: "Thank you."

We were approaching the front steps of the kitchen. I wanted to say something smart, something that would stick in his memory and also make me romantic and mysterious. I could not come up with anything. Mirek opened the door to the kitchen. The fires were roaring under the kettles, Mayer and Ivan stood at attention by them, and a towering man seemed to suck the air out of that dusty space. When he turned around, I felt as I had on the morning of our arrival, when I stepped out of that cattle car.

It was Kommandant Eberle.

The sickly lights and the uneven dance of the fires gave a sinister sheen to Eberle's uniform. A part of me expected him to contort his body or even to change his appearance, like the *sheidim*, the demons I had feared as a child. His hands did not look human: that ramming right fist was red, enlarged, and swollen. The other, clutched like a talon around his wooden stick, flashed on the middle finger a ring embossed with the SS skull and bones.

He had just stepped into the kitchen. Gudrun was stirring on her heap of teabags. "Look how she does her bit for Germany," he chuckled, and poked her with the stick. Gudrun opened her eyes, jumped up, and stood mute and panicked.

"At ease," mouthed Eberle, slapping his stick into his left hand. He turned to Mirek: "*Warum bist du hier, du Verbrecher?*" Why are you here, you criminal?

Mirek, don't do anything stupid, I prayed. Don't show off. Wallow if you have to, but think of your life, think of *me!* Then, I lowered my eyes onto Eberle's boots, just like during the Doctor's selections. But I could not help it—after an instant of waiting, I looked up.

Mirek was not averting his eyes. He replied that he had just handled a power cut up here, and now, with utter respect (he pulled out an official-looking paper), he had to leave the Stelle. The OT Kommandant of camp Mittergars, Hoffman, wanted him to enlarge Mittergars's electrified fence. Mirek was just about to hurry to deputy Rühl, to have him approve Hoffman's request.

"You always have the best excuse to slip out, always get the OT to stick up for you!" Eberle's stare was becoming fierce; he advanced on Mirek, chin jutting out. Mayer and Ivan held their breath. Unexpectedly, what saved Mirek was my presence. Eberle glimpsed me within his peripheral view and stopped.

"Who are you?" he grumbled.

Gudrun stammered that I had just been appointed to run the tea kitchen.

"Oh, yes. Davidovich," he said with a flicker of recognition.

I had been trying to talk to God: Can't You make Your presence felt? But perhaps God did make His presence felt. Eberle momentarily forgot about Mirek. He stationed himself before me and looked at me almost pruriently. "So, Davidovich. What's it like to be alive again?"

I burst into a clamor of gratitude: I was proud to be entrusted with this job. . . . I'd be utterly conscientious and punctual. . . . And I had already started my duties by taking some tea over to the chief engineer. . . .

"Filthy, isn't he?" Eberle grinned, very pleased to be able to badmouth Losch. "Cuckoo here, *na?*" He tapped his temple. I gave out a servile laugh, oh yes, he'd seemed cuckoo to me, too. Behind Eberle, I saw Gudrun gesturing to Mirek: Leave, *now!* But Mirek stayed, maybe to make sure I was out of trouble.

"You make good tea?" Eberle asked.

"Herr Kommandant will judge."

I rushed to the kettle and removed its lid: less than a third was still full, and it was overbrewed. I grabbed a tin cup, filled it while ordering my hands not to shake, *not even a little.* I came back and presented him with the cup. The tea was still warm and looked poisonously dark. Eberle slurped. "*Aaaahhh!*" he groaned, between pain and delight. "Strong tea. This'll put a kick in the workers." Breathless, I waited. He slurped again. He liked it.

"*Geh weg.*" Go away, he threw over his shoulder to Mirek.

Mirek gave me a glance narrowed to a pinpoint. Then he leapt outside and slammed the door shut.

Eberle chewed the dregs in his cup. "The bottom of the kettle is always thicker," I explained apologetically.

"It's good," he proclaimed.

"I'll make it better next time," I promised.

"It's the right strength; we keep it like this!" He bashed the cup onto the sorting table for emphasis.

"You'll serve it to me, too; I'm here with the men every day, to stimulate them to work." (I had witnessed the effects of that stimulation.)

"Come closer, Davidovich. Closer. I don't eat women."

But do you beat them?

I took a breath and stepped closer. His face seemed much jowlier than when I first saw it, and rife with protuberances—even his forehead had two round bumps under his hairline, like a billy goat's sprouting horns. That unevenness of his jaw must have made it hard to shave closely. Clumps of gray hair filled the wrinkles near the corners of his mouth and under his chin.

His mouth, large and wilted, asked, "Do you like my camp?"

"Yes. It's . . . well organized."

He nodded happily. "We have rules here, strict rules, but rights also. Above all, the right to work. And you may be punished, but if the whistle blows for tea, you get your tea like everyone else. Except if you commit a major offense. You know what we do not have here?"

"Favorites?" I guessed.

Bull's-eye. Eberle beamed. "Absolutely no favorites. And no exceptions—that's what makes my camp one of the best. If the Red Cross came here right now, I know that they would write an excellent report because we are a model camp. As for me, I am—" He opened his arms, at a loss for words about himself.

"Fair and equal, Herr Kommandant," said Gudrun.

"Fair and equal," he agreed. "It is hard to remain that way. Everyone tries to take advantage of me, you understand, Davidovich?"

I understood. He was a principled man. He smelled of boot polish and of cologne. And seemed equipped with only two buttons: on and off. Easy to manipulate, if you learned when to press the *on,* and when the *off.* He bared his teeth, laughing, the silver fillings bright. "I did a good thing by keeping you. If you work well here . . . I'll let you clean my own quarters."

He straightened himself. I wondered if he would give me a stretched-arm salute, or . . . pinch my cheek. He only said, "*Weitermachen.*" Carry on. "And remember, I am—"

I blurted, "Fair and equal, Herr Kommandant."

And the would-be human inside him, moved that he was so well understood, stepped backwards with his creaky boots and made it out the door.

I wondered if I had wet my pants. I could not tell. I had sweated the whole length of my body. I slumped onto a stool, while Gudrun's expression told me that today was the birthday of my modest power.

I looked at Mayer and Ivan, who stared back as if I'd grown a foot. I hated myself for it, yet . . . I liked my nascent power. I liked it for a few minutes. Then I panicked again. If I did my best here, I would end up in the lion's den. The only way to avoid that would be to not do my best here, and that I really could not afford!

Thus, I started my job at the tea kitchen.

I had seventeen helpers, but only two from my barracks, Mila the Lithuanian and Eva Lauber—to discourage favoritism. We left the camp at half past six in the morning, on foot, and walked for forty-five minutes on that road running between fields and forests, escorted by two yawning Germans. If we glimpsed a bulbous shape protruding out of a potato field, one of us dived to dig up that potato. The Germans looked the other way because they had to save their energy for dealing with the men at the Stelle. Once we were in our kitchen, our guards joined the other guards patrolling the construction site.

We worked in the old flour mill, breaking tea bags and brewing tea. Mayer and Ivan were always there before us. Mayer was from Romania, but had been deported by the Hungarians when they had occupied Romania's western province, Transylvania. Between him and Ivan, they kept the fires burning so strongly that the kitchen was hot, and we kept opening the windows for air.

At 10:00 A.M. and 3:00 P.M., as always, we went down with jugs and ladles into that deep pit in the rock, to quench the workers' thirst. They couldn't wait for the hot drink, especially those who humped cement sacks weighing two hundred pounds each on their backs. They did it hundreds of times during a shift of twelve hours with a twenty-minute break for lunch and two fifteen-minute tea breaks. But all the men were worked brutally: the rock breakers, who loosened the rocks without drills, just with pickaxes and hammers; the feeders of the bird, who carried boulders and slabs to its hungry beak with their bare hands; the cement mixers—everyone. We descended into the pit by way of an industrial elevator, a platform with iron rails designed to hold fifteen people. We squeezed tight together, burning each other with our hot jugs. The sunlight stopped at the mouth of the pit, and a haze of ground rock filled the air. It was hard to breathe—we covered our mouths and noses with rags. But our eyes remained uncovered, and we watched Eberle punish the prisoners who moved too slowly. He singled them out with his stick, lined them up, and beat them till they collapsed. The elevator's descent was slow, lasting almost one minute, so by the time we touched down, we had plenty of time to see him in action. His most common victims were the Greek Jews and the Russian POWs, who spoke no German and could not figure for their lives that if they fell to the ground after the first blow, that was that— they'd be spared the rest. All kept standing up stoically, in a pathetic show of resistance. I felt like screaming, Dive down, you fools! To whom are you proving your manhood? Don't you have anyone waiting for you at home?

They were men. Maybe being defiant was worth the pain.

Considerate to us women, Eberle tried to beat the prisoners

far from the elevator, by the quarry's opposite wall. When our platform landed, we grabbed our jugs and started to race about (although Eberle never hit us), calling: Tea! Who wants tea? Eberle would hear us and stop. "Tea!" he yelled out, demonstrating again that he was equal and fair; he resumed the beatings after the tea break.

Most often, I was the one who poured him his tea. He ate his lunch here, too, but at lunch he was served by a soldier. He came toward me, taking off his beating glove, grinning, remembering how well I had understood him that one time in the kitchen, and holding out his cup. I filled it, and he sat on a chair, hastily brought by an orderly, and enjoyed his tea.

I kept telling myself, Don't try to understand. Just now, the men are beaten and the women are spared. There is no explanation. The main thing is, we are alive.

After serving the men in the quarry, we went up, refilled our jugs, and then went to the Stelle proper (into which we descended by way of another industrial elevator, larger and in much better condition), to serve the free workers. We had to be careful not to spill tea over the blueprints and notebooks, but otherwise the Stelle proper was a treat—no shouts, no beatings. No blood. On the contrary, we were greeted by the smell of expensive cigarettes, Milde Sorte, and a radio playing symphonic music. After we were done with the serving, I alone ran with two fresh thermoses to Losch's office. My cigarette butts (Milde Sorte) dried out in the sun by the back wall.

I cleaned Losch's stinky lair again. Sometimes he glimpsed me in the fog of his reduced vision. "You smoke?"

"Yes," said I, who had never even put a cigarette between my lips.

"Catch."

He tossed me an unlit cigarette. I stuffed it in my breast pocket.

I began to see what made the system tick. It promoted only two species of people: brutes and bureaucrats, both powered by that pair of essential buttons, on and off. A brute who was also a bureaucrat would rise quickly in this system. Suddenly, I understood this puzzling breed, the frightening Germans. They were themselves deeply frightened, of hardship and hunger, of the lethal air raids, of losing the war. But their fright expressed itself in violence, while their antidote for fright was giving and following orders. In Berlin, at the heart of the octopus, reigned nothing but one man's aggressive improvisation, to which the enlightened Germans (there were some, I suspected Losch to be one) lent their talents of organization, technologic invention, and patriotism. But maybe not their true thoughts; those they hid deeply, from themselves and from their countrymen.

I could never guess Losch's thoughts, and his extreme myopia was the best cover he could wish for. He seemed as dim as a turtle with glasses. And yet, he had to have his own thoughts. He worked too methodically toward a goal I could not grasp, except that it had to do with those incessant phone calls.

I was (forgive me, Mirek) a poor spy. I hadn't yet taken one peek inside Losch's personal agenda, or the other secrets of the camp.

Every couple of days, I added another stash of salvaged butts to my nest egg, which I hid inside my barrack's ceiling, in a hole behind a removable panel. I had discovered that hole lying alone in my bunk one day, recovering from a cold. I trembled that my treasure would be raided by other prisoners— my main fear was Ida Blumenreich. But thank God, she was such a poor cleaner that she took forever discovering the barrack's hidden recesses.

I had not destroyed Mirek's letter. I wore it on my person during the day, and at night I stuffed it in my pillow—we had been issued mattresses and pillows, filled with straw. I reread its cheerful ending and wished he were here to see how well I was doing. My hair was looking like hair again: it lengthened, thickened, and started to hang over my temples and forehead, until my hands remembered the gestures of pushing bangs out of my eyes and of combing strands behind my ears. In short, I looked like a female again—perhaps more ridiculous than attractive, but I quickly found a way to look better. In the effects room, Suri worked under the supervision of that man with a purple triangle, a sweet old man who was German and a Jehovah's Witness, whose church Hitler had almost annihilated because its members would not carry arms for the Reich. I thus discovered that many other faiths and breeds bothered Der Führer, not just us.

As Mirek had predicted, it was incredibly useful to have a link in the effects room, which was crammed with old uniforms, civilian jackets and trousers, Russian fatigues, wool, cotton, yarn . . . I asked Suri to make me a turban, which I could pull over my ears against the growing cold. The one she made me curled my hair up from under it like a flapper girl's. I wore it two days; then a throng of girls lined up by Suri's barrack after the evening roll call, to put in orders for turbans like mine. They bartered their food for the turbans. I had launched a fashion.

I did get my can of lanolin from Otto the canteen man, but after I used it twice it was stolen. But I bought with cigarette butts a pair of leather shoes. In principle, the canteen was only for the Germans, who with coupons bought shaving cream, hand lotion, toothpaste and toothbrushes, aspirin, cough remedies, laxatives, even pipe tobacco. But Otto, like Mirek, had access to the outside, so he managed to bring in dresses, shoes, underwear—all used, but all infinitely better than the fatigues or the stripes. Hulda bitched to the Kommandant, but in vain. Soon, a third of us wore civilian clothes, acquired by trading food. (Otto ate most of that food—he was almost obese—and resold the rest to other men.) Eberle closed an eye. Otto also sold combs, little mirrors, and games of cards and chess, which were tolerated as long as they were kept in the barracks.

In the evenings, if I moved around the yard and happened to have an extra cigarette butt on me, I stuck it through the wire into the begging hand of one of those Greek Jews, who immediately alerted his friends. In no time, a whole bunch gathered at the wire with languishing eyes, waiting for the "cigarette lady" to give them another butt or two. I did, and begged them to keep the secret. Most of them spoke no German at all, so I handed out the butts, then pointed at myself and shook my finger fiercely: Not from me! Not from me! The cigarettes came from God, they had dropped from the sky, but they didn't come from me. They nodded and reassured me in Greek: *nai, nai.* Yes, yes—theirs being the only language in Europe that made *yes* sound like a *no.*

So when I took a long walk along the wire after roll call, I was followed by a shaggy pack of Greeks, avid, excited, and noisily calling me *Schwester,* sister, which in their mouths became *Svester,* as they could not pronounce the Germanic *sch* sound. One Gabi Petilon, in particular, handsome but pitifully skinny, was dying to have me as a sister. I saw him in the daytime at the quarry, humping two-hundred-pound cement sacks, his walk bent and staggering, distorted by those crushing loads. He couldn't be older than thirty, but he heaved and shook as if he were in his last hour, and begged me for cigarette butts. I feared that if he smoked he'd expire in front of me. Instead I gave him bread, crumbling it in small pieces and fitting them through the wire. He gathered them, kneaded them into one lump, kissed that lump, and then ate it. And the other Greeks beamed their dark eyes at me, intoning, "Svester, svester!"

I was being worshiped. I was pleased with my generosity and power.

But one night as I lay in my bunk, I thought about becoming known as the generous cigarette-and-bread lady, and got cold feet. What if someone reported my charitableness? What if Hulda found out that I had, literally, a following? I sweated. I wondered what Mirek would do, and realized that I needed his guidance badly. I thought of him, sailing past murderous fists like Eberle's, past sticks, truncheons, hanging nooses and bullets, and always reemerging alive. What power, what instinct allowed him to play this game so well, making so few mistakes?

Only he could answer that question.

I had not seen him for three weeks now. . . .

I promised myself that if we met again, I would turn on all my charms and prevent him from leaving the camp again. I was convinced that he possessed the tricks necessary to stay here if he wanted to. If he really *really* liked me, he would be here now. In the meantime, as a security measure, I decided to cut down on my gifts through the wire.

That was not so easy. Every evening, the Greeks were out there in force, and Kapo Maurice had given up on hindering them. Every evening, I saw new faces at the wire, begging me, "Svester, svester!" I stopped taking walks in the yard; the Greeks cried for me all the more. Unexpectedly, the walking skeleton, Petilon, put an end to their clamor. I was sitting on the stoop one evening when Petilon staggered over, snapped angrily at his serenading friends, then hooked his fingers into the wire and asked me directly: *"Du nix mehr Svester?"* Which meant: Was I no longer a sister? Was I abdicating my goodness?

I stepped to the wire and opened my arms impotently—I wanted to be a sister. But I was too afraid.

He understood. He gave me a forgiving look and walked away.

I breathed, more relieved than guilty.

My stash in the ceiling got raided, and I decided to rebuild it and relocate it in the safest place possible: Losch's own office. My girls and I, armed with brooms and mops and buckets of suds, had washed the outside of his office; then, after it had dried, we had washed the inside, dried the floors, aired the interior, all during Losch's absences at the Stelle. He let himself be corrupted to cleanliness reluctantly, like a filthy boy hating to take baths, but in a while he started to breathe more freely, to cough less, even seemed to see better. He stepped out of the office with his Agfa and snapped pictures of the quarry himself. I offered to organize his papers, which he declined. I confessed that I was gathering his butts and that I needed a hiding place. He gave me a gift of three packs of cigarettes and an aluminum box, and indicated a spot for the box on his book rack; he did not find it suspicious that I never smoked in his presence. Emboldened, I stole a few more packs. He did not notice.

Now I took a few cigarettes back into camp every evening, like a petty cash allowance.

Amazingly, Losch and I started a dialogue of sorts. As I was subhuman, it was safe for him to unload on the regime in my presence. He told me that the war was going badly because it was run by amateurs; Hitler himself was the most glaring example, and he typically favored and promoted other amateurs, such as Armaments Minister Speer, the ex-architect, who knew zero about armaments and less than zero about fuel, resources, or economic planning. If I believed Losch, anyone who woke up in Berlin with an attractive idea in his head could present it to Hitler (if he managed to finesse a meeting with him), and if Hitler liked it, yet another state agency was hatched, funds were apportioned, personnel was hired, and so on, further exhausting the war economy. Usually the agencies produced nothing, and the funds vanished in Switzerland. Fritz Todt, Losch's dead mentor, a true professional, had died in a suspicious plane crash. What he, Losch, was attempting here, he said once as I mopped tea he had spilled on his chair, could give the war its much awaited "turn"—but would he be allowed to accomplish it? I was stunned, realizing that half of what he said could send him to Dachau, but Losch said it regardless, then picked up the ringing phone. "Losch. Ja. Heil Hitler. Oh, good, you're coming to my meeting, Herr Minister, Herr Kreis-leiter, Herr General, Herr General Inspektor? See you in Jan-uary then. Heil Hitler." Teletype-written RSVPs were coming into the office (I could read the messages; he let them trail on the floor without a care for secrecy), confirming that other high personages would attend that meeting. It seemed that the spec-tacled turtle did have his own thoughts and plans.

Meanwhile, in our barrack, some girl always woke up in the morning without the piece of bread she had saved the night before to add to her breakfast, and there was a storm of curses and accusations, then wise advice about how to hide the bread better next time—useless though, for even if you slept right on top of it, it did not help. The best accomplice of the thief (or thieves) was our own exhaustion. We crashed into sleep so deeply, one could have chopped wood on us.

"If I lay my hands on her, I'll blind her," swore Mila, the Lithuanian I had met clearing rubble.

She often shared her food. Before lights out, she sometimes asked loudly: "Is anyone still hungry? I have a slice of bread here, I'd rather give it away than find it missing tomorrow." Someone always came forward to take Mila's bread. It could have been the thief herself.

For about a week, I tried to not approach the wire.

Instead, I made efforts to reconnect with my cousins. After roll call, I rushed between our five respective barracks and gathered us in a quiet place, by the piles of logs and planks for the water tower under construction. We exchanged the news of the day, so far fairly good. From the laundry, Margit and Tsilka informed us that the work was hard but they were never cold thanks to the steam. From the effects room, Suri reported that she gave out clothes to Frenchmen, Italians, Romanians, Belgians, Dutchmen, forging useful ties—she had given the warmest clothes to two prisoner doctors who worked in the hospital, and they, thankful because autumn was coming, promised their best care if any of us got sick. Many of those strangers Suri would not have figured for Jews, had they not worn the star. Their number and diversity made Jewry seem harder to annihilate, *keneine hore*. Less auspiciously, Tsilka had glimpsed Hulda exiting Rühl's quarters one afternoon, with her stick in her teeth and buttoning her pants. If Hulda had made it with Rühl, she could really unleash her viciousness.

Still, a mood of hope permeated our talks. We babbled, waiting for Manci, who came late from the kitchen (bringing us treats), until one evening she did not show up.

We got nervous.

Then, there was a big commotion at the wire.

We raced over. Lo and behold, Manci was there pulling bread from the pockets of the apron she wore at work, breaking it and stuffing it through to an adoring crowd of Greeks. Gabi Petilon stood some twenty yards behind them, acting as lookout. Manci had brought more than bread—pieces of sausage, *Bratkartoffein* (roasted potatoes), even lumps of cheese, which we had never seen before. More Greeks emerged from the barracks and seemed ready to charge at the fortunates being fed. But Petilon stopped them and talked to them, and they waited at a distance—all under the silent eye of the big watchtower, whose spotlight inexplicably did not come on. "Daviko, Daviko!" Manci crooned. And a little Greek, not much taller than she (Manci was four feet nine; during the Doctor's selections she always stood on tiptoe, afraid she might be selected for her smallness alone), rushed to the fore. She rewarded him with a whole roasted drumstick. He was thin, graceful, with a downy mustache and big brown velvet eyes that looked at Manci worshipfully.

We were panicked. I grabbed her elbow and told her to stop, she would be noticed by Herta the Lageraelteste, who was quickly turning into a second Hulda. Manci could end up swaying from that noose. Manci shook me off and snapped (in Yiddish, which no Greek understood) that she had to finish this. The official calorie count per week per working prisoner had just been posted on a wall in the kitchen: over 1,400 calories, including some cheese and honey. But the SS stole more than half, that was why the Greek cement workers fell like flies. And the girls in the kitchen stuffed their faces. The calorie count had been posted in anticipation of a visit from the Red Cross. Manci had made her decision: she could not save all the Greeks, but she would help a few, and if I and her other cousins were concerned, we should stand around her like a protective screen. While she spoke so resolutely, her gaze stroked the liquid velvet in that boy's eyes, urging him, Eat that drumstick, that one's for you!

He took the drumstick and retreated with the rest of the group. Beyond Petilon's pillar of vigilance, they met the other crowd and shared the gifts. A muffled music of chewing, sucking and burping followed, right under the watchtower, whose light still remained shut off. Then the Greeks started hopping about, dancing for Manci. Dancing the way Greeks do, men with men. Silently. Manci stood at the wire trying to make out Daviko's silhouette—I noticed one svelte ghost who leapt higher than the others. Then Manci turned, led us to our safe spot by the water tower, and opened her apron again. She still had some food in that apron for us.

I was not hungry—I had had lunch from the officers' truck. I chewed a piece of bread, thankful for the darkness. My cheeks were blazing.

"Who's Daviko? How do you know his name? Where's he from?" Tsilka and Margit and Suri pestered Manci. She ignored them and pricked her ears toward the men's compound. Silence.

"He's just some boy," she muttered absentmindedly. "I don't know anything about him."

"Does he speak Yiddish?" asked Tsilka.

"No. None of them do."

"Then what kind of Jew is he?"

"Greek Jews," I cut in knowledgeably, "have their own Yiddish, called Ladino." I remembered that from a history session with Mr. Tauber.

"La-*what?*"

"It means Latin, but it's really a kind of Spanish. These Jews were kicked out of Spain—"

"But they're Greek—"

"That was about four hundred years ago, and they spread everywhere around the Mediterranean, including Greece, and still speak that Spanish at home like we speak Yiddish." I had made a decision, too. I had five *whole* cigarettes hidden in my jacket. In a minute, I would stride back to the wire and sneak them to any Greek still lingering there.

"So, they keep Sabbath?" Margit asked.

"Sabbath, halakah, everything." I touched my cheeks. They were still hot.

We separated, and I went back to the wire. The Greeks trailed about their yard, but one stood right by the wire, and from the bent shape of his body I recognized him. Gabi Petilon. I cursed my bad luck, but a pledge was a pledge. I beckoned, he came over, and I gave him the cigarettes, one by one— with each one, his expression was more enraptured. I could not ask him to share the cigarettes, I spoke not a word in Greek.

He put his mouth to the wire: "*Svester zuruck, zuruck?*" Sister back, back?

What could I do but nod? And he contemplated me as adoringly as Daviko had Manci.

"*Parakalo sas,*" Thank you, he said gravely. He hid the cigarettes and then laced his fingers through the wire, conquering an inch of air from the women's side. "*Was mit Mirek? Was willst mit er?*" he asked suddenly, in his abominable German: What's with Mirek? What do you want with him?

I gawked. What did he know about me and Mirek?

Gabi glared with dark eyes, large and bloodshot from cement

dust. "*Er nix Svester! Nix Svester zu du!*" He is no sister! No sister to you! He shook the wire: "*Ich Svester zu du!*" Gabi was my sister. I laughed; he could not be my sister any more than Mirek. But Gabi became insulted. The meaning he gave to sister had no gender; it was a magical, all-inclusive term for friend, soul mate, sweetheart. To defuse him, I touched his fingers—and cringed. The skin on his fingers, on his palms, on the backs of his hands and wrists was cracked and scabbed with brown hardened blood. Most of the men handling cement had such scabbed paws; the cement drained the oil from their skin, and no gloves or mittens were used in the quarry. At my touch, Gabi quivered. I could follow that quiver along his wiry body. All of him, his stare, his demeanor, even his mangled German carried a male pride that had not been broken, and that pride told him infallibly whom to like and whom to hate or distrust. Gabi liked me. And he hated Mirek.

"All right. You are my sister," I agreed, overpowered. "I'll try to get you some medication for your hands."

We heard the gong for lights out. Gabi hobbled away, and I was grateful for the sound of the gong; otherwise I might have cried.

Then I stumbled to my barrack, concerned—what mess had I stuck myself into now? What was I to expect from that mangy martyr? I couldn't help but savor, in thought, the delight with which Gabi would put a cigarette in his lips, strike a match and light it, puff deeply, exhale the smoke, puff some more, exhale, puff, light another cigarette, until he would finish them all and make the butts into an extra cigarette, to be saved for later. Meanwhile, he would pine for me, not doubtfully now, but with hope. My cigarettes could only be a gift of love.

The following evening the Greeks were back at the wire, and when the five of us appeared they gave us an ovation, yelling "*Penta, penta!*"—meaning "the five," the cousins. Evening after evening, they awaited us at the wire, and Manci continued to be their most generous donor and we her guard. The Germans in the tower knew what was going on, but they kept the light off. We heard them laugh up in the tower, enjoying the break in the monotony. They watched the show, and it was a long one, because the Greeks had dignity and would not panhandle without giving something in exchange—they danced for us, or sang. One of them brought us a collection of miniature birds made from cement paper and passed them to us through the wire. Then again they gave us those worshipful looks, which we began to find intoxicating.

"I like them," said Tsilka, "but I don't know how I'd feel, if I were free and alone with one of them. . . . They're so different." She fought a shiver. "Besides, they're like children, don't you think?"

"Yes," said Suri, watching that huddle of men who arrived together, begged together, sang together, disappeared together. "But when they're not here, we miss them."

True. When the Greeks were confined and their yard was empty, our walks were no fun. We needed that constellation of men's eyes, that bath of male attention, overflowing through the sieve of the wire. We stared dreamily at our worshipers, our minds wandering. Before the war, we knew only of Polaks, Litvaks, Rusnaks, German Jews (*Yekes*, supercilious and snotty—tsk, tsk, tsk, our deportation train is not on time!), Hungarians, Romanians. And us, the best, the Jews who had grown up under the Czech flag. Shaped by a nation that was lawful and courteous. All the others we treated more or less condescendingly. Now we saw some brethren who were truly exotic. And across the Mediterranean, in and around that mythical land of Israel, lived the extreme exotics, the Sephardics of Arabia and Africa. The ones who had endured in the real deserts, the ones who still walked with the cane of Moses. Too different, too legendary. Better leave them that way, as pieces of a legend.

"We're terrible," I said. "We only like our very own. We need to like everyone in this ordeal." I secretly included Mirek in everyone.

I had four inches of hair now. My pubic hair pricked the inside of my thighs until Suri found a way to steal some flannel. A few days later she and I had nice new underpants of flannel and I did not itch anymore. I had thoughts and sensations I had never experienced in Zhdenev. If I wanted to live, I needed to enjoy life. If I let myself enjoy life, I had to acknowledge that almost everything could appeal to my senses. Matter itself was sensual, even if it was a plot of rotting mud. The shoes I bought from Otto's canteen were a feast of forgotten sensations. They were flat-heeled and plain, the kind a saleswoman or waitress might wear, but they were of real leather, properly tanned, and intended for female feet. I sank my nose in them and inhaled their aroma. After taking the weekly showers, I smelled my own body at night, under my blanket, and swore that I smelled not bad. Under the table, Otto sold a tooth-cleaning powder, which I could apply with my finger. Mixed with spit, it brought the whiteness back to my teeth, and if I cupped my hand in front of my mouth, I felt the scent of healthy breath again.

But what was more important, it was the breath I knew. I was returning to my known self.

Finally, there was a day when I realized that I could face a mirror and even feel excited about how I would look.

But I kept avoiding mirrors.

Why?

Because I still carried inside me a terrifying suspicion that none of this was real. That the good camp was not real (and it was good only for us; for 99 percent of the men it was sheer misery), and death might still await us at the other end. So it was smart, as a form of insurance, not to trust my luck. Besides, I did not want to remember too often the moment when Mirek had told me: "They'll let you grow your hair here. You'll be really pretty with your hair grown."

Then he had given me that plum to eat. The first sensual thing that had passed between us. Followed by his gloves. And by my timid hug and peck on his neck.

Now I regretted giving Ida the gloves. I could have fantasized about his hands each time I wore them.

After four weeks of not hearing from Mirek, I began to worry. Where was he? Why wasn't he sending me a message? Maybe I had turned him off by forcing that hug on him. God knew what kind of woman he thought I was. Or maybe his disappointment was physical—he had imagined my skin, my touch, the feel of my arms, my lips on his cheek completely differently. Presumptuous, I had rushed things when they were already going so promisingly. What an idiot.

That thought was comforting: instead of a murderous beating or a bullet, I was the one responsible for his absence.

Still, what had happened to him?

Finally, I put my pride aside and asked Mayer. who was a good source of information because he ran errands all over the camp, whether he knew anything about Mirek. Mayer said no, he hadn't seen him lately. Maybe he had been transferred (permanently) to some other camp. "D'you think he's dead?" I blurted. Mayer's eyebrows went up. Mirek dead? Unlikely. Mayer's Romanian brand of Yiddish was clumsy and reduced; still, groping for words, he managed to convey to me that Mirek . . . was Mirek. He had nine lives, and when someone like him died, everyone knew it.

Then he tried to hug me, perhaps to reassure me, but his hug quickly turned into a clumsy nestling at my chest. He was going through a growth spurt; only a month before he had been one foot shorter than me. But at heart he was still a child who, crimson and confused, could not resist snuggling against an older female.

At my chest, he offered, "I'll go find out about Mirek from Lorentz the Schreiber."

I detached myself gently. "Don't go, Mayer. It's all right."

Safe with me from carrying backbreaking sacks of cement, Mayer was devoted to me like a guard dog. "No, I find out," he insisted.

I did not respond, because I wanted him to learn what he could.

Mayer found out: Mirek was no longer in the subcamp of Mittergars, but in another subcamp, called Waldlager, where he was wiring a new compound. When he was needed elsewhere, he was trucked out of Waldlager—only days before, he had been in our own camp, checking the light towers. Soon, he might be needed at the Stelle again, or even at the tea kitchen.

Mayer's explanation sounded perfectly logical.

I felt so happy that to avoid a jinx I reminded myself that I was being a fool (yet again). It was wonderful that nothing had happened to Mirek, yet Mirek was not bespoken to me; in fact, by shtetl standards, I was bespoken to Boruch. When Boruch had been conscripted to a Hungarian work camp, like my brothers and almost all the local boys, we had met on the shore of the Zhdenevka, "one last time," and I had told Boruch that I would wait for him. Which meant getting married if we made it; there was no other possible interpretation when a shtetl girl promised a shtetl boy to "wait for him." Now, what would happen, if all three of us survived?

That should be my worst fear, I decided.

Another week passed. Five weeks altogether.

Then, one evening after roll call, pacing along the wire to the usual serenade from the Greeks, I was joined by Ida Blumenreich. "What's with your Mirek?" she asked. "I've seen him talking to Herta the Lageraelteste."

I jumped. "When? Where?"

"Last week, right here in our compound. And this week twice already, Monday and Tuesday."

He was back and he couldn't find a way to see me, but he was talking to another woman?

Talking did not mean romancing, but . . . Just as my hair had grown and my figure had improved, so had Herta's. She did no work at all except for reporting every morning: *"Frauenlager Mühldorf, 278 Haeftlinge, alle tauglich und fertig!"* (Women's camp Mühldorf, 278 prisoners, all fit and ready.) Thus, she had put on weight, her breasts poked through her uniform, and her rear swelled her pants. The girls feared and mistrusted her, and whispered that she slipped into the canteen to meet the apoplectic canteen man Otto. I found her pretty in a way that few men could resist.

I told Ida that I didn't believe her. She was making it up. Ida laughed—Herta and Mirek had checked the barracks together for burned bulbs. Spending some time alone in each barrack.

Checking the barracks for burned bulbs. That excuse, identical to the one he had used to be alone with me, hurt worse than anything else. Yet I still fought it. The Greeks' chorus seemed to fade, even though they were cramming the wire just a few feet away, while I said hoarsely, "There's nothing between them. She's the Aelteste, so if he has to check the lights, he has to let her know."

"Twice a week he's checking the lights?"

I stopped walking. Ida had me in her power.

She lowered her voice. "Herta has a lipstick in her bunk, I saw it. Who gave it to her, Otto or Mirek? Blanka . . . You eat up at the Stelle. You have lunch from the Germans' lunch, and fill yourself with water and sugar. Give me half your food, and I'll find out what's between them." Ida's hand felt my waist, caught an inch of meat between two fingers, and squeezed. "You're getting plump, too." She grinned.

"You're getting even plumper, dozing in the barrack all day. You looked better when we came here," I replied nastily.

"What do you care how I look? Is anyone choosing me here? I need more food than you. Besides, you and Mirek would make such a nice pair. It's not right for Herta to have him; she's already got Otto. Of course, Herta's older—"

The implication was: an older woman, trained in sex, could easily service both of them.

I had only spoken a few times to Herta. Working up at the Stelle, I didn't need to make nice to her because she exerted no authority over my detail. But I had seen her close enough to envy her looks. I remembered especially that she had pretty hands (nurtured by Otto with a steady supply of lanolin?). Maybe she could touch, she could stroke wonderfully . . .

I glanced at my hands. The lacerations from clearing the rubble had healed, but my nails were broken, my fingertips singed from handling the hot teakettles, my wrists scalded by hot water. Herta had a woman's hands, a lover's hands.

"Come on. Don't you want to know?"

Ida had won. I did want to know.

So I agreed that in exchange for the information she could have my dinner, and half my breakfast.

he November rain, sloshy and cold, alternated with clear autumn skies of a special chilly beauty, with sunbeams making the muddy roads glitter like rivers of gems. Sometimes I could fill myself with that beauty alone. But I couldn't really. I did not sleep, and despite eating from the officers' lunch truck, I had stopped putting on weight. I kept asking Suri to make me bulkier clothes. She made me a parka and trousers of rayon mixed with wool, from a defective shipment of winter uniforms designed for an SS alpine regiment.

Losch's generator had arrived; now even if he overburdened the circuits, the lights shone in the kitchen, and I had no pretext to call the electrician. Ida kept eating my food and reporting how Mirek had spent another half hour with Herta this week, in an empty barrack. Herta's hair was almost completely grown—so was mine—and she had become a striking blonde; I'd found out that she was twenty-eight and from Košice, a town much bigger than the closest town to my shtetl, Munkács. Ida had told me that Herta had gone to a German school. A refined city girl, friends with the Germans (which meant power); how could I blame Mirek for preferring her?

Losch finally asked me to organize his books. I found two bottles of schnapps stashed among them, one nearly empty, and a framed picture of a woman with plain features but a very determined look, wearing a leather cap that covered her hair completely. The picture was autographed to Losch. When he noticed me looking at it, he made a face as if I was bringing back unwanted memories.

"I was engaged to this woman," he volunteered. "But it didn't work out."

Your smoking habits didn't help, I thought. But I diplomatically replied, "Obviously, she's still your friend."

"*Ach* . . . She has unlimited access in Berlin, but otherwise, I'm among the very few people who can tolerate her." Losch was friendly finally, grateful that I had cleaned his reeking sanctuary. "Most of her life, she is in the air. She's Hanna Reitsch, one of our best test pilots."

"Really." Now I remembered him purring to her on the phone. "A daring woman."

"Women are tougher than they get credit for. Help me with this, Davidovich," he said, handing me his camera. It was fitted with a new lens, long and narrow. Assuming that he wanted his picture taken, I raised it at him. "No, no," he said, motioning toward the quarry. "Is the Herr Kommandant down there?"

"Yes," I said, looking through the eyepiece. Losch's office stood on the pit's edge, and the long lens, like a telescope, brought Eberle right under my nose. I could see in painful detail how he was disciplining another Greek.

"Take a picture," said Losch.

I thought I had misheard him.

"Take a picture," he repeated. "Of Herr Kommandant."

I almost threw the camera back at him. He waved his arms to catch it, then rushed to me, miscalculating the distance and touching me in the face with his eyeglasses. I could not retreat from him, I was backed into the window. "Take his picture, *now*," he panted. "Do you need a direct order?"

"I won't take his picture." I could see down below, even without the long lens, that Eberle had finished one Greek and started another. "Do you want me hanged, Herr Ingenieur?"

"Sshh," he said, as if appeasing a child, and tried to push

the camera back into my hands. "No one will harm you; no one will even know that you were here. These are my photographs. But I can't see enough to focus, not even with a long lens."

I slid around him and grabbed the door handle. He rushed to stop me again. "Nothing will happen to you. You don't understand."

"You're right. I don't."

"Listen," he said, speaking slowly and precisely. "What I am trying to document is very, very important. The way things are going here, we'll never finish this Stelle, and we'll never win the war. Trust me, no one will know that you helped me. That brute down there—"

He started to cough, the cavernous cough of a chronic smoker's bronchitis. In between coughing fits, he mouthed painfully, "Eberle is this camp's biggest problem. . . . He must be removed. . . . You can help me—"

The words came out of me unchecked: "So you can win the war?"

I did not realize the power of what I had said. Silenced, he searched for my expression in that blurred outer world, while his own expression admitted clearly that he hadn't expected me to have a reaction—not being fully human, how could I be interested in the outcome of the war? Speechless, he finally took a clear breath and mumbled, "It can no longer be won, Davidovich, don't worry. It's unwinnable. All I want here is an efficient work camp. I've been trying to take these pictures myself, but I failed. I thought I could trust you to help me."

"Why did you think that?"

He shrugged, looking stupid. "I had assumed . . ." Reminded that we were enemies, he glanced insecurely at the spic-and-span order I had established in his office. "You . . . won't say anything, will you?"

I burst out laughing: "As if anyone would believe me."

He paced: three steps left, three steps right. Like blind

people who have learned their immediate territory. He struggled with himself. Then he whispered, "I placed myself in your power, maybe that was a mistake." He picked up the camera again and stepped to the window: "Would you at least tell me where to point it?"

"No, I don't want to be involved."

"Don't be stupid." He chuckled, but with an edge of anger. "It's in your own best interest. The enemy is getting closer; you think Eberle's kindness to you will last? Meanwhile, we have to complete an important project here. Something that could be useful. . . ." He made an effort to sound sincere: "Even after the war. Trust me."

"I'll tell you where to point the camera," I said. "Then you let me go, all right?" He nodded. "And I want to ask you something, too. Is it true that you're using Jewish blood to give transfusions to your soldiers?"

"Yes," he said angrily.

I managed to sound sarcastic: "You're using 'inferior' Jewish blood?"

"*Ach verdammt,* don't you get it?" Losch took off his glasses, blew on them to clean them, and spoke to the air, not seeing me at all: "The Führer has ordered Total War, without enough weapons, soldiers, blood banks, anything . . . He wants to keep fighting at all cost, and his generals are too scared or too corrupt to kill him." He muffled the start of another cough. "So we need a lot of repaired soldiers, to pit them against the Americans. We repair them with Jewish blood—so what? Those soldiers will be dead in a few weeks, and who will care?"

If they die, their mothers and fathers might care, I thought, surprising myself.

He put his glasses back on. He located me, and said, raising a finger, "I would never, never implicate you. War makes the strangest allies. Tell me where to point the camera."

I took him by the arm and positioned him in the right spot. I even tilted down his camera at the right angle. He started to take shots, fascinated by what he knew was there, and I no longer asked for permission—I ran out of his office.

I was too disturbed to collect my cigarette butts. I made it to the kitchen very slowly. Fear filled me, almost impeding my walk. I was caught in a maze of people moving in different directions, like animals in the dark, toward their own goals, their own exits from the war. Whom was I to trust? Whom could I associate with? Mirek had left, and I had begun to shut down again. I found myself small and cowardly. Was I the one who had vowed on my first night here, after seeing myself in the shower mirror, that my hate would burn and purify, and that my gathering army would be of legions? How much braver I was when I was desperate. No longer desperate, all I wanted was a niche of comfort and a modest romantic fantasy, and Mirek had seen through it. I was too insignificant for him.

I was prepared for anything except for what happened in the next few minutes: a horse's clippety-clop began to be heard among the jagged crunching of the never-satiated Bird. Then Jacek's produce cart appeared on the path running by the tea kitchen, and there was a man sitting next to Jacek. The man had a black patch on his left eye. Together, the two looked like a picture from the shtetl. A world of my own size. The shtetl.

When the man with the black patch stood up in the cart, I jumped. He threw himself over the side, landing roughly, then hurried toward me with a slight limp. It was Mirek.

Jacek stopped the cart in front of the tea kitchen's entrance.

"Hey," Mirek said, smiling. "I was just going to drop in and see if the lights are working."

From under that black patch, an ugly bruise spread onto his forehead, over the bridge of his nose, and back toward his left temple. I felt a violent urge to rush to him, cradle him in my arms and ask what happened. Then, all of Ida's malicious gossip rang in my ears. For over a month I had not seen him, but he had seen Herta repeatedly, and if Ida was right, if Mirek had replaced me with Herta, that made perfect sense. The war was almost over. Caught in its catastrophic end, the fittest would partner with the fittest—someone like Herta could be far more valuable to this little partisan. And then there were her other endowments. Remembering her fleshy body, and the *lipstick*, I became so angry that I could barely utter, "The lights are all fine, and I have to go. Good-bye."

Mirek seemed nonplussed—"Blanka, what's the matter?"

I cleared my throat. "What happened to your eye?"

"I was hit in the face by a live wire. But I closed my eyes that second, so I wasn't really hurt. It's just a bruise. Want to see it?" he asked jovially, trying, I realized, to bring a smile to my face.

"No, I have to go. I'm . . . glad you're not hurt."

"I'm fine. You look good. I'll come see you tonight."

"Liar," I said under my breath.

Then I prayed that he hadn't heard me. But he had; his uncovered eye seemed to want to swallow me whole. I walked away quickly. Go to the camp, Mirek, Herta's there. I did not want to have any more feelings for him, yet as I slipped into the quiet kitchen (the girls were still serving the afternoon tea down in the Stelle), I watched his amazed face until the last second. Then I closed the door. I turned and faced the kitchen.

The place looked as if a storm had hit it: the fires were out, the big vats were overturned, and the bags of tea leaves, some intact and some ripped open, floated in a reddish tide of tea.

From between two overturned vats crawled Mayer. He was drenched, and his face had been lashed open from his forehead to his chin. He mopped the wound with a rag and still tried to gesture reassuringly. "Hulda did this. . . . It's all right, she left. . . . Ivan went out for wood to restart the fires."

I picked up an overturned chair and sat with my feet in cooling tea, thankful that Hulda had not found me here.

. . .

That evening, I did not want to go out in the yard after roll
call. I was sure that Mirek would not show up at the wire. I
climbed in my bunk and started smoothing my straw pillow,
preparing for sleep. From under the pillow, what looked like a
red little animal fell out and landed on the floor. It lay there,
still.

I swung my legs to the floor, bent down, and picked it up.
It was a flower, an artificial one. It was a rosebud.

I raised it under the bare bulb, and turned it in my fingers.
It was small, the kind that peasant brides pin to their gowns
at their weddings, where a fake flower, not a natural one, is
considered distinguished. I chuckled, because a memory of
home seemed to be attached to this flower. Its petals were of
bright red silk, crimped and goffered like real petals, but the
leaves and stem were made from a stiff plastic substance too
green to be natural. Still, under the barrack's light, that rosebud had a gracefulness, an illusion of freshness. I leaned against
the bunk, fake flower in hand, my feelings suddenly uplifted.
Then Ida and Mila appeared, heading toward their respective
bunks, Mila's across the central aisle, Ida's beneath my own.

Ida saw me with the fake flower. Her eyes bulged and she
reached to take it from me. "Who gave you that?"

I swung back from her clutching fingers. "No one. I found
it under my pillow."

"I didn't see anything under your pillow when I cleaned up."

"Some cleaner you are." I lifted the scentless flower to my
face; the feel of the silk petals on my cheek was light and
pleasant. Mila reached for it, too, and I allowed her to hold it.

"Someone put this under your pillow?" she asked incredu-
lously.

"I know I didn't," I said.

"It could be one of the Greeks," opined Mila.

"When? They're at work during the day," countered Ida.

"It's from Gabi Petilon for sure," said Mila. "He found a way."

"How would he get it in here? He couldn't jump over the wire!" snapped Ida, as if the mysterious caller's ingeniousness was a direct insult to her. She reached again for the flower. But Mila shielded it and whispered, "Blanka, this is . . . this is . . . love!"

I had given Gabi those cigarettes. Oh, God. What had I started?

Ida plopped onto her bunk with a surly expression. "What makes you think it's a man that left this here?" she asked.

"Shut up, killjoy!" Mila said belligerently, and although Ida was twice her size, she quickly crawled into her bunk as if seeking protection. I asked Mila not to mention the flower to anyone else.

Minutes later, the Blockova herded the other girls back inside and shouted: "Lights out!"

I climbed into my own bunk. There were a few muffled exchanges, a call for quiet, then we heard a loud *ping* on the roof, then another, then an uninterrupted monotonous tapping. Another cold rain. Tomorrow the yard and the roads would be a giant swamp.

I lay on my back and held the flower to my chest. In the dark, it did not feel like a flower at all.

Underneath me, Ida waited for the snoring to fill the barracks, then whispered, "Blanka?"

I did not respond. But she knew that I was awake.

"It can't be Gabi. He is at the Stelle all day."

I knew that. I had seen him there that morning.

Ida whispered again, "Maybe the flower's from Otto. . . ."

The canteen man? I twitched, revulsed. "He's wooing Herta, you told me that yourself."

"If Herta can handle two men, why couldn't Otto handle two women?"

"Shut up!" But Ida went on whispering—anyone could handle two lovers if the lovers didn't know of each other. I threatened to jump into her bunk and smother her with the pillow, but she talked on as if to herself: "Everything good happens to you, Blanka, I wish I were you."

"Let's switch then, maybe you'll give me some peace."

"You don't want to switch with me." She started crying. While I wondered whether to move to her bunk and try to comfort her, she sank into sleep, and I breathed with relief.

Now I was wide awake. I silently pitied Ida. Trapped in her big body, a pampered city girl once, now a pathetic orphan. But was I any luckier just because of this little tribute lying on my chest?

I thought of Gabi the Greek. I had started to bring him food from the Stelle and even bought him a tube of lanolin from the canteen, while Manci had continued feeding Daviko, and both men had begun to regain their strength—their hair, once lank and thinned, had started to shine, their faces got fuller, they carried themselves more firmly. God, don't let this be from Gabi. I knew now that I had to feel a certain way to want to belong to a man. I owed that discovery to Mirek. Mirek, Mirek, Mirek, who had opened so many doors in me, so excitingly yet so uselessly.

I'll come see you tonight, he had said. Had he approached the wire, he could easily have asked any girl to come to my bunk and let me know.

Liar.

I slept uncomfortably, tossing, waking, dozing off again, finally waking up completely with a choking sensation in my chest and throat.

The little flower was still on my chest.

I sat up, pushed open that panel in the ceiling, and groped inside the dusty hiding place I had not used since I had moved my cigarette stash. A dried butt met my fingers, like a mute welcome. I pushed the flower next to it, and closed the panel.

I still felt like I was choking, so I stuck my feet in my shoes, which I kept in my bunk so they wouldn't be stolen, climbed down and went to the door. I opened it and walked into a rain that pelted the ground and into the beams from the watch-towers.

Maybe I was feverish, for I enjoyed the way the rain cooled my body. I pulled my jacket over my head and stepped behind the barrack. A narrow tract several hundred yards long lay between the barracks, untouched by the towers' beams. I followed the dark tract, my shoes loading up with water, feeling that I had to make a crucial decision, *now*; but what was that decision? Suddenly, I knew: I would give myself to a man, and as soon as possible. I did not want to die a virgin. In the shtetl, like a good Jewish girl, I had saved my innocence—but why had I come into the world, to die here with my precious hymen intact? Even if my parents watched me from heaven, what right did they have to disapprove? They had been luckier than I, they had known each other and had borne children.

I stopped.

There was someone else in that space between the barracks. That person paced along the same dark path, right toward me.

I lowered myself to the ground, unable to think of what I should do. I stared as the solitary walker moved closer, closer, until I recognized a darker spot on that obscure face. Then I thought: I must run back, I must run back, *now*! But I stayed on the ground until the darker spot became that black patch over Mirek's left eye. Then Mirek himself was here, real and silent, and soaked.

He knelt beside me. I got up, but he pushed me down again. I grabbed his wrists, noticing how wide and strong they were, and whispered in his ear: "What are you doing here? Go back to your block!"

"I came to speak to you," he whispered back.

"Go back!" I breathed fiercely. "D'you want us to be caught and hanged?"

Out of that one eye, he gave me a stare that said: Would I play with your life? Then he whispered authoritatively that there was no chance we would be caught; the Germans wouldn't patrol in this rain; they would rely on the electrified wire. Then he looked around and whispered again. The safest place for us would be by the unfinished water tower. Unless I wanted to go back to my block . . .

He waited. I was silent.

He took the lead, and I followed.

Here was the tower: a tarp had been spread over the timber stacked up by it, to protect it from swelling in the rain. Mirek lifted the tarp. We crawled under it and crouched between the timber and the flap of the tarp, our faces almost touching.

He took my hand. I stared at the patch on his eye.

"You didn't have an accident," I whispered. "You were beaten, yes?" He nodded. "Who beat you? Eberle?"

Mirek shrugged—did it matter who beat him?

It had to be Eberle, I thought. I had seen him snarl at Mirek, and I had witnessed how effectively Mirek manipulated the rest of the camp's brass. I wished fiercely that Eberle would die tonight. Then I found myself praying desperately, like that time in Brejinka: God grant me the power not to be frightened, grant me the power to forget all else except this man, for this is the life you gave me. Don't punish us for being happy together for a minute, or two, or five—which seemed like an unending time. If we were found out, we would hang from those gallows together, paired up in death. A warning for other budding romances, like Manci and Daviko. One look at our stiff bodies, and Manci would stop bringing morsels to Daviko; selflessness and courage go only so far.

Grant me the power, God, to become a woman now, with this stranger. Grant me the power.

I put my arms around Mirek's neck, around his soaked collar, and asked, "Did you put that flower under my pillow?"

"Yes." His face widened in a pleased smile. "Didn't Ida tell you it was from me?"

"Ida?" I jumped. The tarp opened, and the rain poured onto my back.

Mirek grabbed the edge of the tarp and pulled it hard. I heard its wet swish as it shifted over the whole stack of timber, until it draped itself around us like a tent. Now we could not see each other at all. I did not care. He lifted me into his arms again. I inhaled the stink of our wet clothes, trying to distinguish Mirek's own smell—I remembered it, it was wired in my brain. I found it by burying my face between his neck and his collar.

"I left you several messages with Ida. For the last few weeks, Hoffman didn't let me stop at the Stelle; every time I finished something here, he rushed me back to Mittergars or to Wald-lager. Then I arranged to come this morning with Jacek, I wanted to give you the flower. But you acted so odd. What happened?"

"Hulda was in my kitchen." Which was almost true. Hulda had been in my kitchen.

But he caught me on the spot. "Hulda was in the quarry. Jacek and I saw her in the elevator, descending into the quarry."

"You're right. She had left the kitchen already. That was not the reason."

"Then what was the reason?"

I tightened my arms around him and buried my face in his neck even deeper. "Ida told me you're friends with Herta."

He seemed stunned. "Is that why you called me a liar this morning?"

"She told me you're friends with Herta, and you went into the barrack with her alone." I sniffed like an indignant child.

His eye blinked innocently. "So?" He started laughing, then

suppressed his laugh. "Herta was nice, she let me into your barrack. I wanted to see where you slept. But nothing else happened."

In the storm in my head, two thoughts obliterated all others: I'm going to wring Ida's neck—but not tonight. Tonight I'll just pray that Mirek makes it back safe, and if someone in my barrack notices my absence and rats on me, I don't care. I'll get the whip without betraying Mirek. Then that thought was replaced by one so excitedly infatuated, it made my head swim: Mirek had worried about how I acted this morning, he had worried so much that he no longer cared about the danger. He just had to find me and talk to me, *me*, the one who wouldn't even look at herself in a mirror! I was the one he missed! I felt a desire to drink him whole, so no one could deny him to me—was this love? I didn't know, but I felt it in Mirek, too. I felt it in his arms: locked around me, they felt hard like beams. Eberle had not really harmed him, thank God. I pressed myself against him willingly, pleased that he felt so strong. His heart pounded like a big clock.

He mumbled that he could not believe that Ida had not given me his messages.

I swore that she hadn't; then I squeezed him to me and cried.

My body felt warm, but below my knees my legs were frozen. My shoes had slipped off, and my feet had gotten lost in that cold tarp. I did not care. Stroking me, Mirek's hand rested briefly on my breast, then withdrew as if he had made a mistake.

I pulled him close to me. *Touch me again, I want it.*

He did not. He asked, his whispered voice tickling my ear, "Did you like the flower?"

"Where did you find it?"

"I ripped it off a display in the Munich radio station. Did you like it?"

I laughed with tears drying on my cheeks. "But it's fake, Mirek."

"So? It will last longer."

I remembered my manners. "I like roses very much. Thank you."

"Blanka . . ."

"Yes?" I also liked respectful men. But he was a little too respectful.

"Do you know the Charles Bridge?"

"What?" It was so wonderful to let my body mold itself against his. I kissed him in my schoolgirl way, pressing my closed lips onto his, then retreating. I wanted him to take the initiative, but he kept talking restlessly. "Charles Bridge, in Prague. If we escape and then get separated, we could meet there after the war. It's a famous bridge; everyone knows it."

"All right, all right. The war's not going to be over tomorrow."

"Two to four months. That's nothing."

"It's still a lot of time. Just don't take any more chances like tonight." *I will be his in the next few minutes.*

"Listen, I have something important to tell you." I waited, wondering what it might be. He had not yet told me *I love you.* "The Allies are bombing everything that has a construction attached to it. There is a construction here. They could start bombing this camp at any time."

"How could they see us through these clouds?"

"They bomb on the map, too. They come high, at twenty thousand feet, look at their instruments, and drop their load."

"Maybe they'll miss. We are together. Kiss me," I pleaded. And he, of all things, gave out a little sigh of impatience.

But then he took me in his arms again and kissed me.

I was kissed in the right way, for the first time. I was kissed with lips open, which was totally new for me, and yet it felt right; it was what I had expected to feel. He kissed me long and thoroughly, as if searching my mouth for a clue of affinity so important and yet so indescribable. Meanwhile, I unbuttoned my jacket and pressed his face onto my throat, praying that his loneliness and the strain of his missions would help and he would lose his control. (Men are supposed to have animal natures, aren't they?) Maybe he would not even notice that I was still so skinny—although Suri had told me that I had put on enough weight to soon need a bra again. Just now I was happy not to be wearing a bra. I wasn't afraid of giving myself, but struggling out of my wet fatigues might be embarrassing. Mirek kissed the skin below my throat. Wanting him to kiss my breasts, I wriggled up in his arms, to bring his lips closer. He suddenly stopped.

"You've never been with a man, have you?"

I felt the cold air entering my jacket and chilling his kisses on my skin.

Find out, I wanted to reply, but I did not have the nerve. "What's the matter?" I asked insecurely.

He whispered, almost inaudibly, "I love you."

He had said it. Fearfully and awkwardly, but he had said it. Now, why was he not kissing me anymore?

He whispered softly but clearly, "You don't want to get in trouble, particularly now. I can organize an escape in about five weeks." So that's what he meant by my getting in trouble— getting pregnant. I stiffened in his arms, feeling that this instant of wonderful and selfish mindlessness was slipping away from me, and I would remain as I was, intact and wondering why I had lived. He went on, unaware of my irritation. "I need two or three other people, otherwise we wouldn't make it. I need to secure a car or a truck, and German uniforms. That's the easy part. It's harder to find safe houses on the way, in case we are pursued and we have to hide. I have one some ten miles from here, a German's farm. I know the farmer—he would help us. But we need more than one safe house. And you"—his eye targeted me—"you want to be in top shape and not hindered by any—" He stroked my cheek. "You understand?"

I pushed his hand away, almost roughly. What made him think I would get pregnant just like that? Like all other men, he was probably so proud of that hairy pouch between his legs. I wasn't so totally ignorant of male anatomy. I remembered overhearing the boastful talk of my brothers and their friends, after they had grown old enough to visit a certain address of ill repute in Munkács. That hairy pouch, ready to score every time, what a marksman. I was angry that I had been ready to give myself to him, and he had guessed it, and rejected me.

"I'm not going anywhere," I said through clenched teeth.

"Don't you want to be free?"

"I just don't want to go."

He opened the tarp a crack and searched my expression in the feeble reflection from the outside. "Are you scared?"

"No."

"Then I don't understand. With a truck we have a chance to make it to the Swiss border, or even to the Rhine. The Americans are at the Rhine."

"Do you really love me?"

Cornered, he coughed throatily. "Ye-es. I mean . . ." He took a deep breath. "Yes."

He had said it now twice.

And I had just given him the chance to make me his.

Then I understood. If he loved me, then the rules were changed. I had hoped for a mindless romp, so I could say that I had lived. But he had not come here for a mindless romp. He was not a man of half-measures, he believed that we had a real chance to survive, and, even more astoundingly, in his mind, he was pledged to me already, and I to him. That was what meeting him on that bridge meant: a pledge of a future together. I had rushed to him as a girl desperate to be a girl no more, but he, even before touching me, had assumed that I would be much more. A committed partner.

I breathed, flabbergasted. Then I felt a deep panic. He probably was . . . the kind of man I would want to marry.

Which meant . . .

I buried my face in his collar again, happy that he couldn't see me, hoping that he would not guess the reason for my shiver, or measure the depth of my fear at losing yet another person I loved—losing him would be as devastating as losing my parents and siblings, perhaps even more devastating, for I was ready to give him what was most essential, my blood. Oh, Mirek, Mirek . . . I had yearned for life. Now I had life right here, in my arms, and instead of bringing me peace, life made me even more frightened, for him, for me . . .

That German boy, the son of the stationmaster, came into my mind: You are Jewish, aren't you? If I decided to escape, even the little children would have their eyes fixed on me. As for the door of my memory, it would burst wide open, pouring out the guilt, the torture: You're still free? Still alive? Why haven't you been caught yet? If I decided to escape, I would have to face my life again, with its frightening balance sheet. How much had I lost, and how much could I still lose?

I shrank back. "Freedom is here," I said, pointing at the narrow space between us. I had spoken utterly at random.

But he whispered in my ear, "You're right. You don't steal freedom. You have to have it whole."

Mistaking my panic for what he was feeling, a momentous commitment, he took me in his arms again and kissed my cheeks, the wet brush of my hair, my forehead, my temples, finally my lips, softer and softer, as if my answer had given him the best confirmation that he was on the right track. Finally, he stopped. The dim cascading of the rain was reflected in his uninjured eye.

He muttered carefully, "I can't tell you everything. If we are betrayed, if you are tortured, you might break. I'll tell you enough so you understand." I clenched my teeth, afraid of any word he might say. "There are Russian spies in Munich. They're there to identify military constructions and call in the Allied bombers to destroy them. They don't care about the prisoners' lives. I don't want this camp to be bombed, so I keep telling them that there's no military construction here, but they probably suspect that I'm lying." He searched inside his jacket and pulled out a cigarette and a book of matches. I had never seen him smoke before. He scratched a match, lit the cigarette, inhaled deeply. Then he put out the burning tip with his fingers and carefully stuffed cigarette and matches back inside his jacket. "If the Allies bomb the camp, they could kill everyone here. You understand?"

I nodded, mute. I understood.

Then I whispered, "So . . . are you trying to stop them?"

He looked at me darkly. "We'll get out of this, somehow." He kissed me again, with lips that tasted smoky, kissed my mouth, then the skin above my breasts. Roughly, greedily. As if to imprint me in his memory.

"We'll get out of this," he repeated.

"I want you to be my man," I whispered.

"I know. I will be your man." I never imagined saying such words or listening to such words from anyone, but from Mirek they sounded sane and reasonable. "Now, you've got to go back to your block, and I to mine."

Don't cry, I told myself. I reached for my shoes and put them on.

I did not want to look at him. I feared I would see a lone man with the whole war weighing on his shoulders.

"Can you come tomorrow to the Stelle?" I asked humbly. "I'll wreck Losch's lamps. I'll do anything."

I could not look at his face, but I felt his gaze. "I'll try."

"Mirek?"

"Yes?"

I wanted to tell him that I loved him. How would I be able to slip back inside my barrack, to lie down in my soaked clothes, how I would survive the next hour, until the quiet on the men's side would signal that he had made it back safely? But . . . he was facing a choice so much more terrifying, a peril so much more real. I suddenly knew that he would not be caught tonight, and neither would I. If God wanted to try us, He would give us a harder trial.

"What are you going to do?" I asked.

"I don't know. But I have to do something soon."

"The Germans are not so stupid. They won't leave the camp unprotected. They'll bring flak guns here if their construction is at all important."

Without answering me, he opened the tarp. Then he held me to his chest, with the rain pouring on our faces. "If something happens and I can't contact you, remember this: Charles Bridge, in Prague. After it's over, go to that bridge, every Tuesday and Friday morning, until you find me."

I repeated, blinking from the rain, "After it's over, I'll go to that bridge every Tuesday and Friday morning, until I find you."

He put me down. In the pale reflection of the camp's lights, I looked at his body, which I had not been fated to share tonight. I touched his chest, swept my palms over his firm pectorals, whispering that I had never liked anyone as much, ever—I was afraid to say *loved*. He did not guess my fear, and laughed quietly. "You like me like this, one-eyed and beaten up?"

"Is your eye going to be all right?" I asked with sudden panic.

"Yes, a doctor in the camp hospital already told me so. Dr. Markus Gudor, a Czech. Go to your block now."

"All right."

He was the more experienced fighter, and I had to obey.

I made the most painful choice of my life, and turned and walked away, not looking back.

· · ·

This did not happen, I thought, opening the barrack door and slipping back inside. I dreamed it. Then I shook myself, like a dog climbing out of a pond, I heard drops of rain fall off my clothes. I froze. Someone stirred in a bed nearby but did not wake up.

Pacing so silently and slowly that the distance to my bunk seemed endless, I finally reached it, climbed in, lay down in my soaked clothes, and breathed, exhausted. My chin was on fire, my lips, my neck . . . Then I realized why. All through those wonderful kisses, he had scratched me with his unshaven chin. I put my palm on my face and smiled. Did I want proof? Here was the proof. Then, I decided that if I opened that hole in the ceiling and Mirek's flower was still there, then that meant that he had made it back safely. Tonight at least, he was safe.

I raised my arm, pushed away that wood panel, and reached inside the little niche. The dust clung to my wet fingers.

The flower was there.

Part 4

LOVE

SIXTEEN

Mirek

*S*he was ready. I realized it as soon as we started to kiss. So why did I not make love to her?

Was I afraid we would be caught? No more than when I slipped under the wire into her compound.

And she was resigned to death striking at any moment, I knew that when I saw her pacing in the rain. Out of her barrack after lights out.

Why did I not make love to her?

Then, she changed her mind, which I did not expect. Something to do with the past? The dead, hovering over us? The word *love*, holding up before us the promise of a future?

Then I started to talk about the danger we were all in, and the magic vanished. We were at war again, after having sneaked a few minutes of ignoring it, like a drag on a cigarette between two missions.

An instant of respite. Then back to the war.

In a way, we already belonged to each other. I did not think that was possible; that's what you read in books. Yet as I crawled under the wire again, flattening myself into earth pounded by the rain, I realized it. For the total time of a few minutes, we were joined more than a man and a woman can be in a bed, in freedom. We were pledged to each other. The spell would be maintained by not accomplishing, by waiting.

Freedom is here, she had said, shaping the space between us with her hands. A few handfuls of space. Amazing how women know such things, instinctively. She was right. Freedom was there. I felt it, I recognized it.

Crawling back with her words humming in my ears, I thought of a day I would never forget. Ten desperate podzemny men were trapped in the cellar of a printing house, in Prague. Ten desperate podzemny men including me. One floor above us, Linotype machines and rotary presses churned out Prague's papers for the next day, special editions of *Noviny* and *Vecerny Praha* printed from typesetting matrices flown in from Germany. The Czech Linotypists and printers worked with Nazi automatics pointed at them, putting out special editions announcing that our country had ceased to exist. The Czech army had surrendered without a shot. A bedroom was being prepared in the Hrad Castle, the home of Bohemian kings, for the visiting Führer.

The SS troops surrounded the block in a steel ring of tanks and armored trucks. We, the ten men trapped in the cellar, stared at each other. None of us were armed—even if we had been, we did not have a prayer. We were here to swear in the new volunteers. I had brought with me the podzemny papers: the membership lists, the maps of the safe houses and mail drops, the names of support groups, even the list of our modest stock of weapons, itemized. And, in a cotton bag, two dozen pins of the athletic club Slavia, to be distributed to the new recruits as camouflaged membership badges.

I had carried all that through the streets in a backpack, ten minutes before the Germans surrounded the block.

Jelinek, our liaison to the Czech army, with his military posture so obvious in his ill-fitting business suit, ordered me to destroy the papers. I said no. I did not have the heart. Jelinek himself did not have the heart. We held our breath, listening to the jackboots crashing above our heads. Then Jelinek started to sing the Czech hymn, in a whisper: *Kde domov muj, domov muj?* Where is my home, my home? The water rustles in the

wild, the forests shiver on the hills / And I glimpse that handsome Czech land / Which is my home, my home.

We started to sing after him. In a whisper we sang, against
the jackboots and the growl of the tanks in the street. I sang
fighting shivers. I recalled trekking to Prague six years before.
Looking at the horizon, letting the sunny aromas from field
and grove enter my lungs, feeling that I was mixing into my
blood that *zeme Ceska*, my country's earth.

It was March 15, 1939. The Germans had taken Prague.

"We don't know how long we'll have to wait," said Jelinek,
"so I think we should proceed. Karel, swear in the new volunteers."

I, Karel, nineteen, a podzemny fighter for five months,
stepped before our new recruits. "This is our oath to our homeland, to all the people and the heritages that made it proud
and free. If you want it to rise from its ashes, proud and free
again, swear, young podzemny fighters, that you shall respond
to our call at any hour, as if the podzemny were the homeland
itself. You shall fulfill any order issued to you by the podzemny.
You shall protect the podzemny with all your strength and
determination, with all your power to withstand torture, with
your last breath. To seal this pledge, young podzemny fighters,
answer me: Where is your heart?"

"In the podzemny."

"Where is your freedom?"

"In the podzemny."

"Where is your honor, your strength, your kin, your reason
to be, until we free the homeland?"

"In the podzemny."

The paper on which I had scribbled the oath for the recruits
to memorize (being an early member, I had participated in
drafting the text) had gone from hand to hand and was crumpled and humid from sweat.

Two unlikely friends, Voricek and Narzissenfeld, stood at the front of the pack. Voricek wore a prankish smile on his pimpled face—working-class kid, suckled on factory fumes along with his mother's milk. Next to him, pink-cheeked and plump, Narzissenfeld—raised in comfort, son of a jeweler. I shook their hands, and Jelinek saluted as if he were still wearing his uniform.

Arnost Lemberger, over two meters tall, fat, with raven-black hair, inspected the recruits cynically. Arnost and Jelinek represented the Underground Committee. Arnost had not joined us in the entire hymn, just its first line. He had quarrelled with the rest of the Committee, suggesting not the Czech hymn but the Communist international as our official song, and had lost. When Jelinek saluted, Arnost raised his balled-up fist.

Then he listened to Narzissenfeld, elated to be a man among men, yet worried—he was raised to go to temple every Friday. If we had actions on Fridays, would his absence from temple betray his new activities? His father did not know of this. His father was in the Alt-Neu Shul just now, praying under its ancient Gothic vaults with a whole crowd of Jews from the Sudeten. They had fled when the Wehrmacht had invaded the Sudeten, not suspecting that they'd be caught again in Prague seven months later. They had swelled the Jewry of Prague to sixty-five thousand. The capital's synagogues had never been so full.

Narzissenfeld added with difficulty, Even Jewish temples were said to have informers now—

Arnost cut in, "You're not here to be a little Yid, Narzissenfeld. We go on *shliches* (mission) on Friday, you come along like any soldier, *recht gezunt*." Arnost showed off his Yiddish and in the same breath discarded his Jewishness for Communism. Not used to being addressed coarsely, Narzissenfeld started to blink fast. "And you begin by dropping that ridiculous name. It stinks of Jewish ten kilometers away." *Narzissenfeld* meant "field of narcissus."

"But it's my name," Narzissenfeld protested.

"Change it. We all have new names here. We're not a bunch of Jews who don't know where to turn. We are Czech patriots."

Recht gezunt. Arnost had a Czech code name now: Loupek. I saw how Narzissenfeld's chin started to quiver. Jelinek, embarrassed, bowed his head. I looked around the room. Three Jews who didn't know where to turn. Seven Czech patriots. But five of them, including Arnost, were Communists. Just now, the podzemny could not afford to alienate the Communists.

When the Germans were done, they loaded their special editions in trucks, then left with a great roar of engines and clatter of tanks, to deliver the evening and morning papers all at once. We waited an hour, then slipped out, one by one, at five-minute intervals. I whispered to Arnost that he and I should be last. He went out before me. After five minutes I followed, found him in the empty street and gave it to him. He was a piece of filth to treat Narzissenfeld like that; we were an army for freedom, not the Communist party. He told me coldly that this was a class war, Nazis against Communists, and the Communists would win. Then, all the old pledges would be swept away.

"All of them? Faith, country, politics—?" Arnost nodded calmly, in sync with me. "Even the pledge to freedom?"

"Freedom is here," he said, showing his heart. "Sometimes. When you're at peace with yourself."

"You're at peace with giving up who you are?"

He looked me straight in the eyes. "For a greater cause, yes. For the pledge of everyone being equal, yes."

"Then why didn't you tell Narzissenfeld to look for another podzemny? He came to us to protect what he is, not to get rid of it."

Silent, Arnost turned and walked away. I walked away, too, into the occupied city.

Five years later, it occurs to me that you can look for freedom everywhere, yet never find it. Freedom resides in the pledges you make, and keep. Even Arnost could be free, as long as he remained loyal to his greater pledge. If that meant dismissing his past, shrugging off his parents, spurning his whole upbringing, childhood memories, if he managed to do it, then he was the free one, not me.

She made me think of all this. As usual. She, who probably never attempted to change, to pass.

She made me think of that Obersturmführer who sat at a bare desk in Warsaw, waiting for me to lay on it the filthy loot from the dead. When I had first met him, I had stood at attention, my striped cap in my hand. "Vencera Karel, *melde gehorsamst, Herr Hauptsturmführer*," which meant Reporting respectfully, Captain.

He jumped like a wound-up devil: Not captain! Not captain! First lieutenant only. I had touched a very sore spot. He contained himself, sat not at his desk but on it, and breathed heavily. You know what this is? he asked, encompassing with a sweep of his arm the whole building. The Warsaw branch of the RSHA (Reich's Central Security Office)? It's actually a Reichskommissariat for Jewish Affairs. That's our expertise, Vencera. I learned all I know from my *Vorgesetzter* (boss—I guessed that he was speaking of Eichmann). My boss should be made Reichskommissar for Jewish Affairs. Maybe those *Scheisskritzeler* (shitscribblers) in Berlin will create that rank someday. Or they won't.

The way things are going, I thought, they won't have to. They'll run out of Jews. But I stood up straight, met his glance, and asked: What is the job, Herr Obersturmführer? And he sent me into the ghetto's sewer. *Suchtkommando*, special search detail. Eight men. Chief scavenging rat: Mirek Vencera.

The Obersturmführer was impressed that we found so many dead Jews in the sewer. Do you think they died fighting, Vencera? They looked as if they did, Herr Obersturmführer. Really? Do you think they had so much character?

The idea made him talkative. He had been sitting at his desk, sorting through the latest sewer harvest. He rose, washed his hands in the metal sink and then joined them behind his back. A race that can never be trusted proves trustworthy in death, he mused.

As trustworthy as anyone else, I muttered.

How many times would I get away with talking back to him? But he laughed—I was such a *Dummkopf*. Did I not know that once every year *they* renounced all the vows they made, they betrayed all their pledges? As he paced before me, like a thin, slinky feline, I felt hypnotized by him. Against my will, against my judgment, a power larger than anything opened my mouth and moved my tongue for me. Was he speaking about the Day of Atonement?

He stopped pacing. Yes, the Day of Atonement. That's what he was speaking about.

The sweat dripped cold on the back of my neck, covering the hot sweat I had shed in the sewer, but I still could not stop. Well then ... As an expert, the Herr Obersturmführer should know that on that day Jews *do not* break their pledges to fellow humans. Debts, business obligations, partnerships, friendship, parenting, marriage, were not affected by the All Vows prayer, which the Jews recited before the sounding of the ram's horn. The All Vows were strictly the ones between man and God, and they were meant to be voided each year only because man, in his imperfection, rarely fulfilled what he promised, even to God. God granted that voiding, so that man could be forgiven his transgressions, and he could start afresh. When you make any vow to the Lord God—said the Jews' sacred book—you must fulfill it without delay. If you refrain from making a vow, that is no sin for you. But refrain from rash vows, even if they are motivated by piousness.

"It's in their book?" he snapped.

"So I heard, Herr Obersturmführer."

He made an annoyed face, then glanced at the photo of his

boss, looming over us. In 1937, on the Nazi party's dime, Eichmann had been sent on a "research" mission to Palestine, which had ended ingloriously a few days after his arrival. It had trickled down among his staff that he was trying to read the Talmud (in German) at his hotel when he was picked up by the British secret police. With due honors to his status. Which meant discretion. No notes between London's Foreign Office and Berlin's Wilhelmstrasse. Silently, he had slipped in; silently, the British had spotted him and expelled him.

Still, from a failed mission, Eichmann had managed to return an expert. So he did not like to be challenged. And he had taught his men not to be challenged.

Had I doomed myself? My mouth kept speaking. "In one respect only, the Day of Atonement can be thought of as a one-sided cancellation. The All Vows, the Kol Nidre, acquired significance in Spain, in the days when Jews were forced to convert to Catholicism. But many still attended the synagogue in secret and at risk for their lives, and used the Kol Nidre prayer as a renunciation of the vows imposed on them by the Inquisition—"

He jumped, with a feral satisfaction in his eyes. "You see?" he gloated.

"With utmost respect, I see nothing. Betrayal of an imposed God in favor of your own seems like no betrayal to me."

He rushed at me. He was a slight man, not given to violence. I stood still, until his face was before and slightly below mine. "Vencera. No Czech boys know such things. You're one of them. You're one of them—don't lie."

There was anger in his voice. I had deceived his instinct, his fine bloodhound nose, of which he was so proud. The sweat no longer dripped on my temples—it poured.

But I stood eyeball to eyeball with him, explaining about my time in the trade school. It was a Jewish school. Director Bobasch had kindly offered me a scholarship. The curriculum included religion. I had listened with one ear, retaining what I, like anyone else, found so intriguing about *them*. That they had been forced to have a secret life, invisible from the outside. I, like so many others, wondered, How did they manage to reconcile how they felt on the inside with how they lived on the outside? Well, their way wasn't so different from fighting in an underground movement. You had to believe in your oath, in your pledge to the underground. That's what enabled one like me to understand them.

For one instant, he was totally silent. Then he sputtered, incensed that I could understand Jews and even sympathize with them without being Jewish—a notion that was an affront to this logic. "Confess it, Vencera, confess it. If you're not one, then you must be a *Mischling* (half-breed). You know too much, you remember too much—"

I yelled from the depth of my lungs: I was no half-breed, just a Czech boy, Cestmir Vencera, a fighter in the underground.

He sat on his desk, not caring that the day's filthy harvest stained his uniform. "Don't you understand," he said, "if you are Czech, you are *germanizable*. Of all the Slavs, we regard the Czechs as forty to sixty percent germanizable. From now on there are only two breeds of people: the Germans and the germanizable. You're a Czech. Do you realize your luck?"

I answered, "Maybe the Czechs are less germanizable than you think."

Surprisingly, he appraised me with a strange, icy good will, and I suddenly glimpsed what he and his boss dealt with every day: the annihilation of a whole people, which was their first experiment of that nature, their first one. Would there be others? They did not know yet. Would this one succeed? They did not know that either. But the awareness of what they were doing was too much; this man who could dispose of me with the blink of an eye was cracking under the strain. The job had turned him into a necrophile, and like all necrophiles he was obsessed with his victims, thinking all day long one thought only: the Jews, the Jews, the Jews. Dead, dying, slated to die, or momentarily spared.

The Obersturmführer's obsession had taken the form of aberrant logic: the Jews were utterly untrustworthy; hence it was good to dispose of them. But that meant the liquidation of millions of humans. Even if they were all proved evil, even if everything about them could be presented as twisted and unhealthy, they were still humans, with faces, eyes, brains, desires, and mouths that opened in cries of pain or calls for mercy. Only an aberrant logic exerted hour by hour could justify killing in such numbers, and that aberrant logic craved rebuttals, in order to reinforce itself.

I had provided a needed rebuttal. And acted wholly ungermanizable, which was the Obersturmführer's triumph. Had I been germanizable, I could not understand the Jews, or sympathize with them. That made his equation correct all over again. Which was why he eyed me with that icy good will.

"Verschwinde, Verbrecher!" Disappear, criminal! he hissed, wasted yet satisfied. And I raced out. I rejoined the others, and we went to the canteen to claim our vodka (for a day's work, we received a bonus of one bottle of vodka per person), while the feeling of the encounter slowly left my body, like a drug.

I went back to the Warsaw building of the RSHA almost every day, always with something to turn over to Eichmann's man. Those linoleum floors shredded by hobnailed boots, the stark and ugly furniture, the guards tired of clicking their heels each time an officer walked by, became familiar. Though we hated and feared this place, it was still our limbo, our alternative destination to Pawiak Prison, or back to camp.

But finally, the mother lode dried up, and the Suchtkommando was disbanded. We could have been shot, but we were scattered among various camps. I left Warsaw alone in a police van closed on all sides except for a narrow grating at the back. After hours of rolling, I felt under me an autobahn still smooth and intact. I was in Germany. We stopped when air raid sirens sounded, which they did much more frequently than in Poland. The landscape became hilly and then mountainous. We pressed on. The air through the grating became strong and fresh, smelling of forests. We stopped in Dachau, where I was to serve the rest of my sentence. We went through the old charade: *Jude?* No. *Beruf?* (Profession?) Elektrotechniker. Good, we can use that. Dachau had made babies tagged *1, 2, 3, 4,* some of them subtagged into *a, b, c,* and so on. I was sent to the growing Dachau 3b, locally known as Mühldorf. An easy camp for someone with my skills.

Two months later, one foggy morning, I glimpsed in the first row of a women's column a girl who walked in her wooden clogs with an odd air of saintliness about her. Both desperate and peaceful. Now, my mind is filled with that woman. I stole a book from the radio station's library. Goethe's *Gedichte.* I cannot write poems, so maybe I will write her Goethe's poems; she wouldn't know that they were not by me—but what would I write them on, bits of paper from cement sacks? I could fold them into balls smaller than the nail on her little finger. I watched her eat a plum. I knew then what all men know when it happens to them: I had become someone else after meeting her.

I'm back in the muddy Opel Blitz truck, sitting next to Ostrander. We are the same age. He is a tall, gangly youngster with oversize hands and feet, and a big blond face. I hear in his laugh the boy that he was. He is over that married woman—he says.

We drive on the bombed Munich streets, passing disfigured old houses, stately public buildings. Ostrander identifies them with his finger: office of the Gestapo, Orpo, Sipo, Kripo,

RSHA, SS, SD . . . "We hold everything in one fist," he explains. "We are the most efficient. Even if we are defeated, our system of organization will be the model for the future."

I ask him, Is there anything, anything at all that he thinks Germany should have done differently?

He reacts with puzzlement. What?

I repeat the question. Anything of any kind that the Reich should have shied from doing?

"We should have left Russia for later. Finish England first. We would have done a better job."

"What about freedom?"

He does not understand what I mean. He is free, he replies, gesturing with his arms, as if testing the air around him for restraints and finding that it contains none. "Besides, we're at war, and I'm a soldier. Freedom's for later, for peace."

Born soldier. Craving commands, instructions, regulations. Without orders, he feels burdened by anxiety, directionless, confined. I never encountered that feature in the podzemny. We, too, are fighting, but we are civilians, missing peace, fighting to reacquire our freedom. We are not happy to fight. Ostrander is happy to fight, and will fight to the end, suicidally. That crowd hypnotist in Berlin already said in a speech—I listened to it on my shortwave radio—that if the German nation cannot emerge victorious, then it's only right that it should perish. What an inspiring prophecy to send to seventy million German civilians, starved, terrified of air raids and of the "people's courts," who are hanging hundreds of deserters and "defeatists" every week.

I cannot save Ostrander. He made his pledges, as I made mine.

But in the name of my pledges, I am brought before a terrible choice. Camp Mühldorf is jammed with thousands of lives—I may not know those people, never learn their names, it does not matter. They are there, and she is there. Camp Mühldorf, or my life.

Of course, I could escape alone. But could I be free alone? She knew that. She said when I asked her if she would escape with me: I'm not going anywhere. She is right. Freedom you do not steal, freedom you have to have whole.

She is free, even in camp. She is free in the one way that counts. She is at peace with her pledges, while I'm no longer at peace with mine.

SEVENTEEN

I brought the radio back into the Mittergars compound hidden in my toolbox. I was already congratulating myself for my cleverness—the Germans' radio-detecting vans roamed the cities and the countryside hunting for clandestine sets operated by spies, but who would look for a spy inside a camp? So I hid the set in the carpenters' shed. A few days later I had a chance to examine it, and I saw that the capacitor was missing. The radio was as good as dead. Someone had torn the capacitor out, someone who knew where the set had been stashed before (in the cellar of the Munich radio station), someone who knew that I could not replace the capacitor in the camp.

Someone. Who?

Kempner.

If it was him, his idea was doubly ingenious—not only could I not use the radio, but I was also loaded with a dreadful piece of incriminating evidence. It's a wonder the Gestapo did not descend on me right away—a fault in communication, a tip relayed too late? I hid in the carpenters' shop after lights out and destroyed the radio piece by piece. The metal parts I twisted and tore with pliers, the wires I cut to bits. I took off my jacket, folded inside it all the debris of what I'd put together with such care, and smashed it with a hammer. The jacket muffled the noise. I crawled into the latrine, poured what was left into one of the reeking holes, and washed my jacket outside, in a pool of rainwater. Then I crawled back to my bunk.

I probably slept one hour.

Someone gave an awesome kick to the leg of my bunk; it broke, and I flopped to the floor on my face. A hobnailed boot crushed the back of my neck, mashing my nose into the floor. I wasn't worried about my nose, but I was terrified that my teeth might be rammed back into my throat; I knew of a man whose vocal cords had been slashed that way.

They wanted the radio. I was pulled up and bounced between three sets of fists. They wore black leather overcoats—Kripo, the Kriminal-polizei. What a joke, but it figured; politikers are criminals against the Reich.

The whole barrack was up, but I did not hear a peep. A fist in one eye clouded my vision, and I closed my other eye and kept it stubbornly closed. You don't need to see who beats you. The three who hit me slackened somewhat, and I became aware of two others, smashing my bunk. No radio. They ordered other prisoners to rip up the floor planks; they yelled for ladders so they could poke at the ceiling. They found nothing. I was manacled and chased outside with kicks. I didn't know when I had made it to the gate. The gates of satellite camps bear no philosophical inscriptions, no ARBEIT MACHT FREI (Work makes you free) or JEDEM DAS SEINE (To each his own fate). This one was a plain iron gate with a bicolored barrier, like at a railroad crossing—railroad tracks, crossties hammered on by my dad the trainman. Dad, Dad! This is me, Karel!

There was a commotion behind me. I turned and saw one agent rushing out of the barrack, frantically waving a book. My copy of Goethe's *Gedichte*. They had found something.

In the car speeding for Munich, they thumbed through the book seeking circled passages, marked pages, anything that might look like a code. I didn't know whether the book was marked in any fashion—I'd stolen it only days before. They found nothing. "You like poetry?" asked the boss, turning from the front seat and slamming the book against my face. It fell on my lap, and I bled over it. The boss spat in my face. "Electrician, ha? We've got something electrical for you. We'll introduce you to Big Heinrich. How many volts on your nuts you think you can take?" I'd heard of Big Heinrich, a high-power wire they clamp onto your genitals, then plug the other end into a socket. Contact. Your brain fills with lightning. Your mouth, dried up instantly, can't even scream anymore. Electricity dehydrates.

They beat me in the speeding car, and I was thankful. Usually their most savage energy takes about forty-eight hours. If they don't get anything out of you in the first forty-eight hours, they know that by then your network has learned of your arrest and has had time to disperse. So it's over. Your network is safe and you, most likely, are dead.

"Who's your contact in Munich? Who's in charge of ground operations south?"

"The Wussians." My tongue was swollen like a sausage. "Want to wrestle with them?"

"Tell us their names!"

Kempner, I wanted to cry out, Kempner.

But what would that do to my fate, and what would it do to the camp?

I swished grotesquely, through lips too torn, gums too swollen to make normal sounds. I was a political prisoner. They had no right to beat me or even investigate me without an order from the Dresden People's Court that had tried me. That was the law. Did they have such an order?

I was clobbered with a pistol butt, and my head fell back on the headrest. Almost unconscious, I glanced out of the car window. White butterflies wheeled and whirled in the air. It was snowing.

. . .

I was dragged into the interrogation building facedown, my hands shackled, my work boots scraping the floors. I was pushed into a dimly lit room; I heard the door opening, closing. A chain was fastened around my ankles, and I was hurled into an icy bath and held under the water. The water washed the blood off my face and cleared my sight. I faced the bathtub's tinny bottom, whose enamel had been almost completely stripped. I used to be able to hold my breath underwater two and a half minutes. I started to count. I got to a hundred, my brain mush, my lungs collapsing. They were not pulling me out. I lost count.

The rusty bottom came alive. Faces floated upward toward mine. Voricek, Narzissenfeld. Dead. Jelinek. Dead. Arnost Lemberger. Disappeared. My father's face floated up, and he looked so sad. Why did you leave home, Karel, why? Why did you have to be so proud? Even if you were to die, you would have died among us. Dad, I did not know. I'm so sorry for all the pain I caused. His face dissolved. I saw my older brother. You still have my knife? he asked me. When I ran away, I took his pocket knife.

They dragged me out of the tub.

"Time for Heinrich," one of them said.

God, don't let this happen.

But it was happening. I was being strapped to a table. One of them grabbed my lower parts, kneading them roughly through my pants. "What we have here is a reflexogenic re-action. Instead of blood swelling up your *Schwantz* at the sight of some appetizing ass, you're responding to a muscular stim-ulus. Makes you ready for Heinrich." He pulled on rubber gloves, held up a thick wire ending in a kind of steel jaw. "Hold him still!" A pain worse than anything stabbed me in the groin, exploded into my legs, my buttocks, my midriff, my heart. I screamed but never heard my scream.

They made me sit up and splashed cold water in my face.

What was left of me down there, *what?* They raised Heinrich again, but the door opened and an SS man called from the door: *"Genug!"* Enough! He strode to the table and looked at me.

"Vencera," he muttered with wonderment.

He had changed. But I recognized him. Rademacher. As a member of the Slavia athletic club, which helped with my cover, I had met him in an amateur boxing contest, in Vienna. Rademacher, welterweight champion of Bavaria, versus challenger Vencera of the occupied Bohemian/Moravian Protectorate. Back then he was a well-built young man, handsome, with quick footwork and a sharp punch; he had good press and a phenomenal gallery of women. He had beat me on points, though I thought I had punched more and harder—but the referees and judges were all German. Fighting him came in handy after I was arrested. My interrogations always started with questions about being in the ring with Rademacher, and although that friendliness was soon dropped, I got off easier than many others.

The war had left its bite on Rademacher. A deep scar, like a trench dug in flesh, split his nose and left cheek.

"Take him to the hospital," he said. "There's been a mistake, he's not the right one."

At the hospital, they gave me water and put me to bed, in a room as narrow as a cell—the bed, a night table, and a closet of medical supplies filled it completely. They tried to fit cigarettes between my lips, but my lips were too swollen. My genitals, too, were swollen enormously, and bandaged so thickly they raised my bedsheets like a tent.

They gave me sedatives, and I slept until it was morning again, and the prisoner doctor, Markus Gudor, stood by the narrow window peering out—grim winter clouds, and the snow falling endlessly. The doctor opened my bandages and grinned.

"Funny spot to get hit by lightning, eh, Mirek?" He applied an antiburn lotion. My tissues would heal, the exposure to that high voltage had been brief. I scanned his face with eyes of terror. He raised his voice roughly. "You'll make babies, unless they finish you here. You can walk, want to try?" He opened the door and called a starched nurse who eased me out of the bed and helped me step around the room. "Bedpan?" I nodded and sat on the bed, bathed in sweat. She brought a bedpan. "It'll feel like you're peeing flames; tinkle slowly," said Gudor. I cried. "All of them cry," he said, and then raised a filled syringe. "Sedative. Helps pass the time and expedites the healing."

He stuck the needle in. I faded out.

When I woke up again, there was a package on my night table: my battered copy of Goethe, stained with my dried blood.

The nurse came in and helped me out of the bed for another walk. She must have thought that I did not speak German, for I surprised her by asking where the hospital was (in Prinz-Regent Strasse in Munich), and what floor we were on. The second floor. From the street came the sound of a snowplow. The agony in my groin was faint now, an echo of the earlier pain.

After being given a sponge bath, I asked the nurse if she had a pen or a pencil. She said it was against regulations, yet gave me a pencil and then looked around for some paper and located a stack of admission forms in the closet. Standing behind her I saw vials of iodine, wads of cotton, a bottle of chloroform. I thanked her for the admission forms, I was going to doodle a little. She put me to bed, and left.

I felt like writing: Who betrayed me and why?

I wrote instead: *Mila Laska*. Dear love.

Mila mila laska. Dear dear love.

Safer than putting her name down on paper.

I had never written those words before. I had never thought that my turn would come, as a man, to say or write or even think such words. But now they seemed so different. I felt as if I'd not spoken for a long time, and now every word could only mean the truth it was supposed to mean.

Dear dear love . . .

On the fifth morning, Dr. Gudor came in and told me that I would be discharged. Destination: back to camp Mittergars.

The nurse brought in my clothes and put them on the bed. Gudor gave me an officially stamped *Weiterbenützungserlaubnis* (authorization to circulate freely), with which I could come back to the hospital for a checkup. Valid for two weeks, and signed by Rademacher. I seemed to be able to make useful friends, Gudor commented while I put on my clothes. Rademacher had asked him to convey to me his regrets about the mistaken arrest; having been athletic opponents, he didn't want me to think him unsportsmanlike. The Kommandant of camp Mittergars had also called and inquired about my state. And there was a man from the Munich radio station outside, waiting to be allowed to talk to me.

"Kempner?" I asked.

Gudor nodded.

I told him to let him in.

Kempner entered, and I gawked. The star announcer wore an elegant gray overcoat unbuttoned over a gray suit lit by a pretty yellow tie. He looked so detached and debonair that I wished I could throw my bedpan at him.

Gudor left, and Kempner picked up the battered copy of Goethe's poems, opened it, and read: " 'What does my heart most yearn to hear? Here is my love for you, please hold it dear.' You writing poems to a camp girl?" He smiled with his pale lips. "I hope she likes your taste in poetry." A pause. "I'm sorry you had a mishap."

"Was it a mishap?"

"Absolutely." He put his palm over his heart for emphasis. "When we heard what happened, we weighed in with all our influence so that you would be treated decently. And you have been." He looked around as if pleased with a personal success.

"Weren't you afraid to cause suspicion by coming here?"

"Our auxiliary personnel is very valuable—why would anyone find this suspicious? Besides, Rademacher knows you. Isn't life full of coincidences?"

"We were once in the ring together. That's all he knows about me."

"Always the fighter, Mirek."

"What do you want?"

Seeming to choose his words, he said in a low voice, "The OT saved you, the OT and us. Now I hope you realize the situation you're in. We need the information on Mühldorf." He spread his arms defensively: "I did try to convince the London man to come to a three-way meeting. He wouldn't do it."

"Who's the London man?"

"You don't expect the British to plop a real Englishman here, do you? He's a relay man. A Czech with a channel to London. I'm not allowed to disclose his name."

"A Czech?"

"Yes."

"A Communist?"

"As it happens, yes. Mirek." He made a pause for effect: "The world has been reorganized already. The Allies met in Casablanca, in Cairo, in Teheran. They settled their matters. You think the Russians will liberate half of Europe and then go home like nice little schoolboys?" He chuckled. "Now, about the camp—"

"If London wants action so badly, why don't they bomb the camps in Poland?"

"Because they're of low strategic priority. They produce, I

don't know . . . truck tires, nets for parachutes—?" Impatient with such trifles, he paced, opened the medicine cabinet, glanced inside. I noticed again that bottle of chloroform; I could stretch my arm and grab it. "Anyway, those camps are Moscow's business, and Moscow is not under a cascade of rockets. D'you know how much explosive the new German rockets pack? A thousand kilograms each, and we still don't know where they are building them. In three weeks, even if I don't have a detailed report on Mühldorf, I'll recommend that the whole area be bombed whether there is a reason or not. You understand?"

"All right. I'll get you the information. As soon as I have it."

I had been sitting on the bed. I got up and felt that my old boots were pinching my feet. After five days of plentiful food and fluid, my limbs had relaxed and swelled.

I clutched Kempner's arm, as if needing support. He trustingly allowed me to hold on to his arm. I rasped, "If someone denounced you, what would you do?"

Kempner's smile returned, very self-assured. "You ever read the Reich's penal code?" I smirked, remembering the Dresden judges, in robes embroidered with swastikas, who had convicted me in under three minutes. "There's such a thing as a special appeal for clemency in the name of the Führer. The propaganda ministry would lodge one for me in the Reich's supreme court, I already got the people to do it. The court would send it to Hitler, who won't ever find the time to review it, and I'd wait in a decent jail till the Russians arrived. Smart, huh? My advice for you is, stop seeing the war as a battle of good and evil. It's a battle of deals, and whoever's left out is left to die from the last bombs and bullets. You're so lucky to be on the winning side." The face of Eichmann's man flashed through my mind. You're so lucky to be germanizable. I was, forever, so lucky.

I hit him on the chin, sending his head back into the open cabinet—it encountered a shelf. To cover the rattling of the iodine vials, in case the guard outside, an aging Volksturm man, was listening, I burst out laughing. "That's a good one, who told it to you?" I already held him limp in my arms and was going through his pockets. I found a pistol, a small Luger with ivory grips, like a dainty revenge weapon in the German melodramas of '37 and '38. I stuck it in my belt, then took his wallet and put in my pocket. Pushing him onto the bed—I wanted to gag him with the sheet—I touched something in the lining of his coat. I ripped the lining and found a second wallet, square and hard, containing an identity card in the RSHA, with the name Kempner, Eduard, SS Hauptsturmführer (captain). Behind the card was inserted a metal plaque perforated with uneven little squares, letters, and numbers. I stared at it, wondering what it was.

Kempner's eyelids beat wearily. I stuck the Luger in his temple. He opened his eyes, and I held the ID and perforated plaque before his face.

"Captain," I said, "Moscow should hear of your advancement in the RSHA, so they can match it. Is this a cipher key? Can I use it to send them a message?"

I thought he would throw up. Then he raised his hands, as if to fight me. I pushed off the toylike Luger's safety catch. "Captain, does this poodle bite?" He let his hands drop. "How long have you been a double spy?" He blinked feverishly. "Did you tip off the Gestapo about my radio?" He crumpled into a silent yes. "Why?"

He shrugged. "You needed to be brought back in line."

"Then you called the interrogation off?"

Another silent yes. Then he spoke, his voice devoid of the trills he used on the radio. "I'll take Mühldorf off the London target list. Is that what you want?"

I nodded, but slipped his ID and cipher card inside my jacket. He broke into a sweat. "I said, I'll discontinue Mühldorf as an objective. Completely. Can I have them back?"

"Sure. Tell me what this is." I held up the plaque again.

He sucked in his lips and stared stubbornly at the wall. Very well. With the gun pointed at him, I asked if he had driven his car here. He confirmed that he had. I explained that we would leave the hospital together, in his car, which he would drive. I took from the closet the bottle of chloroform and a wad of cotton, put them in my pocket, then told him we would walk the hallways abreast, and I'd be holding the gun under my jacket, aimed at him. Then I pushed him out the door. The Volksturm guard rose from his chair and saluted, while we marched shoulder to shoulder past him.

The hallway was empty. Kempner took advantage of that to give me a look as if he saw me for the first time—maybe he was seeing me for the first time. "I hope that whoever you're protecting is worth it," he whispered, and straightened his tie— I had flattened it when I hit him.

I was walking painfully, but I was walking. And I could drop Kempner in the blink of an eye. If I went, he went, too.

On the entrance steps, he started to argue with me. I was insane, my best chance would be to give him back his ID and plaque (I could keep the gun and his other wallet) and walk away. He'd let me reach Mühldorf in peace, or vanish if I chose to, and on his word, Mühldorf would be spared. I pushed him to his car—not a Mercedes but an economic little Stoewer Arkona. More discreet. I forced him behind the wheel. He asked what I wanted to do with his things. Put them in a safe place, I replied. If he left Mühldorf alone, they would never travel on to Moscow.

I ordered him to drive around the Rathausplatz, to get lost in the Christmas traffic. On the steps of the Frauenkirche, kids sang Christmas carols and held out baskets for people to drop in pennies "for our heroes in Russia." I told him to turn west toward the industrial section, and he became very agitated. He begged me to believe him that all our hideouts in that section had been raided by the SS, then destroyed. I told him I didn't believe him. He started to spew like a faucet. All right, he did work for both sides and that plaque was a cipher, but a bank cipher, for depositing money abroad. He and I would make a great team, and we could be partners, fifty-fifty. I asked what we would be selling, and he blurted, camp Jews! The Jewish Joint Distribution Committee was trying to buy out camp Jews, wholesale. Friends of Kempner's in Berlin had already approached the Minister of Armaments—the problem was ensuring adequate numbers of Russian POWs to replace the Jews. Many high-placed officials, including Reichsführer Himmler, found the idea appealing; in fact, rushing between Geneva and Istanbul, a certain Dieter Wisliceny, aide to Himmler, had brokered a two-million-dollar deal for closing two work camps as a tryout. But the money had not been wired because of American objections that it would be used to refinance Germany's war effort. I cut him off. I was no expert, but two million dollars could not finance more than a day of war, perhaps two. He hastened to agree—the Americans probably didn't trust who they were dealing with. But maybe they would trust a new team, particularly if it included a figure "from the inside"—it took me an instant to realize that he meant me.

I looked around. We were on Arnulf Strasse, empty and snowed in, passing bombed warehouses. The area seemed to scare Kempner. "You'd be a great new face on the team," he said, teeth chattering. "And you could get your filly out of the camp. Is she pretty? You done her yet?"

I forgot that he was holding the wheel. I grabbed him by the collar and hurled him into the windshield, which cracked. I tried to squash his foot onto the brake but missed; the car plunged into a heap of snow. He clutched my hand with the gun. I snatched it free but the gun was too light to whip him with it. I grabbed the chloroform bottle, uncapped it and poured it in his face. He gasped like a hooked fish, then started slumping. I staggered around the car, pushed him aside, reversed, and freed the car from the snow. He was passing out, still blathering about camps and deals made in Geneva and Istanbul.

The house, as usual, looked abandoned—shades drawn, an empty garbage can lying on the sidewalk, old copies of newspapers dissolving in the snow.

I pulled Kempner out of the car and dragged him to the front door. I leaned him into the doorbell and heard it ring faintly inside. The door screeched open, and a shot rang, close and hard. The bullet hit Kempner, and though it stopped in his body, its impact punched me in the chest like a fist. Rademacher was standing in the doorway.

Kempner crumpled in my arms. I fired over his sinking body but missed, and the ladylike little Luger jammed. Rademacher plunged out of the door and kicked me between my legs, and nothingness filled my mind.

Was I being tortured again, was I remembering other tortures?

I saw or dreamed a mucky, dark interior, not equipped for interrogations. I faced a stool whose legs were coated in dried blood.

I passed out and became conscious again lying flat on the floor; my elbow was hitting a body that was unfeeling, inert.

Peeping from under my lowered eyelids, I made out Rademacher turning Kempner's plaque in his hand, then staring at his identity card. He threw the card away. Seconds later, I smelled burning paper.

"He was becoming an embarrassment," he said, and I understood that he was referring to Kempner. "After dark, we'll push him with his car into Lake Chiemsee. The bank plaque is good; I already called Geneva. We'll send to Geneva someone we can trust. Now, this saboteur . . ."

He walked toward me. I closed my eyes.

He ripped my right sleeve, lifted my arm and mumbled my tattoo number: "152345. They ashed most of those Czech saboteurs, that's why they gave them numbers. But this one was lucky."

"He was sent out to Warsaw, to dig in the ghetto sewer," said another voice.

Rademacher let my arm drop and stepped away.

I heard chairs being moved. The voices restarted, lower, as if my captors had sat down to take a break. "There was an *Aufräumungskommando* (cleaning detail) in Warsaw," mused that other voice. "But I thought it was made of Jews only. . . ."

"Who knows?" grumbled Rademacher. "This one's bobbing around three or four camps now. Maybe he's looking for something."

"Then we should put him back where he was. If he's looking for something, maybe he'll take us to it."

"If we send him back, Eberle will kill him."

"And if we don't, what good is he outside? We send him back," Rademacher decided.

The body beside me was Kempner.

I moved my arm as gently as I could, thankful for the darkness that concealed my movement, and poked him. No reaction. He was truly dead, he had even stiffened in the past few hours. He had told the truth about the house being raided. For once he had told the truth, and I had not believed him.

Part 5

THE SPRING

EIGHTEEN

EARLY MARCH 1945

Blanka

*T*here was a snowstorm outside our barrack. The wind moaned down the banks of the frozen Inn River, while from the Alps, gusts of icy air lashed the camp. The winter clung to the gelled earth, stubborn like the war.

I got up before all the other girls in my barracks, shaken from my sleep by Gudrun, who stepped in and gave my shoulder a tug; when I opened my eyes she had already vanished. I remained in bed another minute, trying to delay reality. Then I sat up, slipped into the winter suit that Suri had sewn for me, pulled on my boots (all those winter clothes I kept overnight in my bunk), dropped to the floor, and touched the shoulder of Margit, who had taken Ida's bunk.

Sometimes Margit returned the touch in her sleep; her fingers clasped mine. She didn't really wake up, but her touch was enough. Ida was no longer in that lower bunk because she had started to vomit incessantly one day and had been taken to the infirmary with a high fever. She was still sick, and the doctors could not diagnose her ailment. (In my opinion, it was the result of her overeating.) As soon as she had left, I had brought Margit back.

In my boots and alpine coat, I hurry out of the barrack. With the freezing wind in my eyes, I run blindly through the blasting snow to our compound's gate. In less than a minute, I'm there, passing a sentry who checks me with eyes barely visible in a crack between his helmet and a scarf pulled up to the root of his nose. He opens the gate. At the end of that minute, maybe a few seconds over, panting hard, I'm stamping the snow off my feet in front of the door leading into the officers' quarters.

There are fireplaces in the mess hall and in each of the officers' rooms, and Mayer is here, feeding the fires. Good. Gudrun has already vanished into the officers' kitchen. If Mayer is alone by the smoky mess fire (the firewood, no matter how carefully sheltered under tarp, always gets wet from the snow) I might touch him quickly, by clapping his shoulder. He's almost a man now—the dark fuzz on his upper lip is almost a mustache, and a curly little beard is beginning to dress his angular chin. I managed to bring Mayer here when Eberle promoted me to cleaning his room. So Mayer works in the mouth of the lion just like me, but this mouth is warmer than the tea kitchen, and its jaws are not snapping down—sometimes I cannot take that feeling, and I almost yell, deep within myself: Do it! Kill us already!

I go into the kitchen, where Gudrun hands me a tray with a mug of hot tea and a bowl of hot water for the Kommandant to shave, which he likes to do while sipping his first cup of tea of the day. I rush into Eberle's room without muffling my steps. He told me to thud hard, I would be his alarm clock.

The room smells unclean.

I set the tray down and move to the window, open the blinds, then the glass panes. A gray shaft of morning light thrusts in, together with the snowstorm's moan. The light falls on a few framed photographs lined up on the top of a chest of drawers. One is of Eberle thirty years ago, on a motorcycle. He had the same stocky build and the same jowly smile, proud and a little dumb—except that youth, which gives a glow to everything, gave the younger Eberle a coarse charm. What was that charm, exactly? Life, lying before him, still full of undiscovered mysteries. Where has that life disappeared, which mysteries has he pierced and which has he passed by, trampling with his soldier's boots? I don't want to know. For me, that younger

Eberle is a complete stranger. To disconnect myself from the current Eberle, I glance at that picture often, and he believes that I like him as a young man—each time I glance at his picture, he grins.

Here he is. He moves with the stiffness of an aging man, lifting his puffy face off a pillow marked with spit dribbled in his sleep. He gets up on his elbows and watches as I bring the tea literally to his lips. He isn't the Kommandant now, but an aging man pleased that a young woman serves him. He smiles benevolently, while I wonder (I have this thought every morning): How badly would I scorch his face if I scalded him with the tea? Could I blind him at least?

I always fear that my yearning to kill him might show on my face. But he sees nothing and knows nothing of what goes on inside me. He reaches for his underwear, while I take the hot water into the bathroom, put it on the rim of the sink, and turn on the light above the mirror. As I exit the bathroom, he trudges in past me, boots already on, like a true soldier. He carries in his cup of tea and sets it on the shelf with his razor, his aftershave, and a tube of acne lotion, which he rubs over the pimples on his upper chest and shoulders. He washes to his waist, with cold water, every morning, while I straighten his bed and collect his pajamas and yesterday's underwear; I'm the one who will send them to Tsilka to the *Waescherei*. Tsilka told me how disgustingly filthy the Germans' underclothes are, especially the NCOs. I collect his underwear and remember that I stood right next to his open razor just a minute ago. Washing, Eberle makes noise. He splashes and sings the waking song of an optimistic Neanderthal: *brum-brah-brum, brah-brum-brah-brum*, and then a long ecstatic *braaaagghh*. He's throwing cold water at his face, cupped in his huge fists, over and over.

He also drenches his hair with cold water and combs it back flat and shiny, black with salty white streaks. He takes a brush, but instead of exerting it on his hair he uses it to prick up his eyebrows. With quick upward strokes, in seconds they are twice their former size. That mark of manliness restored, he steps back bare-chested, and I present him with the day's fresh body vest and shirt. He puts them on.

He sits down to a breakfast of more tea, two slices of bread, an apple, and three spoonfuls of walnuts. He is an ardent vegetarian. Meanwhile, I take a quart-size bottle from under his bed. Lifting it, I feel by its weight that it is over half full. It's the urine he voids at night, too lazy to get up and step to the bathroom. I take the bottle under my arm and rush out, trying not to think of it, of the rusty deposit on its bottom, of the disgusting, wet cork that he caps it with. It's my duty to wash it, but I give it to Mayer, who goes out and empties it in the snow; then he goes to the galley, asks for some hot water, rinses the bottle, and slips it back to me. When I return with it, Eberle nods, pleased. His bottle is ready for duty again, and I'm taking good care of him. He was right to bring me over from the tea kitchen.

He says, as he does every morning: "Take some apples and nuts, Davidovich."

"Thank you, I will as soon as I'm done cleaning."

"You can take as much as you like, when you like. But never—"

"Never take any out of this room to the other prisoners. I know."

"You should be a vegetarian, Davidovich." At lunch at the Stelle, he eats the broth and the vegetables, never the meat. "When I became a vegetarian, my entire thinking changed." For the better, no doubt.

"Maybe I'll try to become one someday," I say, ignoring the grotesque humor of this exchange.

And I go on about straightening up.

He will soon leave for the cement quarry. And I will steal apples and nuts and load my parka with them, for me and the other prisoners. Some I'll keep for the girls who work outside the camp's enclosure, clearing a long narrow band of earth, flattening the snow on it with shovels and setting oil drums on its edges every hundred meters—empty oil drums now filled with wood sprinkled with gasoline. Markers for what they are building: an airstrip. I will be finished here in one hour at the most and will catch a ride in a motorcycle to the tea kitchen, where I'll work along with Margit, but before the end of the day I'll make it to the airstrip, and work next to Manci, who no longer works at the camp's main kitchen. (Teams are rotated, no favoritism.) We'll shovel and flatten together. The Kommandant knows that I still work at the Stelle although I'm no longer required to, and at the airstrip, and he likes that; he likes us to give of ourselves.

"These Greeks are very musical," says Eberle, chewing on his walnuts. "I heard one blow into a piece of cement paper; he was making the most incredible sounds." It's not unusual for him to muse out loud in my presence, but mentioning the Greeks as human beings, especially gifted ones, is very unusual. "I asked him about it—he almost creamed his pants at first, he didn't understand what I wanted. I had to bring an interpreter. It seems that Greek shepherds can play a whole tune on a leaf held to their lips. You want an apple, Davidovich?"

"Thank you, no, Herr Kommandant."

"Aren't you hungry? I know you haven't eaten yet."

"I'm never very hungry in the morning."

Lie. I was, until a few weeks ago, starved every single morning. Ravenous. I ate anything. Now my weight is down, and I often feel nausea. I wonder if the food contains some subtle poison—but if so, why would the poison spare the Germans, or my cousins? The food I give away or don't eat is devoured on the spot.

"I decided to let the Greeks give a musical concert, right by your compound, so that you women can hear it."

How very nice of him. I almost say it, but the oddity of his decision makes me suspicious. I finish making his bed with frantic, uneven gestures.

"They could do it the first Sunday it doesn't snow. I think it's a good idea for the morale. It would inspire the prisoners to work."

More than your fists, you bastard. But what I say out loud is, "Does Herr Kommandant need anything else?"

"No. Where are you rushing to?"

"To the tea kitchen. One girl in my block is sick, and I promised to put in her time."

"You put in time there yesterday, too, and the day before. Hulda told me."

I'm in a situation in which I have to take his grandfatherly manner, and it keeps getting friendlier. I'd rather empty his bottle, make his smelly bed, even wash his underwear. I loathe everything about him, even the crop of tiny gray hairs left on the blade of his razor, which I have to wash every day; also the hairs left in his lathering bowl, glued to its rim. Suddenly, I'm in the bathroom. Instead of washing the razor, I grab it and bring it into the room, held behind my back. I slash Eberle's neck, severing his throat swift and clean, pushing that blade into him with those little hairs still glued to it. A child could do it. The intensity of this fantasy is so strong that I have to be careful if he speaks to me, so I can answer him. I hear his yell of pain, turning into a pitiful gurgle as I sever his vocal cords. I see his massive body crashing to the floor, his hands holding his butchered throat. I feel healthy when I imagine all this. I'm not passive, not compliant. Too bad that I still fear for my life, but I fear for it so much less now, I'm really quite close to the edge. And too bad that the SS would kill a hundred of us at least, in retribution. I put the razor blade back on the rim of the sink.

What I loathe most is that he knows so much about me. How can he not? He knows all my movements. He can look

at my file anytime, he can look at anyone's file. He can ask
me anything he wants, and believe it or not, questions asked
without hostility are hard to leave unanswered. But I'm lucky.
All that knowledge enters his head, but once in there, nothing
happens.

"Yes," I say, trying to sound very casual. "I like working by
the Stelle, especially now. I like the snow—where I'm from, it
snows a lot."

"But then you're not working very hard." He looks at me,
relaxed, which means that his eyelids droop—his whole face
droops, and I could, if I didn't know who he was, mistake
him for just an old man harmlessly ogling a young woman.
That scares the wits out of me, that proximity, that line
which I know I would never cross, I'd rather die—but would
he cross it?

"The other girls can use my help," I answer, surreptitiously
retreating toward the door.

"You'll go to the airstrip after that," he predicts. "What's the
matter, you want to win the war by yourself?"

Like Losch, he makes no distinction between his war and
mine. That should reassure me. I'm subhuman, unable to root
for any side other than my masters'. But I am frightened: Losch
confuses my silence with allegiance because he is too self-
absorbed to really wonder about me. If he did, he could guess
so many things. But Eberle's appreciation of who I am, of what
I might think, is different. Polishing a window last week, I
spotted him in the glass—he stood right behind me, scanning
me from top to toe. Then he uttered a strange cluck, as if of
surprise, and turned and stepped out. I shivered with my hand
still pressing a rag on the windowpane, for I had seen myself,
too, and I looked . . . good.

Maybe that's why I stopped eating. I want to make myself
ugly again.

No. I know it's not that.

I clean the razor, the shaving bowl, the sink, and then I'm

out of Eberle's room. I throw my cleaning bucket with its rags, soap, brushes, mop head, and toilet plunger (the water in the toilet drain freezes often and clogs up) into a communal cleaning closet. Letting out a big breath, Mila exits Rühl's room and puts her bucket next to mine. I'm the one who brought her here. She works harder than I do, because she has to clean after the nightly romps of Rühl and Hulda. I clutch her shoulder. Hey, still holding on?

Yes, her eyes reply. Still holding on.

The wind has stopped howling. I wait under a light snowfall. March 8. The buds, bulging with sap, are freezing on the branches.

Soon, a truck appears. I wave to the driver, and he slows down enough for me to jump onto the cabin's step. I'll hold onto the door, and he'll give me a lift to the Stelle. You see, I'm still a slave but I'm also a house servant to the *power*, which makes a whole lot of difference. When Eberle ordered me to work for him, I immediately felt the benefits of my promotion: friends, even strangers, gave me hopeful looks or whispered to me so that I would remember them in a fix. Even my cousins, bless them, doubled their attention toward me. I moved Margit into Ida's empty bunk and neither Herta the Lageraelteste nor Hulda objected; in fact, Hulda stopped hitting me altogether, while Herta, as a personal gift, issued me a new blanket and mattress. But then, why am I rushing to do work not demanded of me? And why am I not eating? Here comes the lunch truck at the Stelle, and one of my cousins, or Mila (we have included Mila, only her, in our tight sorority) has to shake me by the sleeve. Where's your spoon, your bowl, eat, what's with you? What are you doing *tones* (fasting) for?

What am I fearing?

. . .

The truck races against the snowfall. Because of the speed, the lovely little flakes become cold and vicious, stinging my cheeks. Of course, the truck driver could let me sit in the cabin—he is alone, no one would know. But that would be expecting too much.

I hold on as best as I can. The road has been gutted horribly by trucks and tractors pulling big flak guns to the Stelle. During the tea breaks, my girls serve artillerymen who walk around the Stelle looking for emplacement sites for those guns. They select the sites; then the Greeks are brought out to dig the emplacements and the nests for the crews. They are always yelled at and lashed because they don't understand what the artillerymen want. Finally, they spread camouflage netting over the guns. The work in the pits has accelerated. Several thousand prisoners have been added, and also fresh guards, young Germans, many of whom don't even look eighteen yet. Kids out of high school. Scared. They know some of them will die before it's over. I'll die, too, most likely, but I've accepted it. The young Germans have not accepted it; they are too young, too close to their childhoods and the comforts of their homes. So they guard the big guns with a glaze of dread in their eyes, while I almost don't care. There's power in not caring. I'm no longer scared of every little trifle. I bang on the cabin's window, and the driver slows the truck and lets me off on the rim of the cement pit.

I stand on the rim, staring down at the men working in the pit. Trying to locate Mirek.

I think I see him. But no, I'm mistaken. During the last seven months, the cement pit deepened by fifteen meters or more. Now the features of a man wielding a pickaxe in that depth are indistinguishable—I have to rely on the way he moves, on the strength he shows as he breaks the rock.

I strain my eyes, check a few workers. One is too skinny, another has extra long arms, hanging almost to his knees. Mirek is well proportioned. . . .

There. Someone is standing by a rocky crag, cleverly hitting it at its base, which brings it down suddenly—the man jumps back just in time. He's made it easier for other men, who rush to grab the loose pieces. He takes a breath and inspects the rim of the pit. He can see me, equally anonymous at this distance. He wipes his face, moves on to the next crag. I hurry off to the tea kitchen, where seventeen girls with cheeks red from the fire's warmth get ready to serve the eleven o'clock tea. Margit is one of them; she works here now because the old tea detail has been rotated, too. She knows that I stopped on the lip of the quarry to look down; she knows why I'm here. She made a special jug of tea, double strength, and kept it apart from the other jugs—some of them are just hot water with a pinch of sugar in it. The girls are stealing tea leaves, and sugar. The tea leaves go to Otto at the canteen, where they are traded; the sugar goes into the girls' stomachs. They have learned the ways of survival. I taught them those ways myself. Margit stares at me as I step in and then hands me my special jug.

At eleven, carrying that steaming jug, I board the crowded elevator with Margit and the other tea girls, and we all descend into the quarry. We get off, and the girls hold up their steaming jugs, while the men drop their tools and cluster around them. I keep walking, even though men on my path pull out their tin cups and are confused when I refuse to stop. Some scowl or curse. I keep going. I know where I'm going. The first familiar face I meet is Jacek, who used to bring in the produce from the other camp, but now the produce is out of season, and Jacek, like Mirek, has been added to the cement detail.

Jacek—tall, emaciated, forever unshaved—has an icicle under each nostril. *"Wus is naies?"* What's new? I ask him. He answers the same thing each time: *"Mi mer noch Hitlern shive sitzen."* We'll soon sit shiva for Hitler. When he says it, I shiver from top to toe. Shiva is a piece of me, of home, it means my parents (even though I couldn't sit shiva for them), it means Judaism. It means God. Yet Jacek connects it to our archenemy with such obstinacy, with such a toughness of his soul, that I feel a hellish sense of hope. If Jacek can be so unyielding, maybe I can be, too. If we are all so unyielding, maybe we'll tip the scales, and God the incomprehensible will crush our enemy. Maybe.

Jacek and I head together toward those rocky crags.

"Mirek is fine," Jacek volunteers. "We have a pair of Americans in our block now, pilots. Mirek's teaching them a little German. Mirek made cards from cement paper, and we're all playing cards together."

In other circumstances, I would have been keenly interested in those Americans. Now I couldn't give a damn. All I want is for Mirek to smile when he sees me.

"Did they come for him again?" I ask Jacek.

He answers yes, they came for him again. But it wasn't serious this time, they just roughed him up a little. Look, he's able to work—that's what matters. Work, the passport to another day, hour, minute. Aren't the Germans perversely accurate when they say that *Arbeit macht frei*? Jacek is about fifty. He was captured in '39 in the uniform of the defeated Polish army, first interned with Polish POWs, then identified as a Jew and sent to Dachau. Meanwhile, his family was deported; he doesn't know where they were sent, or if they are still alive. Often, he seems barely aware of what's happening around him. When he drove that produce cart, I could tell that the horse trotted the road by itself; Jacek was in his world of shadows. Yet, each time I come down here, Jacek tries to reassure me in his cranky monosyllabic way that Mirek is better, Mirek can take it, he is taking it. He's doing it for Mirek. Jacek cares about Mirek, not about me—in the dark of the men's barracks, the same bonding occurs as in ours. He's doing it so I won't break down when I see him. Because that, in turn, would erode

Mirek's strength and power, and I've learned that everyone here survives as part of a chain of reinforcements that cannot afford to lose one link, not one.

So I force my lips into a smile even before Mirek sees me. I force my heart into a state of pained confidence; he's alive, that's what counts—he works, that's the proof that his luck is holding.

Mirek is near one of the last standing crags. He measures it with a practical eye. How many blows would it need before it collapses?

Then he sees me and forces himself to smile, too. "Hey," he calls a little sullenly. "What are you doing here?"

I hold up the jug, and my heart sings a little song of hope. He's getting better, he's getting better. Even when he looks worse, I borrow from my bank of faith in tomorrow. Last week, they hit him on his lips. He's healed now, but he doesn't smile like before, not as broadly. But I'll take any kind of smile because I'm the one who said no to his plan of escape. I should have let him take me out of the camp, innocent or not, who cared, and none of this would have happened. Or if we were to die after a frightening manhunt, we would have died together, which would have been tragic but right.

Mirek blows his nose in a handkerchief with a square pattern, which I brought him last week from the effects room. I also brought him a scarf. He is wearing the scarf.

"Nice morning," he says, glancing at the low sky, which ought to open and send down spring's first rays of warmth instead of this icy tide of snow.

I nod in agreement. It's nice: I'm here and you're here, and we're still alive.

Both he and Jacek pull out their cups. I fill Mirek's first. They both sip, slurping, burning their lips, too eager to have that warm drink inside them to care if it scorches their throats and drops into their stomachs like fluid fire.

Jacek says "*Aaa-HA!*" with almost masochistic contentment.

Mirek indicates the lip of the quarry, where I stood about an hour ago, and the bruises on his face are not so bad this time, not so bad at all.

"I saw you up there."

"How could you tell it was me?"

He glances at Jacek. Jacek grabs the jug, refills his cup to the brim, and then shuffles off on the filthy snow. He knows that this is our time together. Mirek looks at me with those eyes which from the beginning made everything else disappear. Even his face disappeared—I no longer noticed whether he had shaved or not, or whether he looked fresh or tired. I just saw his eyes.

He says, "Of course I can tell. I could tell which was your bed in the barrack, when I brought you that flower."

Of course he couldn't have known that—Ida or Herta showed it to him. But why would I protest this romantic declaration, especially if it's meant for me?

I see that they haven't knocked out his teeth yet. He's still handsome, even with those bruises. He knows I'm staring at them, for he whispers, "I buried my face in the snow. Ice would have been better. When I was boxing for Slavia, I used to put my face in an ice bucket after each fight. But snow's all right, too." He pauses. "Am I putting you off?"

Nothing of yours puts me off, nothing—that's how I'd like to answer. But I can't do it. I feel that every word I say has to be filled with truth, otherwise it would be offensive and empty, and what would he take back with him, until our next encounter? He's not putting me off, but he makes me feel pity for him, and that's hard. He reminds me, involuntarily of course, that any of these encounters might be our last.

So I force a strong answer: "No, of course not." I clear my throat. "How long are they going to keep coming for you like that?"

"Not long. They'll get tired."

"What do they want from you?"

He shrugs. "I don't really know. They're after things they can sell—they have this idea the podzemny is a bunch of criminals, like them. Stupid."

Another sip. I watch his lips closely. He doesn't act as though he's in pain, not at all.

He just burned himself with the hot drink. "Nice tea. You made it yourself?"

"No. Margit made it."

He looks right and left. The open-faced mine is dotted with groups of men gathered around girls with tea jugs. They drink and let out thick puffs of breath warmed by the tea.

Mirek looks at them and seems content, and I manage to feel almost as if we were in a street, or in a public square. Somewhere open and harmless. With other people like us. It's winter. We sip hot drinks that make our breath steam.

"I felt some buds on a branch this morning," he says. "They're very heavy. Another week, then the thaw will start."

In my mind, a clock ticks the seconds. I must reply; I must say something. I say something. "What's the first thing we're going to do after the war?"

He smiles so widely that my heart sinks—a big scab at his mouth corner cracks, a drop of blood starts rounding up, and it freezes instantly. A tiny bud of blood. He's not aware of it. "We're going to find each other, what else? Remember, we meet on the bridge."

"*Kadosh kadosh kadosh*," I recite. "*Adonai tz'vuot*." Holy, holy, holy, Lord of the hosts. The Hebrew words written at our appointment site, around that bronze crucifixion that I've never seen.

"That's right."

I wonder as I often do: If I did survive and he did also, if I did marry him, would I always think of our difference? Would that strange, unnecessary sense of divergence forever flit through me as I touched him, or as he touched me? Would I always remember that it was there?

Probably. So?

I'd learn to live with it, I tell myself. God, just save him. Save him! It's not right that he dies. He is . . . he is deep down one of us, whether he knows it or not, whether he'll ever acknowledge it or not—and he might feel that way himself. I can tell that he doesn't hate, it's not in him—

"Come over here," Mirek says.

After deepening the quarry, a collection of irregular pillars, like petrified tree stumps, has been left in this area, and Mirek knocks them down one by one. When I come with my jug, he and I step into what's left of the petrified forest. Soon, he will knock them all down, there will be no more forest, and I will have to find another way to hide down here with him. Since there are now a lot more workers, the tea breaks have been lengthened to twenty-five minutes; we may have ten, perhaps twelve minutes left, which we'll spent together. It's safe, relatively. These days, Eberle doesn't go down into the quarry anymore. He comes to the Stelle but spends his time chatting with the artillerymen, trying to impress them with stories about his first year of war, in Poland. Then, he descends into the main construction site, which, under its lid of ferroconcrete, glows festooned with wreaths of red fabric. The underground city is almost finished and ready to be opened for work.

It's also safe because Jacek sips his tea ten meters away and keeps watch. So I'm free to lose myself with Mirek for a few minutes, like a village girl and boy hiding in a grove. That's the most astounding part of our encounters—we put a few stone crags between us and the rest of the quarry, and everything else vanishes.

He tells me, his palms hugging his cup, "You know, that first time I saw you—when you marched in a row with your cousins—even then you stood out."

I giggle, almost. "Really? Shaved like that, I must have looked—"

"You looked fine. The boys ahead of me were panting, 'Let

us see the girls, too, Mirek, let us see them, too'—so I moved ahead and let them take my place in the last row."

I remember every detail of that scene. I almost see myself, one of a throng of hairless mannequins, and cannot believe that he found me attractive.

"Then I got back to my place." I remember his sideways, crablike walk. "We were cutting through fog, remember? But even then I could tell your face. And I had no trouble spotting you anytime after that."

So, I was already carved in his mind?

I don't believe him—what could have been more anonymous than those androids in stripes? But Mirek chuckles. "The mind's like a radar, you know? It catches something, it doesn't let go—"

We are so close. I could touch him. I could rub my palm over his shoulder, lower it onto his arm, feel under his thick ugly sleeve the hardness of his muscles. But I don't want to take the chance. Absurdly, my mother flashes through my mind. The days when she could not touch my father. A different reason, a different feeling. And here comes the question that has been haunting me, the reason for my guilt, the true cause for my crazy behavior—I don't eat, I work maniacally. It forms in my mind, it rolls out of my mouth, my lips can't stop it.

"You think we could've made it, if we tried to escape?"

His face gets a shade darker, but his voice is cheerful. "Don't think of what didn't happen. Maybe it's better like this. Can you hold on another month?"

"Just one month?"

"Maybe even three weeks." His eyes sweep above me, along the quarry's rim. A frosted gun barrel rises by the tea kitchen, another one by Losch's cube-shaped office. He shakes his head. "They won't have the time to produce anything here, it's too late."

"Mirek . . ."

"Mmhm?"

How can I tell him? How can I tell him that guilt is in my heart, flooding it? I see the purplish marks of yesterday's fists on his cheeks, healing so slowly. I see a cut on his forehead, a long cut that disappears into his rich hair. It's an older cut, the scar covering it is beginning to peel. He was ready to fly to freedom. He would never blame me, but I know that I'm responsible for his change of luck. Before I arrived here, he was darting about, needed and important and privileged. Look at him now.

I cannot live with myself. I come here hoping against hope that seeing him would bring me some sort of peace. But when I see him, when we manage to be "alone," I cannot even cry. I am gripped by a horrible conviction that my own life is over. Fear of the frozen desert I'd have to face after he's no longer alive paralyzes me. All due to my error. I said no to his plan of escape.

I have to ask him. I have to ask him what he really feels.

One minute out of those precious few minutes passes. He searches my face. "What's the matter?"

"Maybe we could have made it—"

"Well, we didn't try. And maybe that was best for this camp."

"For this camp?"

"Maybe," he says. "I'm not sure."

"What are you talking about?"

Mirek does not look me in the eyes, but he speaks very hurriedly, which is not like him. "Maybe after the war, I'll tell you. But if I don't get to tell you—" Now he looks me in the eyes. "—then it won't matter anyway, right?"

Right. The pain that he *won't be anymore* clutches my heart. I cannot take one more death, one more disappearance, doesn't he know that?

"But that won't happen," he adds. "We'll make it. If the ground gets too hot under me in Mittergars, I can still escape. I can always escape."

Can you, Mirek?

"You better go now. You coming tomorrow?"

"Of course. Don't you want tea tomorrow?"

"Absolutely." In his usual cheerful tone.

I carry in the breast of my coat my day's gift for him. It's usually bread and an apple. (A girl from the infirmary told me that the cement workers suffer from severe vitamin deficiency, so I never fail to bring that apple.) Today, I have something extra, a pair of mittens, knitted from black yarn—I knitted them myself, which took longer than if I had asked Suri, but I wanted to make them myself. I quickly pull them on and stroke Mirek's cheeks with them, to show him how warm and light they are. Then I peel them off and hand them to him. He puts them on, breaking them in, widening them, pulling at their cuffs because—oh, damn, I'm so stupid!—they're too short. But he keeps pulling at them till they cover his wrists. "They're great," he says objectively. "Could you make Jacek a pair, too?"

"Huh? Of course." I would ask Suri to knit another pair. "But don't give him yours."

"Don't worry." He winks. "I'll sleep with them on. That way they won't get stolen, and besides it's pretty cold in our barracks."

I whisper, "I wish I could kiss you."

"We'll have the time. Take this, quickly."

I don't know how he did it, but he's suddenly holding another one of his notes written on cement paper. Crumpled into a ball which I take and hide in my sleeve.

"Don't do anything stupid," he says authoritatively. "It's going to be over before you know it." Yes, but in what way exactly? "So don't take any risks, especially not on my account.

I'll be fine." Really? Can you promise me that? "How is working for the Kommandant?"

"All right so far."

"Good. Stay with him, it's the best protection. . . . Blanka—"

I still start when he says my name. "What?"

His gaze is different now, it's . . . proprietary. Maybe this would be the way he would appraise me after he knew me as a woman. This feels like that gaze *after*. After doing things that I don't know how to describe. My blood shoots into my cheeks. How can I think of such things, like a tart, like a strumpet, while the marks of those blows are still on his face? But—he might be thinking about the same things, because his voice changes, becoming low and throaty, the way it was that night in the rain. "You look so pretty. . . . And you learned how to stay alive. I never thought you'd learn so well. . . ."

The scent of the rain, of the wood. Of Mirek's skin and of my own, wetted by kisses. It rises in my nostrils.

"Remember the rain?" I whisper.

He bows his head solemnly. "Yes. I learned so much about you that night."

"What did you learn?"

"That you wouldn't have anything halfway."

Sometimes, I wonder about God's jokes. I remember that night in the rain, too, every second of it. I remember the awed surprise with which I discovered that Mirek would not take the woman he loved, not like that. He was the one who wouldn't have it halfway, but isn't it funny, he remembers that I was the one. So what can I do but smile my warmest smile and say, "But you wouldn't either."

He thinks for a second. "That's right. That's too bad, sometimes . . ."

His stare becomes too intense. I don't want him to feel pain or become weaker because of me. I say quickly, "Remember the bridge. Good-bye."

"What, good-bye? I'll see you tomorrow."

"All right."

I pick up the jug and realize from its pull on my arm that I feel drained, even though the jug is almost empty.

I step out of the petrified forest just as a sharp whistle signals the end of the break. I almost bump into Jacek, who nods his good-bye as he wipes his nose with the back of his hand. His hand is bare, cracked, bitten by the cold. He needs mittens; I'll get him a pair as soon as I can. I start running because I'm at the opposite end of the quarry, and I see the elevator's platform filling up. When I reach it, its cables are already taut. I hurl myself in and crash into Margit. The cables make a grinding noise and jolt us up.

Margit whispers, blowing warm air into my ear, "How is he?"

I shrug. "Holding on."

NINETEEN

I turned in my tea jug, left the kitchen, and walked along the rim of the quarry, peering down. This time, I could not identify Mirek. He was lost among those rock pillars. Then another pillar collapsed, sending up a cloud of snow and a flurry of rock chips. Men with barrows advanced to smash the pillar into smaller pieces and haul them away.

I waited, but Mirek did not reappear. Maybe he was taking advantage of that natural cover to sneak a few minutes of rest.

I felt that the world was absolutely empty, empty even of me.

I tried to collect myself. I tried to take comfort in that balled-up paper inside my sleeve. But I felt no desire to look for a quiet place to read his message. I could no longer take his messages, or our encounters. I could not bear the thought of having been his misfortune, even though he denied it, or precisely because he denied it. I could not bear the longing in his eyes, almost surely fated to remain unfulfilled. What had I done to him? And what was I doing to myself?

I trudged on, until I came to Losch's cardboard cube, surrounded by piles of snow and with snow curling over the edges of its flat roof. I heard Losch's voice—as usual, he was on the phone. Then I stopped and I tilted my head back.

The snowfall had not thinned, and the clouds hung low, still banishing the sun. And yet, right under the clouds, I sensed a passage. An invisible river was flowing up there, a river of souls.

It was flowing in from the east, and it was so overpoweringly wide. This was what I needed to see.

This was the end: the heavens replete with souls, brimming with souls to their distant outer limits. But some of us would still die, even though this was the end. The immediate reality, like a lingering nightmare, refused to change. Inside that office, the phone rang again, and the turtle grabbed it: *"Hallo? Losch hier. Heil Hitler!"*

The growling of a truck slowing down by the cube drowned out his voice.

The driver had recognized me. He allowed me to jump on the step; then we hurtled off with a big metallic rattle. The truck carried a supply of brand-new shovels for the airstrip.

The snow was easy to flatten with a shovel; what was hard was to keep it flat.

There was one, only one, snow plow, which took almost an hour to level the airstrip from end to end. Meanwhile the snow kept falling. Fifty girls beat it flat as it came down, while a kapo kept yelling through a bullhorn, look, over there, there were footprints, over here, the flat surface was less than flawless. The girls rushed back and forth, working like devils to erase their own footprints, while the snow, like a tool of torture, kept falling, kept spoiling their work. I worked next to Mila and Manci, each of us in a bath of sweat despite the cold. In an hour, we would stop and gather around oil drums filled with crackling burning wood, to warm up our hands. In about three hours, the airstrip would be snowed in again, but by that time it would be dark. The much-anticipated landing had not occurred today. Why? No one knew.

I worked and did not feel the weight of the shovel in my hands. I patted flat my own steps and did not remember how many times I had done it already—it was all a blur. I talked to Manci and Mila, and they trailed behind the others so we would not be overheard, while I talked and talked with the snow gusting into my mouth. I talked about Mirek; I talked about my heart being skewered by guilt. I started to weep, and my tears formed icicles on my face. I told the girls that all I wanted was one day of peace, one day when Mirek and I would stand before each other dressed in clean clothes, our feet not bleeding or frozen, our bodies at rest instead of frantic all the time. Our words uttered freely instead of being whispered. Like a regular young couple. Like a man and a woman for whom life still held promise.

All I wanted was one blink of time, to reverse all the strain and misery of how we had met.

I broke down. Manci and Mila realized the condition I was in. Holding me between them, they waited for the order to form a column and return to camp.

My cousins and Mila gathered in my barrack. We asked Eva Lauber to be our lookout, then I pulled out that tiny wad of paper. I was afraid to unfold it and read it myself. Margit did it for me. It contained two lines:

Don't worry.
  Everything will turn out all right.

I breathed. The innocuous text calmed me down a little.

The scrap of cement paper passed from hand to hand. My cousins read it and reread it. Then they looked at each other. Then they looked at me.

Tsilka was the most straightforward. "You met with him, you let him kiss you . . . at least you got something out of this place."

I heard her real meaning all too clearly: You got a rich and undeserved gift. Why are you complaining?

"Why are you beating yourself up?" asked Margit. "You're

not the one who got him into trouble." She didn't know, she didn't know! "You don't eat, you toss all night . . . You want to wake up on a Zugang back to Auschwitz?"

"What are you going to do?" asked Manci, the elf. So little flesh, so much spirit.

Faltering, barely stringing one word after another, I explained that I had thought of begging Eberle to intercede on Mirek's behalf. But I knew his animosity toward Mirek, so that could backfire. Besides, Mirek was in Mittergars, so Eberle would have to negotiate with the Kommandant there, Hoffman. But the problem was not Hoffman. The problem was those Gestapos who played with Mirek's life.

Tsilka spoke again: "If you live, he won't be the last man in your life, Blanka."

I nodded. Yes, that was true. My fingers started to tear the little letter. But the cement sack paper was tough, designed not to tear easily. The little letter fought for its life in my hands.

"Do you love him?" Manci asked.

Mila took the note away from me and smoothed it. "Aren't you going to keep this?"

I shrugged. The danger of keeping it was self-evident.

"Didn't you keep the flower?"

Yes, I had kept the flower. It was hidden in that niche in the ceiling, no longer in danger of being found by nosy Ida.

But . . . a flower was a flower. The letter was a "contact," proof of a forbidden liaison.

"Do you love him?" Manci repeated.

I sighed. Afraid of what I might answer, I muttered, "He's not even Jewish—"

"So? You getting married?" asked Suri with irritation.

"Some of the Greeks are only half Jewish," said Manci.

I laughed. So what did that mean? A half betrayal instead of a full betrayal?

I was trying to rally them to my one logical reason to forget Mirek: We were of different faiths; we could not have a future together. Yet amazingly, passing between them that scrap of paper, they were so free of shtetl thinking—none of them seemed alarmed that if we did survive, Mirek would come to claim his rights over me. And his rights were not just the rights of a loving heart, but the rights of the pleasure and fun of living that he had rekindled in me, even here. Sensing the tenuousness of my argument, I turned to Suri, pleading with the oldest and wisest of us: "We *are* different, Suri. . . . Think of what our parents would have said—"

Manci threw the little paper at me. She thudded out the door.

All five of us became again that multibodied creature incapable of living without one of its segments, as we rushed to bring Manci back. We found her sitting outside, her face turned toward the finished water tower. Built from the timber near which Mirek and I had huddled, it had been completed exclusively by the camp's women.

Suri hunkered down by our tiny cousin. "What's the matter? Come back inside."

"I want to talk to Blanka alone."

"Very well," I said. "Just come back."

Manci pounded the wooden floor, her steps heavy from sheer energy. She pulled me between two bunks. I knew that the others were listening in, but I had to confront that little face alone. "You *tsedreiter* (idiot)! If he dies, do you think he'll still be different? What about if you both die?" I babbled that it was not dying but surviving that concerned me, but she blurted out, her scorn thick: "You should be so lucky! You should be so thankful that after the war he would still come looking for you. Who do you think would disapprove, our parents in those clouds of smoke?"

Then she cried tearlessly, tiny shoulders twisting so hard they seemed ready to break off.

"Manci, Manci!" the others cried rushing to us—they had heard everything—and in that outbreak of concern for the youngest of us, my scruples were swept aside. Yes, I was a *tse-dreiter*, and I was a liar. I did not really fear Mirek's faith, I feared loving him. Only seven months had passed since we had arrived here, but in seven months I had lost my armor of numb-ness, my every defense, and stood utterly naked before love and pain and guilt. And not even that clear principle, faith, could give me guidance. God was incomprehensible even in that respect. There were people in this world who were good, and *some were not Jews*.

Mirek's power of sacrifice had melted my cousins. Mila, not a crier, wiped a tear, then whispered: "Have you ever prayed for him?" She was intense, passionate—ugly with passion. "Pray for him and for both of you together!"

Then she handed me back my letter.

Gratefully, I heard Herta's yell for roll call.

We hurried outside.

Most of that night I lay sleepless, trying to reassert in my mind what I had always believed but apparently couldn't believe any-more. The unspoken.

We were Jews, and all the others weren't. After two thou-sand years of woe, we were to be eliminated from the planet as Jews, not as Germany's war foes or as her rivals to world supremacy (even though Der Führer kept barking about a world conspiracy of the Jews, which must have been the most inept conspiracy in history seeing how it had delivered us to him tied hand and foot!). But now I knew that others could be treated as Jews or almost, that the Nazis had made "Jews" of anyone they disliked. That complicated my equation; but I still had the deepest fear and suspicion of Christians, of all Chris-tians, in response to the ancient and stratified anti-Semitism I'd encountered at home. The suffering of non-Jews had not made my feelings more flexible; quite the contrary, I was de-termined to remain uncompromisingly distrustful. But now, after half of Europe had made such an obsessive investment in our annihilation, a Christian (what else could I call Mirek?) had suddenly turned to me not just with a good word or a gesture of help, but with his heart.

I tried to imagine him as he was growing up. Being dunked in a baptismal font, singing in a boys' choir, being confirmed. Praying on his knees, kissing icons and plowing the air with vast and zealous signs of the cross. I tried thus to make him alien and unlikable, only to notice that those rituals seemed far less alien if performed by him. In fact, they seemed unimportant. I panicked—were my own rituals equally unimportant? I felt anger, shame, a sense of near-sin when I thought about Jesus, because I thus acknowledged his importance. Yet he was important. He was too ingrained, too present. Being from a shtetl, I could not have a complex understanding of Christianity, but I had seen the Nazarene's statues and images. His grimace of suffering, his blood seeping from under the crown of thorns and from the holes in his open palms, his eyes closed comatosely, his skinny ribs gashed by the spear—they were in every church. Even tiny Zhdenev had two churches, and Munkács, that citadel of Judaism, easily had a dozen. The face of Jesus hung in the Ukrainians' homes; it watched from behind the counter in Stefi Arendatzki's tavern and abided in the store of Mr. Mallinich, the grocer, glued to the poorbox by the till. No matter how gaudily portrayed, so much suffering had to be effective. Was it that the Christians, forever bound by the guilt of his death, could only void it in violence? Was that what had started the Crusades, that subtle endless guilt, rather than the greed for power and territory? But the Nazarene had died out of love, and for *everyone's* sins. Ironically, there were no Jews and Christians at the time, just different kinds of Jews. So what had happened to *everyone*? Jesus' suffering was reenacted at every Christian mass, and the worshipers chanted our psalms, proclaimed laws patterned on our laws, filled their sermons with our proverbs and parables, and we who opened their path to God, they put us in their liturgy as the *perfidi Judaei* (Latin for "the treacherous Jews"—Mr. Tauber had taught me that, and I had not forgotten). We had given them their book, and their martyr and inspiration, and we were still at fault!

That hypocrisy choked me. Even Hitler had been more honest when he had called Christianity *verjudet*, jewified. At least, by lumping both faiths together, he had achieved a perverse restitution.

It was all very simple. It was the right of numbers.

I remembered a saying that I'd heard in Zhdenev, usually muttered by older Jews: *"In goolis, man miss shvaigen."* Goolis, from the Hebrew word *galut*, meant "exile." In exile, you keep your mouth shut. For centuries, we had been in goolis, and we still were, always being tested, questioned, forced to pass, to prove loyalty, to pay dues. We lived in dread of disappointing, of annoying, of antagonizing the Christians. We lived in great fear that any deviation, any misstep, even being a drunk or a womanizer, could cost us our life as a people. We needed protectors, but were ashamed to have them. We had secrets. We talked carefully. We were Jews on the inside and Czechs, Poles, Hungarians, Romanians, even Germans on the outside. Christians never knew how hard it was to have two names: one for inside, one for outside. To celebrate two weddings, one with a rabbi, the other at city hall. To go to school, walk down the street, enter a shop, board a train, visit a friend's house, or defend the soil we were born on, always cautious of who might jump us, grab us by the collar, and blurt in our faces: You're a fake!

All that turmoil and ambivalence were inside me. All that conflict I had lived, and would live again—if I survived.

But now I was presented with a simple issue: a man, unknown, different, and yet connected to me, had saved my life. Now he was in danger, and perhaps I had caused that danger. He might die loving me. No, I cried with all my being, not

him! It was him I wanted as a mate. I did want him to be like
me. If we were blessed with children I did want him to play
the role my father had played in Zhdenev, but . . . I knew (from
Mirek) that the Russians had occupied Poland and Hungary.
Fierce fighting had raged around our shtetls, and maybe there
were no more shtetls at all. There was no more Zhdenev. The
world of my childhood had been destroyed. So what difference
did it make if Mirek was not a Jew? Was I still a Jew without
the world that had shaped me?

I groped for that niche in the ceiling. I moved away the
wooden pane.

I felt for that little flower, and touched a handful of dust.
Maybe the flower had disintegrated, it had lain hidden there
more than three months. . . . Then I felt its shape, I recognized
its shriveled petals: the dust had permeated the flower, adding
a fine graininess to it. It was a flower of dust now. I pushed it
back inside and closed the pane. Then I touched the little
letter that I had not managed to tear up. I had hidden it in
my pillow.

Thus, having tried to discard Mirek on grounds of irrecon-
cilable faith differences, and failed, I finally did what Mila had
suggested.

I prayed for him, and for me, and even for us together.

I fell asleep still praying.

I woke up with a high fever.

I was taken to the Revier, the infirmary that frightened me so
deeply, as a sure dead end for anyone who entered it.

But what I found here were four crowded wards, two of them
occupied by men, the other two by women. Most of the patients suffered from dysentery or bad frostbite. I was practically
force-fed and told by a prisoner nurse that Kommandant Eberle
wanted me back on the job quickly, so it was my duty to get
well fast.

I found out that Ida was in another ward. It was suspected that she had diabetes.

I ate broth and bread, and my fever dropped. The ward's window was broken, and the last wintry wind howled over the hard beds and the patients in them. I pulled the blanket over my head, and again I fell asleep praying.

I woke up in the middle of the night, deathly thirsty.

I got out of my bed to look for water. There was none in our room. I stepped into the hallway separating us from the men's wards, and stopped dead. A young girl stood in the hallway, her eyes down, her expression pensive. She was stark naked.

To avoid looking at her face, I stared at her body. But I knew that body as well as I knew the face. I knew the budding breasts, the thin waist, the innocently flat womb . . . She was five feet only, and had a teenager's body. Her shoulders had little dimples. I looked at those dimples and I thought I would go insane.

"Rivka?" I whispered.

Rivka gave me a smile of recognition.

Some part of my brain was still rational. It told me that this was a hallucination. Yet I could not remain silent. "I'm sorry . . . ," I whispered. "Rivka, I'm so sorry . . ."

Rivka smiled. An expression of kindness, of protection toward the confused older sister spread on her face.

"It's the way it happened," she said, and my hair pricked up on the back of my neck. What did she mean—was I responsible for her death, was I guiltless? My teeth were clenched so hard I heard their loud grinding. Rivka kept smiling and said in a voice that sounded like her voice, my other sister Manci's, and my mother's all in one: "Don't feel guilty about him."

She was speaking of Mirek.

"Love is not guilt. Love gets poisoned by guilt."

"I . . . I'll remember that . . . ," I said, in tears.

"Then I will be happy."

I prayed. If I could hold up my hand and somehow bring her back here, then I would go in her place, without regrets, without fears. And leave her in my place.

"Don't cry," said my sister. So gently. I had never experienced such gentleness.

"I can't help it."

"Then cry, for God preserves all the tears."

God preserves all the tears. It was written so in the psalms.

My heart was in such pain. And the pain was so thorough and endless, how could I live after this encounter? How? I wanted to crawl and kiss her feet, bluish as if from the cold, and I was afraid—maybe God would strike me with his thunder. But God seemed to gather in Rivka's small face, in her immature breasts and small feet. Her breasts, her feet, the whole innocence of her body became God, and He lingered in my dead sister, sad, disappointed, and holding back His power for a reason I could not guess.

"I'm not cold," said Rivka. Her face acquired a glow of contentment. Had I contributed something, no matter how small, to her peace? I closed my eyes and prayed that those little feet would step closer again. They didn't.

"No one knew," she repeated. "That's the way it happened."

There was a strange noise in the hallway, like a big intake of breath. A core of air being sucked away, into a cold and alien height. The little voice echoed: . . . *it happened, happened, happened . . .*

TWENTY

I was out of the Revier after another day.

The last gasp of winter was over: a bright morning sun thawed the snow on the infirmary's roof and melted the dirt roads into rivers of mud.

I walked to the officers' quarters. When I stepped into the mess hall, Gudrun rushed to me, almost knocking me down: "*Da endlich!*" Finally! She thrust me into the kitchen. Tea needed to be brewed right away.

From the corner of my eye, I glimpsed that the mess hall had a festive look. Two tables had been joined and covered with a starched tablecloth, and several Aufseherinnen, not in uniforms but in white frocks that made them look like waitresses, lined up on them bottles of wine and cognac, and clean glasses, and plates loaded with cold cuts. In the kitchen I bumped into Mayer, who carried in a load of muddy firewood. "See that it doesn't make smoke!" was Gudrun's order to him; Mayer hastened to dry off the logs with rags before throwing them on the fire. Setting the kettles on with gestures goaded by Gudrun's frenzy, I heard her back in the mess hall, booming: Plates there, glasses here, *los, los!*

The tea bags, already out on the counter, were of a much nicer brand than what we brewed at the Stelle. I asked Mayer what the occasion was, and he pointed at the window—the muddy airstrip swarmed with men and women who were trying to pound it, as much as possible given the sudden thaw, into a hard top. A group of civilians was setting up a motion picture camera; they wore thin city clothes and mud-splattered shoes. Eberle and Rühl and the other officers and NCOs, plus a big collection of OTs, were heading for the airstrip, followed by all the guards not on duty. The turtle himself was rushing over, standing in a motorcycle's sidecar and squinting to assess the state of the preparations; he wore a pressed OT uniform and looked far less sloppy than usual.

I guessed that this was it, his long awaited event. Being sick, I had missed the preparations. But Mayer had been in the thick of them. He whispered to me that a special guest was to descend from the sky any minute: Hanna Reitsch, Germany's top test pilot.

The fires in the gasoline drums burned brightly.

Eberle acted nervous. He yelled unnecessarily at the guards to form a square—they had formed the square already. Losch got off the motorcycle and took his place next to Eberle. Then everyone was so quiet that I heard a bird chirp.

Then from the sky descended a plane like I had never seen. It was long-nosed like a shark, and I could not see its propellers. It had no propellers. Yet it uttered a high whine from an unusual engine—two tubes opening under its belly. Something inside those tubes sucked in the sky and then churned it out.

The plane turned for another approach. Waving its wings, it seemed unsure of whether to risk a landing; all the SS and OTs squinted nervously as it rose again, right above the strip, glinting in the sunlight. Losch grabbed Eberle by the sleeve, either arguing with Eberle or urging him to describe the plane's performance. The plane passed over the crowd again, so low that the high brass clutched their hats and caps; Losch, nearly blind, gesticulated at the sky. Out on the access road, I heard the laboring of an aging vehicle: a fire truck from Mühldorf fought the mud, then mired itself right by the camp's gate. It was overtaken by a fleet of expensive cars, all caked with mud. They skidded to a halt by the gate, and guests in suits jumped out and sank their polished shoes into the mud, trooping past the sentries. One guest, the only one in uniform, was the Mühldorf mayor—I recognized him from that rubble-cleaning day. The others looked like business types.

Finally, the plane determined its best mode of landing. It touched down at the far end of the strip and dragged behind it a foaming whirlpool as its engines kicked back flurries of slush.

All the kitchen windows were loaded with faces. The Aufseherinnen let out *ooohs* and *aaahs*; Gudrun, right next to me, sighed with relief and pride. On the strip, the plane stopped before the officers and OTs, its peculiar engines still whining. The glass shell of the cockpit moved. A short, small-boned pilot emerged and stepped out onto the wing. As she took off her dark leather helmet, the civilians aimed their camera at her and started filming.

"Hanna!" Losch welcomed her. She trod the mud toward him, quick but mindful of the camera, for she smiled and patted her short hair with a gesture that seemed well rehearsed. "Alfred, Heil Hitler!" she greeted Losch.

"Heil Hitler, Hanna!" He kissed her, and then clung to her, for he had slipped on the mud. Holding him up, she smiled: "Gentlemen, Heil Hitler! I give you our last invention, the ME-262. Let's hope its new home will bring it luck!"

A couple of OT men stepped closer and clicked still cameras. Eberle advanced, saluted, then kissed the ace aviator's hand. She traveled the length of the crowd and started toward the mess hall.

For the next half hour, while my hands moved like quicksilver—brewing, pouring, and brewing more tea, which the Aufseherinnen took away in steaming cups on trays—I knew what went on from the reverberation of the voices in the mess hall, they were so loud. The guests streamed in, and Hanna greeted them in a high, slightly grating voice. (I peeked once through the kitchen door: she bobbed about like a high-strung insomniac.) There were some noisy toasts for the incredible new plane—a great progress in aeronautics—for the Reich, for Hanna, even for our camp as the plane's production home.

I managed to produce enough pots of tea for that thirsty crowd, while Mayer kept nursing the fires almost without smoke. Gudrun anxiously wandered in and out. The Aufseherinnen broke glasses and cups, so a few prisoners were hurried in to clean the mess—but nothing broke the spell that the ace pilot had thrown over the guests. Losch spoke emotionally. There on the mud strip glowed the secret unveiled, the prize he had worked so hard for. This superplane would be assembled right in the heart of our Stelle. He described its engine as a "Strohm" or jet-type. Hanna took over, praised the new plane, too, mentioned that the Führer had personally given her the green light to supervise its production. This could bring about the much awaited "turn of the war." But she said that quickly, stressing again that jet engines heralded an incredible progress and would be even more valuable in peace. She raised a final toast. *"Für die Zukunft und für Frieden!"* To the future and to peace! And everyone chorused, To the future and to peace!

In the adjacent room, a situation room Eberle had not used for years, hammers thumped, nailing a big screen to the wall— a team of OTs was setting up a slide projector.

Busy brewing more tea, I could not see Hanna, but I heard her clearly. She was impressive. And the word *peace,* even from a German pilot, was soothing to hear. How unusual that she talked of peace, instead of "victory at all costs." And now the production conference would kick off immediately. "Come, Alfred," I heard Hanna say to Losch, and he giggled like a little boy on his birthday, as she led him and everyone else into the screening room.

· · ·

Mayer, Gudrun, the white-clad Aufseherinnen, and I cleaned up the mess hall.

Now we could hear Losch in the screening room, explaining the camp's work capacities. The atmosphere in there was relaxed, with frequent laughter. Many guests had carried their drinks with them. The bluish mist of good cigarettes seeped out whenever another Aufseherin with a tray slipped inside to refresh drinks or cups of tea.

We finished cleaning, and I asked Gudrun if I could have a few minutes to myself. Generously, she gave me an hour—the conference would not break till midday or later.

I stepped outside. I tilted my head back to look up at the sky.

"Hey," said a woman's voice.

I started. It was Suri.

"I was looking for you," she said. "Can you come to the effects room now? It's ready."

"It" was a bra. Despite my fasting, my breasts had fleshed out again.

TWENTY-ONE

*F*ive people worked in the effects room, but only Suri, who did not hand out clothes but repaired them, had her own separate working space: an enclosure of bedsheets hanging from the ceiling, hiding a sewing machine, a chair, a tall upright mirror, and a table. Suri had enlivened her sanctuary with cutouts from the magazine of the German Fashion Institute, affixed to the bedsheets with safety pins. They featured frigid-looking blond women and male models with blue eyes and square jaws. Smelling pungently from unwashed fabric, this little nest was among the warmest places in camp, and when Suri did not have a visitor she was all alone in it. Unwatched. Private. I wondered if I would ever recapture my own sense of privacy.

My new bra, made of plain white cotton, was just a set of cups joined at the front with a patch of fabric and hooked at the back with a strap with snap buttons—nothing like the one fancy bra I had owned before being deported. That one had side bones and underwiring for added support, and I had bought it in the best women's store in Munkács. That bra had stayed in my mind as the epitome of intimate elegance, and even though I did not expect anything similar, the austerity of this one shocked me. But I swallowed my shock. Suri's creation was clean and new, and would make me feel comfortable. Suri fussed as she fitted the cups over my breasts. She had lined the inside of the cups with a layer of flannel: "This will feel so nice and soft."

"It'll feel hot. The weather's getting warm really fast."

"God, you're right. I didn't even think about that. We've been cold for so long."

"It doesn't matter." Feeling guilty that I had complained, I pulled on the shoulder straps. "Can you close it for me?"

She closed the snap buttons, and I examined myself in the upright mirror, which was dim and spotted where the silver coating had worn off. But it was perfect for disguising my new undergarment's plainness. I saw a woman before me, a real woman wearing a real bra. The straps cut into my shoulders.

"I made it too tight," said Suri. "What's with me? I'll have to make you another one. But I measured you . . ."

"Maybe I'm still growing," I joked.

Suri grinned and undid the buttons of her blouse. "Want to see something?" She had made herself a bra, too, which fitted better than mine. But her shoulders plumped up under the straps, and her breasts, though not large, had gained a slight pendulousness. Taller than me, she stood behind me, and the green mist of the old mirror made us look almost like two models in an ad. "I'm growing, too!" Suri laughed.

Such talk was not our usual talk, so she moved about nervously, as if expecting to be punished. She threw her sewing kit onto the table loaded with fabric marked with chalk. "I'm making caps for the OT civilians. Caps, vests, soles for their boots. When they signed up, they wore new clothes, but now they're in rags, and they keep asking me to take in their pants. Most of them lost five, ten kilograms. . . . There's an Italian who keeps coming here, he told me that they want out of their contracts, and if the Germans won't let them, they'll have a riot on their hands."

"Really? Good, good."

I locked my arms around her. She squeezed me back and we stood like that, heartbeat to heartbeat. Then she, four years my senior, which had always seemed to me like a cosmic difference, whispered, "Blanka, do you realize how young we are?"

"Yes." I squeezed her harder. We were so young. And my sister Rivka had been even younger.

"What are we going to do about these bras?"

"Wear them, what else?" I whispered to her. "This war must end someday."

We stood quietly, bonded by that incredible notion. All our expectations, all our desires were connected to the end of the war; and yet we could not believe that it would happen, we could not imagine it. But Mirek believed it—he always mentioned the end of the war as if it were a solid chronological date. "What are we going to do after the war?" asked Suri, with a mix of hope, bafflement, and fear.

"Buy ourselves some decent bras."

There is a time when whoever has cried enough must finally laugh. We exploded into laughter. Bras as our first priority after the war—that sounded pretty funny. Then, Suri clasped my arms, and I felt that silent flood of souls. It was no longer circling in the sky. It seemed to enter Suri's precarious sanctuary; we were bathed in them, gasping, not daring to breathe. I felt that they would never leave. Then, suddenly, they were here as us. They suffused our beings. I felt the weight of the question Suri had asked, casually, unaware of its hidden meaning: What are we going to do after the war?

We would always carry those souls inside our own. I would always carry my little sister, and all the other kin I had lost. We would be surrounded, never alone, yet paradoxically we would feel the loneliest on earth. We, the innocent, would feel the guiltiest. The real culprits, the killers, would claim that they were blameless. But we would carry the eternal blame that we had cheated death and lived.

"Are you thinking of them?" I whispered to Suri.

She knew who I meant. The ones we had lost.

"Yes."

"Me, too. All the time."

"Yes, all the time," she echoed me. "I thought about them when I was making these bras."

"Why?" It was painful to ask, but I was curious about the connection.

"Because of my mother. She was wonderful with a needle, and she taught me everything I know. . . . Even on the train to camp, we knitted. Although it was summer, we expected to be cold . . ." She grew silent so abruptly, I realized that she wasn't pushing her memories away. But she couldn't talk about them anymore. "God, how we laughed," she marveled.

The door of the effects room opened; then a man in an OT uniform lifted one of the bedsheets. *"Permesso?"* he intoned to Suri, as Italians do, chanting their vowels endlessly. He stepped in. He had a long nose, was very thin and barely in his twenties, but he radiated strength. I threw on my jacket while Suri quickly buttoned her blouse. *"Dov'è il mio cappello, bellezza?"* Where is my hat, beauty? Suri rushed to choose a finished cap from the table. The young man put it on in front of the mirror and seemed pleased. He danced around, cocking his cap, taking it off, sticking it on again, and then blew Suri a kiss. *"Grazie mille, bellezza."*

He slipped her a little wad of coupons exchangeable at Otto's canteen and hurried out. Suri lowered her eyes, moved a stool around without reason. "I fixed everything he wears. He works as a draftsman at the Stelle. He comes here all the time; today he came for his cap, but other times he just walks in and says that he wanted to warm up."

I had been missing from the mess hall for almost an hour. I had to hurry back.

I tramped in the mud anxiously and then noticed that the guests' cars were still parked by the main gate. Good, I wasn't late.

Then I began to hear a man shouting.

The mess hall's door opened, and the guests started walking out, their faces tight. Hanna stepped out, head high, followed by Losch and the mayor.

Then Eberle emerged. His face was crimson and his chin shone with foamy saliva. He was the one shouting—*"Nie ohne Disziplin Grund! Nie ohne Disziplin Grund!"* Never without disciplinary reason! He repeated it several times.

Losch turned to him and yelled, too. I'd never heard the turtle yell. "You will stop mistreating the prisoners or you can start seeking a transfer!"

Which made Eberle so enraged that he hollered: What kind of Schweinerei was this, what did these liars try to turn him into? A scapegoat for Germany losing the war? When Germany was victorious, did anyone mind how brutally—?

Hanna cut him off loudly. "Brutes always make scenes!"

"I'll give you brutes!" Eberle shouted back. "Did you ever see a camp in Poland?"

Hanna didn't shout, but her voice was piercing. She had, she snapped back, and the conditions in this camp were still appalling. Rühl rushed to Eberle and pulled on his sleeve, and the Kommandant managed not to shout his next answer: Conditions here were much better than elsewhere. "Oh? When did they change from the normal barbaric standard?" she countered. Dumbstruck, Eberle looked around for allies. But no one came to his rescue. They all stood with blank expressions, as if confronted with something to be ignored or denied, and the mayor of Mühldorf (in SS uniform!) even stepped forward, as if to protect Hanna.

I could not believe my eyes. I had never seen a high-ranking SS being disgraced publicly. I was terrified.

The commotion had awakened the drivers dozing in those expensive cars. Seeing their passengers, they all turned on their engines at once, and the guests stepped into their cars through exhaust fumes that made them cough. Honking and spinning their wheels in the mud, the cars headed off toward Mühldorf, until Eberle stood alone. His arms were flexed at the elbows, and his oversize fists closed and opened, closed and opened, gradually slower, like a diminishing heartbeat.

At the mess hall door, there was a scurrying movement— Mayer slipped out and fled, right in front of Eberle, who was climbing the steps. Rühl made room for Eberle; then Gudrun motioned for me to get back inside because someone had to clean up the kitchen.

I moved. But when I stepped in, I gasped in astonishment.

The door to the conference room was open, and there was a picture frozen on the screen, a still photo of someone bashing the face of a shadow in stripes. I knew instantly whose photo it was, and who had taken it: the turtle. The picture was out of focus—the turtle had messed up even though I had pointed and focused the camera for him. But the outline of the body, the tall cap, the jutting jaw, the size of the fist, left no doubt: the one beating that prisoner was the Kommandant.

I raced into the kitchen, empty now, and hid behind its door. But I could hear every sound in the mess hall. Eberle lumbered to the table and poured himself a big drink. I heard him gurgle, draining the glass. "Brutes!" He poured another glass. "I could've shown them real brutes! How the hell did Losch take those pictures? He's blind as a bat!"

He drained the second drink. "We must stop this damn conference," he rambled. I peered through the crack of the door. Rühl looked stupefied, but shook his head slowly. "You don't think so?" Eberle asked, aggressively insecure.

"They've got that damn plane," said Rühl. "It's impossible."

Eberle collapsed on a chair, and his face crinkled up, as if ready to cry. "I was never a harsh Kommandant," he moaned. "I've always been good to the women, I spoiled them . . . Even the men . . . This coming Sunday I was going to let the Greeks play music. . . ."

"You should let them. And increase their food rations."

"Maybe give them some cigarettes, too . . . ," said Gudrun, forgotten by the table. "They're smoking the straw in their pillows, Herr Kommandant."

Eberle reflected, then nodded. "*Überhaupt.*" Definitely. He pulled at his jacket collar, as if choking.

Then he muttered that he wanted a report on the state of the camp's supplies. Rühl promised one by the next morning. "And I have a suggestion, Herr Kommandant," Rühl said, with fear in his voice. "When the conference resumes tomorrow, maybe you should . . . apologize to Fräulein Reitsch and the other guests. Tell them that from now on everything here will be as if ready for a visit from the Red Cross."

Eberle did not react. He was beaten.

"*Raus!*" Out! he said. Rühl led Gudrun toward the exit, while I escaped out the kitchen's back door, without cleaning up.

Outside, I wondered what I'd witnessed. The fall of a god? But it was just a slide, a partial loss of power, not a crash. And, as Rühl had suggested, Eberle could regain the lost terrain by apologizing. Why, then, did Eberle act so defeated? Was it the public humiliation? Or was it prescience that a bigger collapse would follow, and it would affect not just him?

That collapse Hanna had referred to as peace.

I stood staring at the mud outside the gate, rutted by those automobiles departing. I remembered Hanna saying that sweet word, *peace.* I remembered the guests listening to her in awe, and I suddenly saw her as an even more stunning individual. She had come here empowered by Hitler, she had said so herself; she had tested the Reich's deadliest planes, and she was, according to Losch, one of the Führer's intimates. Yet somehow . . . that did not matter! Hanna talked of progress, and of peace. She was no longer accountable. Losch, who had presided unmoved over the camp's misery, was no longer accountable.

The guests who had drunk and laughed with them were not accountable either. There was a river of souls circling in the sky, asking mutely, Who is accountable? But everyone in that mess hall, through the way they had toasted the future and the peace, had pleaded back toward that tribunal—I'm not part of this! Don't you see how humanely I'm eating, drinking, and preparing for the peace? Can't you hear what I'm saying? It isn't me! It was never me!

What this party had tried to launch, along with the assembling of the plane, was a Big Cheat. I sensed it in that talk about peace, in the readiness with which the guests had gotten the message, and sided with Hanna against Eberle. They sensed the Cheat, too, and rushed to join it, knowing that its occupancy would be limited—for the Cheat to work, some culprits would have to be kept out, some henchmen would have to be declared unacceptable. I had seen one. He had stormed out of the mess hall with spit on his face, yelling his outrage. Then he had controlled himself and accepted Rühl's suggestion of meekness, in the hope that the Cheat might still find him eligible.

The Cheat might still accept Eberle; that depended on a multitude of factors as yet undefined. If it didn't, Eberle would have to put his hopes in something he never had to experience. Survival.

TWENTY-TWO

*E*arly the next morning, I found Eberle passed out on the floor of his bedroom, among torn sacks of walnuts, pools of vomit, and an empty bottle of vodka. I woke him up by wiping his face with a rag dipped in cold water. Then I got down on my knees to clean the mess he had made, keeping my eye stubbornly on the nuts and the vomit, because I was afraid of some unpredictable violence on his part.

But he managed to shower and dress, and then, like a somnambulist, attended the conference's second day.

It lasted three days altogether. On the last day, an almost lukewarm rain melted every vestige of snow, turning the camp into a giant swamp. I brewed the last cup of tea before the last guest's departure and then asked Eberle to transfer me out of his quarters. I wondered what excuse to invoke, but he did not ask my reason (which was that I was terrified of him). Again, like a somnambulist, he agreed and gave me to Gudrun, who put me on a maintenance detail.

That meant work in the mud—we had to maintain the road to the camp, because the parts of the planes to be assembled were already being brought in, by truck. Hulda beat me the first morning she found me working with my new detail, punishing me because for a while she had not been able to touch me.

The men's food rations were increased. I could tell by the renewed energy with which they marched out of the camp in the morning. After the evening roll call, we saw lit cigarette ends crisscrossing the air on the men's side, like fireflies. They no longer needed my butts, now they had plenty of their own. The temperature jumped ten degrees, and the bird calls were so loud they woke us up before the camp's whistle.

And the following Sunday, the Greeks were allowed to put on their concert.

About three in the afternoon on a day so cloudless it was a wonder that the Allies were not bombing, six Greek musicians marched solemnly out of their barracks, led by Gabi Petilon, who carried no instrument but was the *Kapellmeister* of the band. The others lined up, holding an accordion, a zither (which I saw for the first time), a violin, a guitar, and a piece of foil paper which, held between the teeth, moaned like the wind through the caves of a deserted island.

The other Greeks gathered in thick crowds and leaned against our wire, joined soon by the Italians, whose operatic chatter fought for space with the Russian bassi, with the hurried sputter of Hungarian, and the endless throat-clearing of Dutch. The gates between the men's compounds had been opened, and everyone was pouring in to attend the concert.

Not one woman, except for the ones who were sick or on duty, was going to miss this. The Greeks could have staged their show anywhere, but the spot they chose was right by the wire, where they had serenaded us and begged for our sistership. We were not just their audience, we were all the women they missed or had lost. They started with a series of love songs which were slow and melodious, but grew increasingly more nervous and lustful. Soul was the focus in those songs—*psychi mu, psychaki mu*, my soul, my little soul (that much Greek we had managed to learn in seven months) was what the beloved was called in most of them.

The other Greeks hummed the tunes and clapped; here and there, two or three men threw arms around each other and started hopping about, their expressions serious, ritualistic. Finally, the whole sea of Greeks rolled into waves of dancing men. Even the German guards, stunned at first that the concert had been allowed at all, started to beat time with their boots.

The girls had jammed the wire and clung to its mesh with hooked fingers.

The love songs ended with a huge ovation from the Greeks—to themselves. Then all their faces turned toward us. There was another huge ovation, and the Greek with the guitar said something. None of us understood it, but he opened his arms invitingly toward the wire loaded with women, and Eva Lauber was the first to guess it: the band was welcoming our requests.

" 'La Paloma'!" she called out excitedly. "Sami! 'La Paloma.' "

Sami, the Greek with the guitar, smiled contentedly. He strummed the guitar, and the band joined him in "La Paloma."

Standing in the crowd, I played hide-and-seek with Gabi Petilon's stare. In his mind, after I had given him those cigarettes, I had become his beloved, his hope for a matrimonial future. I knew that from the speed with which he materialized, as if warned by a sixth sense, every time I happened by the wire. Aware of it, I made sure to be always accompanied by Tsilka or Suri. Tsilka had even indicated, greeting Gabi by his name or slipping him bread, that she would be interested in him. But Gabi was Gabi—he had made his pledge, to me. Thus, I was both uncomfortable and flattered when I saw him step to the front of the men's crowd by himself. He waited for "La Paloma" to be over; then he opened his arms and burst into song, for me.

He sang forcing his voice. His passion was in his unmelodic intensity. *Adio*, he started, lengthening the word, making it rip the air: *Adiooooooo. . . . Adio, queridaaa / No quero la vidaaa / Se m'amargarces tuuu. . . .*

Tsilka poked me. "He's singing for you, but what is he saying?"

"It's in Latein," said Eva Lauber, who had become an expert on the Greeks.

Yes, Gabi sang in Latein, or Ladino, as the Greeks themselves called it. The language his ancestors had brought from Spain. Eva ventured a translation: Farewell, farewell my beloved, I care not for living, if thou embitterest me. . . . So did Gabi complain to me of his unrequited love, and soon the other Greeks joined in, some standing on tiptoe to spot me behind our wire, then knitting their brows at me, to signal their reproach. Gabi, emboldened, leapt and danced by himself, one step forward, one back, bursting into another tune. *Por ti, me muero yo*—from loving you, I'll die. Another Greek picked it up: *por ti, me muero yo*; then others continued, not in a chorus but passing that declaration back and forth. Whereas Gabi, both happy and anxious about my reaction, danced his heart out, kicking off clumps of mud, until all the Greeks started singing together again, throwing little bits of paper over our wire, for us. Paper ripped from cement sacks. Camp confetti.

Someone grabbed my arm. It was Mila.

"Suri's waiting for you in the effects room," she said urgently. Loaded down with a big order for the OTs, Suri had been forced to miss the concert.

I wanted to ask her what the emergency was. But Mila fought her way out of the crowd. I fought my way after her.

Seconds later, we passed the guard at our gate. Too busy craning his neck to catch the last of the concert, he paid no attention to us. Mila almost ran; as I ran after her I fought my fear as best I could. Had something happened to Suri? Here was the low, peeling building of the effects room. Mila opened the door. The man who ran the place was not in sight, nor were his helpers. The sheets sectioning off Suri's work area were flapping gently, and Suri stood by them and seemed fine.

I had no time to breathe in relief. She raised a finger to her lips, then parted the sheets to her sanctuary: I saw Mirek inside, his back to me.

I stepped inside. He heard me and turned, and I stifled a whoop of excitement. His face was clean of bruises for the first time in weeks.

"*Ahoy*," he said, in his best Prague intonation.

"What are you doing here?"

"I wanted to see you, because I'm going to leave."

I felt as if he'd hit me: he did not mean that he would leave the building. He meant that he would escape. He took me in his arms, and I closed my eyes. Then, aware of Suri standing on the other side of the sheet, I opened them again and put my palm on Mirek's lips. He took my hand away and kissed me, eyes wide open, in broad daylight. I did not even feel the taste of the kiss.

He whispered: "My *babicka* (granny) is still in Prague. I just found out. She lives in Dejvice, on Krasna Street. Mrs. Novakova. She runs a grocery store."

Novakova. Could it have been anything but the most Czech name, Novakova?

"How did you find out she's there?" I whispered back.

"Never mind. Now listen. The first rainy night, I'm going to cut off the power in the Mittergars wire fence." He made it sound like such child's play! "They may not even notice till a whole day later. But if you hear the Mittergars alarm, don't be afraid; we'll still be a long way out by then."

"We?"

"There are two Americans who want to go with me, and . . ." He put his lips to my ear, whispering very softly, tickling me: "There's a German farmer not far from Mittergars who will give us shelter."

"You trust him?"

"Yes. He's a hundred percent safe. You don't need to know more."

"That's right," I muttered. "I don't."

"Everything's a hundred percent safe," he repeated. I looked up, realizing how many times over the last weeks I had winced when closely inspecting his face. Now his face was clean, un-hurt, normal. I raised my hand to touch it, and he smiled. "They left me alone for a whole week. Maybe they got tired of me."

"Then why are you leaving?"

"Because the front will be here in a few days, and then they'll come back. Maybe they'll think that they can trade me, or they'll kill me just like that, for revenge. . . . I can't let that happen. I think you'll be all right." He took a step back, as if to assert that our fates were separate. "They'll try to build some-thing here until the last minute, so you have better odds than me. The Americans will probably find all of you right here."

"They're building a plane," I said, fulfilling my promise to spy for him for the first and last time.

"I thought so. I saw a plane out on the strip."

"It's got a very peculiar engine. . . ."

"It won't help them. Nothing can help them now."

I said nothing. The debacle hovered upon us, yet he would not be here to protect me. I'd have to face danger alone—a sensation I had almost forgotten. His presence had been my security even when I poured him tea in the quarry and cringed at the marks of beatings on his cheeks.

"It's all right," he whispered forcefully. "This is the best way."

"Then go away," I said. Angry, scared for him, scared for myself. Angry that I had kissed him, and yet his choice was to disappear. "Go. You know what will happen if someone finds you here."

"I'll go in a minute. Remember, Novakova, or the bridge."

"I'll remember."

He looked at me longingly, not trying to hide his feelings at all. I felt ready to run off with him *this time*—which was, of course, impossible. We weren't even in the same camp any-more.

"Are you going to wait for me?" he asked. "You might get

to Prague before me . . . and every man's going to chase you, you know?"

"I'm not a strumpet," I said tightly.

"That's not what I meant."

"How long shall I wait, two, three weeks?" I sounded angry again. I found it easier to be angry. "Longer? If I don't hear from you, what am I to believe?"

He nodded, granting me that point: "No one can guarantee anything, there will be fighting till the last minute. If you feel too alone . . . or you meet someone you knew before. . . ." He cleared his throat. "I can understand . . ."

I whispered harshly, He did not understand anything. What if I waited, and he wasn't alive anymore?

The mocking little flame was back in his eyes. "I got through so much, you think I won't get through this?" He sized me up from head to toe: "And you waited so long, you're not going to wait a few weeks more?"

He was amazing, a monument of confidence. I pursed my lips and turned to leave, getting tangled in one of the sheets. He instantly pulled me back, turned me around with those arms that exuded reassurance. "Blanka . . . I've been thinking of a little place in Prague for us. Rain on the roof, like that night . . . It rains a lot in Prague in the spring." He brought his face close. "I know you so well," he added simply.

"I don't know you at all."

"Of course you do. God, it's going to be so wonderful to walk on a street, and stop when we like, and start walking again when we like. . . ."

"Yes," I agreed in spite of myself.

"I'm going now."

"Then go."

This time he did not kiss me, and I was not bold enough to initiate a kiss. He just put his hands on my shoulders, squeezing gently, as if to absorb the feel of me in his palms and fingers. Then he turned, slapped the sheets aside, and headed for the door. He opened it enough for a shaft of sunlight to surround him incandescently—and that was how he remained in my mind, like a man stepping into a tall flame. Then he was gone, and Suri moved toward me, looking at me with a stare that was beyond curiosity. The inexperienced female inside her sought clues about something I was experiencing ahead of her.

A minute passed, maybe a few minutes. I expected to hear yells, even shots. I heard nothing. I told myself that I had been a fool again. I should have kissed his mouth, his face, his forehead, his eyes—every part of him that I had not touched enough, which was truly all of him.

Suri spoke, "He gave me this to give you, in case Mila did not find you."

And she opened her hand. It contained another note on cement paper.

"How many of these did he write to you?"

"Six." An enormous number, given the risks involved. I opened this last one and read: *Pockei na mne. I spal ten dopis. Nashledanou.*

Wait for me. And destroy this letter. So long.

Suri watched me quietly, then asked, "What are you going to do?"

"If we make it, I'll . . . go to Prague to find him."

I expected the roof to collapse, or the walls to shut in on me, blotting me out. I still felt it was that dangerous to assert that there would be a world after the war, and that he and I would be part of it.

But the roof held, the walls did not move, and I folded his last message and stuck it in my sleeve.

TWENTY-THREE

*I*t started to rain again two days after our encounter in the effects room. A scant and spitting drizzle, pricking at the camp's roofs, stopping, starting again. As if playing with me. Would it grow into a full rain? Would it provide enough cover for Mirek's escape?

When I fell asleep that night, the hesitant rain was still tapping on the roof.

A few hours later, a wail pierced the night. It faded, then pealed, then faded again, choked by the foggy night. In my sleep, I mistook it at first for an air raid alarm. Then I realized what it was. A steam whistle. In a nearby camp—probably Mittergars, but I couldn't be sure. Someone, probably Mirek— but again I couldn't be sure—had attempted to escape.

I raised myself in my bunk, moved the wood panel, and touched what was left of Mirek's flower.

TWENTY-FOUR

APRIL 25–29, 1945

I counted the days. Thirty-two days since I had heard that whistle in the night.

April drew to its end. The world was ripe with life that was bursting into being at the close of the biggest human slaughter.

The Americans kept pummeling the Mühldorf area. They came with big Liberator bombers accompanied by small, swift Mustang escort fighters, and seemed to be on a search-and-destroy mission. They left nothing intact—they demolished the railroad tracks as soon as the maintenance crews (swelled with men from our camp) managed to put them back together. Maybe they were still looking for our production site, but by now its camouflaged lid blended into the surrounding forest so well that the German flak guns, on orders not to betray their presence unless hit directly, had not been fired yet. Still, many nights we jumped out of our barracks barefoot and wrapped in our blankets, and dived into ditches because of bombs shaking the earth so violently that they threw men and women to the ground if they tried to stand up. However, most of us were convinced that the Americans could distinguish us from the Germans, even at night and from thousands of meters up in the sky. The Germans themselves made us believe that. In mid-April they suddenly ordered us to turn in the civilian clothes we had enjoyed so much, and the Russian fatigues, too. We were reissued stripes brought in from another camp— bloodied, torn, smeared with feces. Which meant that the Germans themselves counted on the "Haefting look" as a form of protection.

As we boiled the stripes and fixed them as best we could, Tsilka said, "You'd think that when the Americans march in, the Germans would present us looking as human as possible."

"They won't have to show us as human," Margit said, "because they'll ship us out of here to the nearest functioning oven."

"They won't have the time . . . and how are they going to get us out of here? The railroad's all smashed."

"Want to bet?"

A strange bet, on which maybe no one would collect.

Hideous rumors circulated regarding how we would be disposed of. Since the Germans were counting every drop of gasoline and every bullet, we would be made to dig our graves and then buried alive: or we would be marched to the Alps, where we'd be locked in caves without food, to eat each other. I hoped that these horror stories were nothing but a gruesome form of catharsis on our part. We did fear death, but we were forced into a strange optimism by the daily spectacle of the Nazis falling apart. The Aufeherinnen no longer cared who heard them, and, after the Munich radio station ceased its broadcasts, they became the camp's main rumor mill. The Americans had taken every city around: Munich, Düsseldorf, Köln, Koblenz. Now they were advancing on three fronts, from the north, west, and south, on what was left of the Mühldorf Kreis. And they were led by these colored soldiers with mammoth genitals who looked to rape anything that was blond and spoke German. At the hospital, a prisoner girl informed us, they were all out of cough syrup because the German nurses put it on their hair; they were putting anything brown on their hair, to make themselves brunettes. Why don't they use their dreck—it's brown and available every day? We laughed with the ugly joy of pain that could finally inflict pain in return—even though, of all the Germans, the nurses were probably the least guilty. But there had to be, we sensed it in our bones, a time when all of them would have to pay, even in humiliation alone, for all of us.

There were also rumors about Berlin having already fallen. The source of that intelligence was Otto the canteen man. The Russians had seized Hitler's bunker but found in it only a dummy of cardboard and a stack of recorded speeches. Hitler had flown to Berchtesgaden (over our camp most likely) and barricaded himself at his eagle's nest. Thus, some eighty kilometers south of us, the Führer was still the Führer; but there was also another Führer somewhere in the north: one of the German admirals, who was trying to negotiate with the Allies. Swapping such news, we stayed up half the night, buzzing away even though we were dead tired. For despite the imminent collapse, the camp functioned. The kitchen staff still cooked, the Wäscherei still washed both the guards' and the prisoners' clothes, and all of us were marched to work daily, the men to a new line of fortification which was being built (uselessly) only a few miles to the west, the women to maintain the access road. Inside the finished Stelle, the production continued, although it was utterly senseless to pull an airplane out of there and send it up into the already conquered sky. And next to the Stelle, the Bird still ate rocks.

Hope, conflicted and hesitant but real nonetheless, occasionally became sheer torture: Should we try to escape? Or should we wait for God to kill us in this filthy pen, where so far He had spared us?

Meanwhile, a few of those baby recruits guarding us tried to desert, and one morning we woke up to the sight of three young Germans being lowered dead from the "soccer gate." They had been hanged at night. The execution in the night, cruel but cowardly, reinforced our hope. The Reich was in such disarray that it wavered about its own practices—ordinarily, the deserters would have swayed from their nooses, as an example, for days. Still, in its collapse, would the Reich pull us down with it?

I cried. I cried for Mirek.

I had no inkling of what had happened to him.

Through Mayer, through Otto, through Lorentz the Schreiber, I had tried to find some information. But I dug up absolutely nothing. Except that he had not been dragged back to Mittergars. So, was he still alive? Was he free? Had he made it to the Americans' side? Or (a dreadful thought that crossed my mind all the time) was he rotting somewhere, eaten away by the bugs of spring?

Wait for me. And destroy this letter.

I had not destroyed the letter.

Mayer told me that Eberle and Losch were fighting. A team of Wehrmacht engineers had driven over to the Stelle, in a truck stuffed with packages of what Mayer took to be dynamite, and boxes with wires sticking out of them. The Stelle was set to be blown up. Losch protested that order, had a shouting match with Eberle, then sat in the mess hall and acted catatonic until he was practically carried to his own quarters. A reinforcement of younger SS was brought in, the remnants of a division decimated by the Americans in France. They had wolves' eyes, wore battered uniforms, and seemed ready to shoot anyone, even fellow SS. They were posted in the watchtowers, doubling the number of our guards.

The days had become indistinguishable from one another. It did not matter whether it was Monday, Thursday, or Sunday, because Sunday's rest had been canceled. Time was stagnant, yet the hours passed. Then, around noon on one nameless day, a strong breeze arose, and we smelled that nauseating stench again. Human steak.

The word spread from wire to wire: Check the next compound, check the next compound. Look in the distance, climb on your barracks' roofs, look for human pyres. Where's that smoke coming from? Have they started on us?

Slowly, from compound to compound, the answer filtered back. The smoke came from another camp.

They had not started on us. Not yet.

Then for two days it rained torrentially, washing away the stench of burning corpses.

I thought of Mirek practically every minute. I thought: Why had God been so stingy on the night of his escape, and given him as cover a measly drizzle, while now He opened the sky's sluices? Who was He saving this flood for?

I looked at Mirek's last note every day. I almost did not hide myself anymore. The note wore away a little more each time I looked at it. And yet the repeated unfolding and refolding did not erase his writing, nor did the paper sever along the folding lines.

Wait for me. And destroy this letter.

On April 26 (I calculated the date later), in the grayness of predawn, the Americans hit Mühldorf again and a straying Mustang fighter bomber spotted the camp through the scattering clouds. The American pilot probably mistook it for German army barracks, for he came sweeping low and strafing angrily. We had all poured out of our bunks and flattened ourselves to the ground. But as we eased our faces up, we saw a hallucinatory scene: Some of those crazy-eyed SS started grabbing terrified women, pulling them up from the ground and stripping them of their striped jackets. *Schnell, schnell!* They wanted them to climb on the camps' roofs, all the roofs— barracks, offices, the kitchen, the infirmary—and spread their striped jackets on them to signal to the American pilot that down here were *prisoners.* They were so demented with fright they would use anything as cover, even our rags.

That was so funny. As the Mustang swept low for another strafing, I started chortling out loud, and someone caught me by my sleeve and yanked hard. It was Hulda. My jacket's buttons popped open, and Hulda peeled it off me.

I was wearing that bra tailored by Suri; in five weeks, it had grown even tighter on me. Mirek's letter was tucked inside my bra, showing through the thin cotton like a kind of oversize mole.

Hulda's eyes focused on my chest.

"*Büstenhalter!*" Bra! she squealed as if noticing an enemy infiltration, and she raised her stick. The SS were leaning ladders against the barrack walls, yelling for us to go lay our jackets on the roofs. I ducked Hulda's stick and climbed up the nearest ladder. On the roof, with my jacket in my hands, I waited for the flying machine to rip through the clouds again, straight at me. I screamed at its silhouette, already showing through the clouds' lower layers: "Do it! Kill them! Kill them all!"

More than ever, I had the insane conviction that the pilot would know how to spare me.

The plane dropped a bomb that fell outside the camp's enclosure, then soared to the heights in less than a minute. I climbed down without my jacket. I ran into my barrack, scrambled onto my bunk, and moved that wood panel. I wanted to hide Mirek's letter in that dark space between the roof and the ceiling. I did not get my chance. Hulda was rushing in after me, bawling: "*Alles kaput, und die verfluchte trägt Büstenhalter!*" Everything's lost, and this wretch wears a bra! As if my bra derided Germany's disaster. The plane dropped another bomb, closer, and I fell on my back in my bunk. I heard Hulda crawl into the safest space available: against the back wall there was that little stove of cement, and between the stove and the wall itself there were some fifteen centimeters of space. Somehow, she fitted herself in there. The plane dropped one last bomb. It hit the new water tank. In an explosion of water, the shell of the tank fell onto the barrack's roof, crashed right through, and pinned me under a ceiling beam.

I felt pain in my head and shoulder, but I did not pass out. I realized that I wasn't seriously hurt.

I heard the bunk creak as it gave way under the weight of the beam. Then, another explosion shook the earth and flipped the beam upward, just long enough for me to roll from under its weight, onto the floor. I crawled on my hands and knees, seeking anything that I might use as cover.

Then I saw Hulda. Crashing in through the roof, the water tank had destroyed half the bunks, then met the stove and flattened it into the wall. Caught behind it, Hulda's body looked now like a squashed cockroach, with only the head intact and hanging from an almost severed neck. Her eyes were glazing over: I watched how they went from clear to murky red, from internal bleeding.

I had wished her dead so many times; now she *was* dead, right in front of me, my first gift of liberation from the Allies. She had died only a minute before, but in that minute eternity had opened up before her—and in a strange way for me, too. I would never have the chance to kill her myself, or just to hurt her. To hit just once, just once, this creature of harsh, wound-up anger, this being of my own sex, with a body like mine, with hormones like mine, who had been put in my life to make me aware that even women, the vessels of birth, could be killers and demons. That unknown American pilot had robbed me forever of the chance to take my revenge.

I shrank back. Without words, I sensed the unhealthy twisting of my life. If I lived, would I be able to reconcile this unfulfilled revenge and my guilt for having survived while others hadn't, with a sense of joy, a *future*?

In Mühldorf, a siren sounded the all-clear.

I staggered outside.

I thought I was dreaming. Our yard was packed with German soldiers mixed together with half-undressed women. Hoping to escape the bombs, some of the Germans had put on striped suits, which contrasted absurdly with their hobnailed boots. Now they were taking off those stripes and slipping back into their uniforms. Beyond the wire, other Germans were stripping the Greeks. From the effects room soldiers raced over with bundles of Russian fatigues, which they threw at random at the seminaked prisoners, while all the striped suits were gathered carefully as shields against future raids. I caught a flying Russian jacket and pulled it on.

One German had gone crazy: he ran around blindly shouting *"Fliegeralarm! Fliegeralarm!"* Air raid!

A deafening chain explosion shook the camp: a cascade of giant bursts that slapped the air into our faces over and over. Then, in the direction of the Stelle, a black pillar of smoke split the sky. That crazy German screamed, *"Das Flugzeug!"* The plane! and I recognized him—it was Losch. Hearing his plane blow up, he dived to the mess hall, screaming, "Eberle, Eberle!" The explosions continued, the Stelle was a volcano gushing up mangled plane wings and flak guns that had never been fired. Losch was about to burst into the mess hall when the *whak* of a gunshot made him jump grotesquely and crash on his face. I ducked, then jumped up to see who had shot him—I was convinced it had been Eberle.

But I didn't see Eberle anywhere. Gudrun raced into our yard dragging a bedsheet smeared with an unevenly drawn Red Cross. When she saw Losch, she started to shake, then threw the bedsheet over him. She spotted me and stammered, "Where is Herr Kommandant?"

I shrugged. I had no idea.

"Lorentz!" she yelled. "Where is Lorentz?"

Lorentz, too, seemed to have vanished.

A German jumped me, pulling at my Russian jacket. Before I could shove him away, Rühl boomed through the bullhorn—the soldiers were forbidden to shed their uniforms, that was equivalent to a desertion and punishable by death! I wrenched myself free and saw the one who had attacked me. He wasn't a terrified youngster; he was one of those fierce-eyed SS. Rühl boomed on, The camp would be evacuated *now*. We had two minutes to gather in rows of five. There was a train to transport us to safety.

I fell in next to Margit (as usual) and waited for Hulda to sweep down our row and give me the customary lash, then remembered: Hulda was dead. And I started to laugh crazily. Gudrun was calling for fifteen volunteers to step forward, but for the first time I remained in my row. She needed fifteen volunteers to carry those life-saving striped outfits.

The tightness of my bra made me aware of Mirek's letter. If I rolled my shoulders to ease that tightness, the wad of paper bit into my skin. But my feet hurt me much worse. In the chaos of leaving the camp, I had lost my own shoes and grabbed another pair at random. They were two sizes too small.

We trekked out of the camp. Reversing our direction of eight months ago, we headed for Mühldorf.

I turned and looked behind me, at the huddles of barracks fading with each of my hobbled steps. I had spent eight months of my life in this place. Eight months out of nineteen years—that seemed brief. Yet how many time spans that felt endless had I lived in those months? How many days, hours, even minutes had seemed impossible to survive? Crushed by the water tower, my barrack looked as if it had trapped a monster and choked it in its clasp. My bunk was gone. The barrack's roof was gone, and my little hiding place with it. Amazingly, I felt a loss. Eight months spent in and around this place were gone, and I was being delivered to the future almost as hopeless as when I had arrived.

But I wasn't as hopeless. I had cheated death for eight months. And I still carried Mirek's letter on my body.

You said that you knew me so well, Mirek, and I replied that I did not know you at all.

I lied, though I wasn't aware that I was lying.

Now I realize how well I know you.

My revelation was obvious and profound and illuminating—life meant *knowing*. And of all experiences, love was made of knowing more than any other experience. One couldn't love another human without knowing him or her to the deepest core. Love was the knowledge of others, the understanding of what they were made of, what activated and satisfied them, what goals they were bound for. Even more, what was not quite formed inside them, but still taking shape, love could detect that, too. Love was the microscope and the telescope into every creature and every facet of life.

I knew Mirek, whose arms had held me only a few times, and whose lips, after he had kissed me, scratching my face savagely, had uttered, You've never been with a man, have you? I knew why he had asked that, and why my silent confirmation had been enough to stop his urge. He would not take me (even though I wished it), other than in freedom. Not just with my looks restored, but with my dignity returned. Otherwise he would not do it, because he was not a man of half measures. He took completely, and he gave completely. He had given completely since that first night when, pretending to be coarse and uninterested, he had thrown that toolbox at me and maneuvered to be alone with me. He had already laid out the plan of an encounter; and as we sat and talked in that untransfigured sanctuary by the wire, that oasis of dirt under the shadow of the gallows, he was already planning my job with the tea detail, my endowment of cigarettes, my training in learning the secrets of the camp.

He had pretended to ask me for help—I knew now that he never needed my help; it was his way of making me feel necessary and valued.

Then his feelings for me had overpowered him, and he had confessed them to me, in total sincerity. Then he had tried to keep himself away, but had not managed—so he had returned, offering himself with that silly flower. And then his feelings had overpowered him much, much more. He had suddenly re-alized that if there was to be anything between us, even here, then it was a crossing of fates, nothing less would do. And he had accepted that, as serious in the depth of his commitment as he had been in everything. And if he was to suffer or even die, he would blame no one, he would burden no one. He would remain the joy he had always been, for me, for his friends, for all that his humanity had touched on his passage. Consistent, unchanging, till the last minute.

He was like that.

He could not be any different.

I knew the key to his strength now.

The Greeks walked behind our column, and we could hear them talk vivaciously as if life had completely returned to them. The SS yelled at them to shut up, and finally loosed a few bullets over their heads. The Greeks reluctantly grew quiet.

Rühl was somewhere ahead, leading us from a motorcycle's sidecar.

We passed the charred ruin of the train station, which no one had tried to repair or even clear away.

We passed the end of a devastated street, and I could not help thinking that it might lead, across the town's wreckage, to the street where Mirek had given me his gloves. I wanted to stop thinking about Mirek. I was afraid, now that we had left the camp and I had no inkling of my future, that I would be even more at the mercy of my feelings for him. I had to separate myself, I had to.

We heard Rühl's voice through the bullhorn: Our train waited for us two kilometers ahead. Once we arrived at the train, we should embark quickly and without chaos, starting with the men. The last three cars were reserved for the women, a hundred per car.

Behind us the bombing started again, the bombs falling closer, closer, until we finally started to run ahead of them, soldiers and prisoners together. Then we saw the train waiting at an arbitrary spot on the repaired tracks, cattle cars open. Margit's eyes swelled in her sockets, she gripped my arm, motioned toward the car roofs: every inch of their surface had been covered in prisoners' stripes.

I thought, Who had those stripes belonged to?

The bombs were still falling close, about a half kilometer back, making craters in an empty wasteland. And what could have happened at any time happened now—we met a horde of German refugees, grimy, tattered, pushing their valuables in carts and barrows, even in wheelchairs. They were astoundingly many. I would have thought that the bombs had killed all but a few of them. They saw the train at the same time we did and rushed forward, only to face our guards and their lowered rifles. Desperate, stunned shouts exploded: "*Und wir? Und wir?*" And us? *Whizz-boom*, a bomb erupted the earth right at the back of their crowd. Humans were whipped into the air, screaming, dying as they were hurled up. The refugees dropped their belongings and rushed to fight for access to the train. Rühl tried to stop them with his bullhorn. Overwhelmed by their tide, he vanished. SS soldiers fired into that horde, at close range, *rat tat tat*. Screams of death and agony. The other SS beat us into the cars. As I stumbled in, I glimpsed with the corner of my eye the open platforms between two cars: packed with German soldiers. In their gray uniforms they looked like large huddles of gray rats. Then the car doors were pulled shut.

We heard more shots. Squeezed into a window's grating, pushed brutally into rusted bars that reeked (the whole car reeked, even the metal stank of filth), I saw what I never thought I would see: the German refugees, grimy, betrayed, and crying, were left behind, and the bombs started decimating them, while our train escaped eastward, flapping those striped uniforms.

TWENTY-FIVE

*W*e kept hearing planes and explosions. But no one knew where we were going.

I sat with Margit on the floor, our faces squeezed between standing women's thighs and buttocks. Then the train stopped. We heard car doors being opened. Our car door opened with a jangle like hell being unlocked, and voices shouted repeatedly: *"Sie sind frei!"* You are free! The women closest to the door hesitated, but the ones behind them were pushing. Several fell out of the train. The row behind jumped out and into a resplendent field of blooming poppies.

To my astonishment, despite the movement and commotion, Margit had dozed off. I shook her. We were free!

The two of us were the last in the car. We jumped out, glancing ahead, right, left, everywhere. Where were the Americans?

Lagging behind saved our lives. As the throngs of stripes scattered into the field, there was that *rat tat tat* again, and I saw people being shot, growing monstrous flowers of blood on their striped suits, then collapsing among the poppies, the red of their blood mixing with the red of flowers. Turning to run back, a man met a burst of bullets and his face seemed to pulverize.

"Back in the cars! Back in the cars!" the Germans shouted.

The men and women rushed into the cars mixed together. A girl fell, rose, and ran and fell again, until a man, stocky, big-boned, his eyes shaded by his low, heavy forehead, caught up with her and almost carried her to our car. He lifted her inside, hopped in after her. The door slammed shut, the engine jolted us all to the floor, the train raced forward again.

I fearfully examined the girl's clothes, finding no spots of blood, no obvious reason why she lay on the floor teary-eyed and gritting her teeth.

The stocky man reached for her striped pants. "Maybe you sprained your leg, let me see," he urged her in Hungarian.

"I'm all right—let go of me," she answered, also in Hungarian.

"Where does it hurt?" He reached again, above her knees.

"Let go of me!" she repeated.

He raised his palms above his head. "I'm not even touching you!" Again he reached for her, but she started sobbing aloud, and he drew back and cursed her under his breath. "I got you back on the train, didn't I?"

"Leave me alone," she wailed.

Other voices, both male and female, snapped at him to stop pestering her. He cursed her again, then staggered aside, and I realized how empty the car was now. We had left crammed like sardines; now we were barely fifty, men and women mixed together. The ones left behind, were any of them still alive? A man seemed to recognize me and crouched next to me. "You're the girl that Greek sang for," he said. "He made it, he's in the next car."

I nodded just to put a stop to his attention and crawled to the crying girl. She allowed me to roll up her pants. Some shrapnel hidden in the grass had lacerated her legs.

I tore off my sleeves at the elbow and helped her bandage her legs.

TWENTY-SIX

*T*he train was stopping almost every hour, moving in reverse then heading forward again, as if changing tracks, until we realized that we were on the old track, passing the same railroad crossings back and forth, the same German trucks and tanks destroyed from the air, and as the darkness fell, the same stars.

The fear crept back into us. A whisper went around the car: They're choosing a spot to finish us.

Mila got up. "If it's meant to be, let's choose the time and place ourselves!" And she started pounding on the door.

From the nearest other cars came the same pounding, but we heard no curses in German, no shots—as if the Germans had either vanished or decided to ignore us. The men in our car got together and tried to open the door by rattling it hard, hoping to unhinge the heavy latch from inside. The latch did not give way. The men drew back, exhausted. Then someone by the window shouted that he saw trucks rolling on a parallel road, headlights on. Could they be American? It seemed so, given those daring headlights. The Americans would not fear strikes from the sky. We lined up at the window and stared in turn at those lights until they vanished behind trees. We smelled a body of water. Its cool humidity filled the car, tinged with a slight rottenness, as if from wilted weeds. Then we saw a lake: about a dozen boats were burning in a small marina, illuminating a string of houses that faced an empty beach and water that rippled and played with the flames' reflection.

The houses were small, summer houses, and all of them were dark, as if abandoned. The moon lit the lake even more clearly, and the isolation of the place scared us more. The train would stop any minute now, and we would be ordered out and murdered under the glow of the indifferent moon.

But the train did not stop until the morning.

I had fallen into a semiconscious sleep. I was jolted from it when the train stopped for the last time. Framed by the grated window, there was a dented, smoke-smudged sign. Clutching the rusty bars, I got up and read: SEESHAUPT.

The name meant nothing to any of us. The train was motionless and quiet. Then we heard a car door open, but still no orders to disembark. A man squashed his face between the bars, peered out as if to say farewell to his life, then started to cry.

"It's over . . ." he gurgled. "Come look . . ."

I pushed him aside, peered, and saw a burned train station, a row of buildings, and, about a half kilometer beyond them, the lake. In between, on a pitted street, a German policeman rode a bicycle with a white flag stuck in its back rack. The buildings were white with bedsheets and tablecloths hanging from the windows, overlapping, reaching to the ground, as if from a frenzied effort to cry surrender as clearly as possible. A gigantic tank rumbled into view and honked like a car, shooing the bicycling cop away. On the tank's turret, a dozen American soldiers, the chin straps of their helmets loosened, shot curious glances at the little town, which was not abandoned—those bedsheets could not have rolled out the windows by themselves. But the Germans were staying hidden, even though the policeman turned his bike and rode in the other direction, as if to demonstrate that the street was safe.

Then we heard the sound of English. Shouted commands and shouted answers. Loud but without the shrieking tension of German commands. We heard the Americans' boots approaching the train, and even their boots sounded softer than the thumping of German boots. I gripped Margit. We all gripped each other, incapable of living through this except as a crowd, a sum of creatures too often tested together to face this moment individually. The car doors on our right and left jangled open. Ours jangled open, too. We saw our first Allied soldiers. They were gesturing for us to come out. One American was whistling softly. Then he stopped whistling.

We jumped out. Our liberators gaped at us almost like Eberle and his soldiers on the morning we had arrived in Mühldorf.

I could not tell what happened in the next few minutes. The need for this not to be some trick was so powerful in me that I broke across a circle of Americans and stepped away backwards, staring at them as if I could sustain the miracle of their presence by my stare alone. Then I closed my eyes. When I opened them again, the Americans had not disappeared. I saw a Greek kneel before an American, who was so stupefied that he staggered back. A medic with a red cross on his arm tried to help the Greek to his feet, but the Greek kissed the medic's boots, then sat on the ground and cried.

More medics hurried over. The last prisoners straggled out of the cars, staring at the Americans as if they were a mirage, then scrounging up the courage to touch them. The Americans let themselves be touched. Then an American NCO hurried over and asked the crying Greek, "*Wo ist der Deutsche Solda-ten?*" Then he questioned the whole crowd in stripes: "*Wo ist der Deutsche Soldaten?*" Where were the Germans? I remembered those gray-clad rats packing the train's platforms, and looked, and saw not one German Soldaten. The American NCO gave an order, and several soldiers ran, with rifles pointed, to the train's locomotive. They cautiously climbed and peered inside the cabin. Then they jumped down and walked back, gesturing that they'd found no one.

I closed my eyes again and waited for that huge blast from heaven, that deadly hellfire that would punish me, and our liberators, too. It did not come. I remained like that for at least a minute. The punishment still did not come. I felt a tap on the arm, and I jumped. I was facing a woman in uniform, with a cap on. All the uniformed women I had seen before were German. But this one was an American, tall, freckled and toothy. Moving carefully in case I might panic, she held up a tin cup filled with water and spoke nasally and softly, probably encouraging me to drink. Then she said the first three words in English that I understood right away even though I spoke no English: "You are free."

I was alive, and free.

I had tried to imagine the liberation. I had expected an immense relief, a transfiguration of everything: the sky, the earth, the other people, me. Everything would be transformed beyond recognition. If that metamorphosis occurred, it lasted so briefly that the next moment I could not even remember it.

I was aware that I had finished the water and was signaling by poking my finger into the empty cup: more. I received more water. The woman with big teeth and freckles motioned me to sit on the gutted pavement and took my pulse. She seemed reassured, for she tapped me on the shoulder, then offered her hand, and I trustingly put my palm in her palm.

Then I leapt to my feet.

Where were my cousins?

I yelled, "Margit! Suri! Manci!"

Thinking I'd seen Margit, I bumped people off my path, Margit! Margit!—till I fell on top of a stranger. I stopped, panting, alive and free but missing four-fifths of my familiar self. Where were they? Other liberated Haeftlings overran the

street, outnumbering our transport; here and there, Americans
with their helmets on, brandishing their rifles, swam in a sea
of stripes. Suddenly, again, that terrifying *rat tat tat*. From a
nearby wall, a big chipping of plaster flew above the crowd and
then broke, hitting bodies and faces. The Americans shouted
at us to dive to the pavement. Somewhere, some Germans were
still fighting the war. People ducked on top of each other, using
as cover a hay wagon in flames, a crushed streetcar, a fallen
tree.

An American tank ground to a stop right by me, erected a
thick and ugly cannon. *Ssluckk*—I heard a shell leave the barrel—and then *boom*—far ahead, the shell blew a hole in a
hillside dotted with puffs of gunfire. Those puffs looked harmless, but the bullets fired from that hillside whizzed right above
my head. The tank shelled the hillside again, then rumbled
toward it, fearless, while the infantrymen jumped up and over
the prisoners they had freed, and rushed to follow the tank.

I could not lie on the ground—I bolted and raced after my
saviors.

The sea of stripes, terrified yet indifferent to the gunfire,
followed in the same direction, and we were suddenly outside
the town, in a field imprinted with tank tracks. We tripped on
dead German soldiers, severely trampled, killed perhaps days
before.

"Margit!" I hollered, meaninglessly, for the noise of the gunfire drowned out everything else, and if it was her this time, I
could not reach her. She was running off to my right, where
buildings enclosed with wire fences burned brightly.

The wire fences had been torn by the tanks. Other Americans, scattered among the buildings, returned the hillside's gunfire. More humans in stripes, skeletal, skulls shaved, ankles
caught in clinking chains, limped painfully toward the Americans and the battle in progress. They engulfed the Americans,
forcing them to stop firing. The Americans flailed their arms
as if not to drown, and shouted another line which I under-

stood without translation: "It's over, it's all over!" But the Haeftlings did not understand, did not believe that it was over; and when they did, they wept, hugged the Americans, fell off them from lack of strength, and tried to kiss their boots or the dirt they were treading. Several Americans pulled back the chained men, gestured as if inquiring about the keys to unlock their chains; then one of them raised a handgun and set it on the support of his folded left arm. He shot the chains off like a marksman, while the Haeftlings stood still with childlike trust; each time a lock popped open, they moaned as if in veneration. The marksman raised his pistol as if it were the tool of a sacred deliverance, and just then a burst of shots from the hill punctured him across the chest. A huddle of bodies formed over his collapsed shape.

"*Achtung! Achtung!*"

The sound of German made me cringe.

But it was an American, rushing around with a bullhorn, shouting in broken German: All prisoners is freed and now pull back, off from line of fire! For your own good, back into town, German Soldaten are not defeated yet! An engine's growl made me spin around fearfully. A tank rammed a burning building, from which I heard screams. The wall gave in: nude skeletons, sexless, featureless from incredible loss of fat and tissue, still had enough life in them to crawl out. The tank moved on to batter another building and open it up.

More stripes were staggering about, while heaps of stripes lay lifeless on the ground. I was in a huge unknown camp, invaded by the battle. Packs of Americans cut paths among the prisoners. I leapt to avoid a plot of smelly vomit, then saw many Americans doubled over, retching. The stench of burning flesh hit my nostrils—what I had taken to be a hut in flames was a stack of bodies layered over wooden logs, crackling and smoldering. And—I froze, maybe I voided my bladder—out in the open, on a wooden board, a naked man had been impaled with steel spikes. He could not move or scream, for he had a deep gash at the neck, probably where his vocal cords had been severed.

But he was breathing. He was staring down at his own rib cage, which had been split open—his lungs showed, foamily purple, expanding and contracting, as if he had been dissected alive. Between the lungs, a darkly red heart still pumped, crumpled, small, ready to give out. But the man, since he could not make sounds, blinked desperately, rolled his almost severed head, and his eyes scoured the nearby space: Help me! Help me!

Oh, Lord . . .

Those words came to my mind without my wish. They sprang forward, for want of any other words, for want of any understanding, any explanation, anything that could somehow reverse what I saw.

Nothing could reverse what I saw. Not the words: Oh, Lord . . . Oh, Lord . . . Oh, Lord . . .

Someone called: "Doctor! Doctor!"

A ring of Americans gathered up from every direction. As they saw the man nailed to that board, the vomit burst out of them, with coughs and yells of horror.

I fell. When my body hit the ground, I saw the sky, thick with the smoke of artillery, but those pulsating lungs were imprinted on it. In a desperate attempt to forget them, I decided: that image just could not be real, I had fabricated it, I was insane. And since I was insane, I could expect other hallucinations.

I staggered up. And, right on cue, I saw Hulda Braun.

She was alive, and there were six of her. Six SS Aufseherinnen marched in a double file, herded along by an American soldier who was black and whose eyes were so fiery I wondered if he had gone crazy. His fingers were jiggling the lock of his rifle. The Aufseherinnen had a strange expression, a kind of dazed smile, but their cheeks rippled like gelatine from fear. Stepping closer, they revealed the sight of gallows from which naked dark-skinned men were hanging contortedly. The men had been hanged by their necks but also by their wrists tied behind their backs. The nooses around their necks hadn't broken their dog tags, which dangled on their chests, glinting in the sunlight. They were colored American soldiers. Other soldiers ran to the gallows, then stopped. It was too late, the colored prisoners were dead. Then someone yelled at the Aufseherinnen, in German: Why had these men been executed? Why? They were prisoners of war!

None of them responded. A soldier grabbed one by her collar and swatted her on her quivering cheeks, palm and backhand, palm and backhand, palm and backhand. I thought he would draw blood, but her cheeks just quivered harder. She sniveled that the Americans had been brought in only a few days before. This morning, as the order came to douse the locked barracks with gasoline and set them on fire, starting with the Jewish barracks, one American yelled out, "Assassins!" And the camp Kommandant got very upset and ordered the colored Americans hanged as a warning. Then all the Americans started shouting and screaming; the Kommandant lost his head and ordered the American Jews killed, but the others had swapped their dog tags with them, so the Jews couldn't be identified by the H on their dog tags, and since all Americans were circumcised, there were no other means of verification. So, as the sounds of the battle approached, the Kommandant ordered all Americans killed. Now they were lying in the yard with all the others.

Raging shouts silenced her, gun muzzles poked her in the cheeks, poked the other Aufseherinnen in the breasts of their uniforms. A few voices pleaded, perhaps arguing that the Aufseherinnen should be spared as witnesses.

I found the strength to turn away and bumped into a limping skeleton. "What camp is this?" I asked him. I feared it was the place Mirek had tried to flee from.

He looked at me out of the mists of total exhaustion. "Dachau Four," he peeped, feeble as a fledgling bird.

I shivered. "Is this also called Mittergars?"

"Mittergars? No . . . ," he peeped uncertainly.

"Waldlager, then? Waldlager?"

He blinked, but very slowly, as if every blink required a lot of energy.

"Can you hear me?"

The man did not answer. Like a ghost, he floated past me. Mirek . . . Mirek . . . Are you alive?

I remembered my pledge to myself: I will drag myself away.

The disoriented prisoners finally found their way back into town.

I sleepwalked with them down the main street, passing another American with a bullhorn, stationed there for our benefit. He informed us, in good German but hitting his rs very strongly, that the bulk of the American forces was one day away, but when they arrived, a camp would be erected for us, a Displaced Persons camp. Meanwhile, we should be wary of German civilians; some were SS wearing belt-buckles with built-in barrels, compact little guns that could be fired at the touch of a button. Others hid charges of TNT in their shirts, looking to take with them as many Haeftlings or liberators as possible.

I shall walk. One step. One step.

A man blocked my path, and his face seemed familiar. But it wasn't Mirek. It was Gabi Petilon.

Away from the battle, the Greeks had used their time well. They had investigated the area and found a row of summer houses lying empty, some of them unlocked, on the shore of the Seeshaupt lake. A dozen of Gabi's friends had selected a big house, found axes, and hacked the furniture, and when Gabi helped me step stiffly down to the lakeshore, a fire was crackling on the sand in front of the house. The Greeks had confiscated food, mostly cans, from the nearest terrified Germans. The smell of beans rose out of a pot hung over the fire.

I turned away, shaking. I could not bear seeing flames. Gabi guessed something, for he put his arms around me and rocked me gently: "Svester, Svester . . ."

I heard a whoop of joy. Tsilka was running down from the house. From her voice and self-assured steps, I knew: she had missed what I had seen.

My cousins were in the house. They had accepted the Greeks' hospitality.

TWENTY-SEVEN

*A*ll five of us slept that night in the master bedroom, grateful to be able to squeeze together in a big bed abandoned by the vanquished, grateful for that skin-to-skin security we had learned in camp.

We barricaded the door with chairs. But the Greeks never tried to bother us.

A moon stained with artillery smoke beamed into the bedroom.

Cradled between two cousins, I slept fitfully, now and then hearing explosions, then the sleepy caw of a bird, or a fish's splash in the lake. The noises of nature had a puzzling perfection. I woke up in a puddle of my own tears, remembering those beating lungs and heart, seeing the hanged colored soldiers. Adonai, you created the wonder of those lungs and heart, and left them undefended. Why did that man have to die, and not me? Why those black men, who had fought to free us, and not me? Why my parents, and not me? And Mirek . . . Oh Mirek, Mirek, Mirek, he could have died in so many ways, I pictured him trampled, hanged, split open . . . I knew he had not made it—how could he survive that murderous hell? Adonai, why have you allowed the grass and stones and birds and beasts to remain innocent, but not the humans, whom you endowed with knowing good from evil? Adonai, why did you leave me so alone, alone, alone and unworthy, needed by no one, able to help no one, even on the cusp of peace?

My tears streamed into my pillow until I lifted the pillow, drenched, and threw it out of the bed.

Then I gently patted the faces of my cousins. I touched their hair. Margit mumbled something, but slept on. Suri turned on her back, and her body, the most mature, even in its unconsciousness gave me some hope.

Part 6

THE SEARCH

TWENTY-EIGHT

FOUR MONTHS LATER—AUGUST 1945
SUBURB OF DEJVICE, PRAGUE

*G*ranny Novakova's house consisted partly of a grocery store with empty shelves, with a sign in the window that read: WE SHALL RECEIVE NEW SUPPLIES SOON. All grocery stores in Prague carried similar signs, and since the end of the war all had been mostly empty. Granny Novakova's apartment was on the floor above the store, and it was reachable via a shaky outer stairway. The upper floor sagged as if ready to collapse over the store and crush it; inside the apartment, the floors were uneven. The humble, precarious look of the house had helped when it was an outpost of the underground. Novakova was an "underground granny," the keeper of a reliable place through which people, weapons, and messages had transited safely, unknown to the Gestapo.

When Mirek had told me to go to Prague and look him up at his granny's (*Babicka*, as Mirek called her), I had imagined that I would meet his real grandmother. But Novakova could not have been his grandmother—a slight woman under five feet in height, she was in her late forties and not related to him at all. At first glance, she appeared stern, like a schoolteacher who could discipline unruly kids with one stare, despite her size. But that sternness, too, was deceptive.

When I told her that I came from a camp and was looking for Mirek Vencera, she walked with me up into the ramshackle apartment at the top of the stairs, put two cups of chicory coffee on a table covered with newspapers, then sat with me and took my hands in her hands.

Having not expected the gesture, I tensed up. Then I gave in and left my hands in hers.

She asked me to describe Mirek physically. I did, and she nodded—yes, that was him. Meanwhile, her hands, warm, dry and bony, worked some spell of their own, for after a few minutes I was confessing everything to her, including Mirek's letters on cement paper and the tea breaks we had shared in the pit. Gradually, Novakova's hands tightened over mine, her eyes took on a fixed look, her shoulders bowed in, as if doubting my revelations. But as I kept repeating, Mühldorf, Mühldorf, her forehead wrinkled up. The name was ringing a bell. Then she sat up in her chair. Yes, that was the camp of Mirek's last mission. Where the Germans were building a new weapon.

Yes, what I had told her was credible.

"By the way," she said. "His real name wasn't Mirek."

My hands tensed up in hers.

She smiled appeasingly. "My dear girl, we all had to change our names. He came to us as Karel, but he became Mirek when we disbanded our Prague unit because the Gestapo was after us. But Mirek or Karel, it's not important. He's the same one. My dear girl . . ." She squirmed a little in her chair. "I haven't heard from him yet."

I had been in Prague for only ten days. I was almost convinced that I would find him at the address he had given me, perhaps eating *knedliki* prepared by his Babicka. Or gone for the day or maybe for the week, but still within accessible distance. Mute, I tried to free my hands, but Novakova firmed up her grip, and I panicked: She thinks he's dead. She thinks he's dead and is trying to break it to me gently.

"My dear girl." In that formal tone, I heard a different woman, a lady. The war had also made her a grocer, and a fighter. "Mirek is a man of his word. If he said he'll look you up, he'll look you up—and thanks to you, he'll look me up, too." A little titter softened her lips. Then it faded in a strange way, as if retreating inside her to join her memories of Mirek.

"The little rascal," she said with affection. "How could he endanger you like that?"

I bolted up. "I endangered him, too," I said, almost offended that she considered him alone responsible.

"Of course, of course. But he'd been in eight prisons and camps; he should've had more foresight." Silent, I decided not to mention our most dangerous moment together, that rainy night. "Anyway . . ." She pondered, then rose, beckoned me over . . . and opened the wall.

That was exactly what she did: she pressed the wallpaper at a particular spot, and it gave in, revealing a camouflaged doorway.

Stunned, I followed her into a command post that had outlived its use: a room without windows, and no larger than four feet by six. Novakova stood on tiptoe and pulled a cord, shining a hanging fifty-watt bulb on military maps tacked to the walls, field radios stored on narrow racks, even a couple of rifles and ammunition belts hanging from pegs. And a fantastic array of clothes of all sorts, including German uniforms, which had been used as disguises. Novakova touched them. "Mirek wore some of these when he went on missions."

Then she pulled out a plain binder that could have contained the grocery's record of sales, and showed me one page of handwriting that would have confounded a graphologist: "I developed my own shorthand. This is Mirek's file."

Mirek's file.

I looked at the disguises, maps, and weapons surrounding that frail lone woman. They looked real and yet hard to believe. Novakova, too, was the real thing, but did not look it one bit—thank God, otherwise she wouldn't have stood a chance with the Gestapo.

She walked back into the kitchen with the file, laid it on the table, and after following some passages in it with her finger, looked up at me. She explained that Mirek had had a number of "inside missions," including the one in Mühldorf, monitoring the building of that underground plant. Which was exactly the reason that she couldn't predict when Mirek would return. After he had escaped from his last camp, taking out two Americans with him, the podzemny had expected him to find his way to Prague fairly quickly. But he hadn't, so the podzemny had sent a man of their own to track him, who had reported that after escaping, Mirek had vanished somewhere in the Frankfurt region.

I was following all this with my heart sinking lower and lower, until it beat somewhere near my ankles. Mirek's disappearance could mean two things: the Americans had rescued him, and then sent him for debriefing to a regimental or divisional HQ, where they might hold on to him for a while, depending on the value of his information. The other possibility was . . .

She stopped. We knew what the other possibility was. Mirek had broken out of Mittergars a whole month before Germany's capitulation.

Her eyelids blinked quickly, very quickly. "I loved Mirek," she whispered. "He was always more than just a good fighter, he was so lively and full of hope. He would've made a joke even in front of a firing squad, made those bastard Germans laugh and given them that laugh as a present. That's the way he was." She sat down, lifted the cup of cold chicory, set it down again, prey to a nervousness I had not detected before. "That's why I'd like to know . . . You're here because you're grateful to him . . . or is it more than that?"

"It's . . . more than that," I said, blushing.

"For you only, or for him, too?"

I blushed harder. "I think we felt the same way."

"Humans are so incredible," she marveled. "In the direst conditions, they still yearn for love."

Novakova got up. Fully standing, she was slightly taller than me sitting down. "My dear girl, the secret of life is life itself. You can't do anything to get Mirek back faster. You have to wait, but you also have to go on with your life, you understand?"

"I understand . . . but can't you find out if he's alive?"

My voice was hot and scratchy. I hoped that I would not cry.

She shook her head. She whispered that she couldn't find that out without asking the cooperation of some people she no longer trusted, because . . . Not because of fear. Because of bitterness and disgust. Over the last year, the podzemny had been totally infiltrated by the Russians. A man named Arnost Lemberger, a Communist and a former comrade of hers and Mirek's, sat now in a big office at Prague's Police Presidium and made lists of his old comrades, for the Soviet MGB. Key members of the underground had been arrested by the MGB and were now being tortured at Prague's Pankrac Prison, on suspicion that they had been British or American spies. Mirek had helped the Americans, he was hopefully with the Americans now, why make him a target for the Russians? "Do you understand that, my girl?"

I nodded. I understood.

"You came here with love in your heart, but it's best that you muzzle that love, at least for now. Try not to think of Mirek. The biggest gift from God is to live. Don't betray Mirek, but live. Can you do that?"

I felt that the walls of the little kitchen were leaning in on me. The air itself had become solid and was squeezing my temples.

But Novakova's eyes had a commanding power, and I felt that any other answer would disappoint her. I answered that I would try.

"Good girl," she said. "I'm trying, too, you know?"

And she put her arms around me. Small and frail, she felt like those tiny creatures whose heartbeats are more palpable than their bodies.

"If he does contact me, I'll let you know right away. What's your address?"

The newspapers had announced that the mail service would restart soon, but only the domestic mail. I gave her my address.

"I'll drop you a note," said Novakova. "And if you're impatient, you can always visit me again."

Parting with her, I felt like kissing the little hands that had held mine with such trust, but I did not dare. I wanted to ask more about Mirek, but I did not dare. I left and took the streetcar back to the heart of town. On the streetcar, I glimpsed myself in the car window. I still did not look in mirrors very often—one minute in the morning, washing my face and brushing my hair, that was all. But random reflections seemed to follow me, as if pleading with me: Look, you are here, you exist. My hair was brown and wavy and rich as if to make up for all the hair of my lost kin. I used no makeup or lipstick—I didn't own any. I was thin as a rail, though perhaps moving with a certain gangly grace. I noticed that men stared at me. But when they did that, I looked away.

To meet Babicka, I had put on my good attire for going out: a plain white cotton dress, yellow leather sandals whose soles were getting thin, white socks, and a beige purse that almost went with the dress and the sandals.

The ticket collector stepped up to my seat, and I showed him my ID: a Displaced Person's card issued by the Americans. He nodded, and I didn't have to pay for my ticket.

Now it was the end of August. I had not seen Mirek for five months. My last month in camp, and the four months after the liberation.

I was visiting Granny Novakova for the fifth time since my arrival in Prague.

At first sight, things had not changed much in her apartment. Yet the disguised command post was gradually becoming empty. Unable to make a living as a grocer, Babicka was selling off those unconsecrated war trophies, the equipment, and the weapons.

Each time I came here, the first part of my pilgrimage was the most optimistic and energizing. On the streetcar, then walking to Granny's store, then knocking on the door of her apartment, I sang a song of hope: Mirek is here, he just arrived. Or, he arrived a few days ago and was simply too exhausted to travel downtown. Or he had just sent a message for me: I'll be in Prague in a week, in two weeks, in a month at the most.

Then the door opened. The older woman looked me in the eyes, affectionate and helpless, and I knew. She still had no news for me.

She made the obligatory chicory coffee, which was the first step in my ritual of settling into my next stretch of waiting.

"I can't come to your brother's wedding tonight," said Novakova, setting the cups between us. "I think I found a buyer for my store. He said he'd come to look at it tonight, and I don't want to miss him."

I was disappointed. An uplifting change had happened in my life: I had found my brothers. They had survived, all four of them. The older ones, Leizer and Pepo, had been in Hungarian work camps. The baby brothers, Henju and Mechel, had also been in work camps, but for the last two months of the war they had been transferred to Mauthausen. Even there, death had spared them. Which prompted Babicka to say each time I mentioned my brothers: "See how much God gave you back already?"

"I see, I see, Babicka."

The eldest, Leizer, was getting married tonight. I had invited

Novakova because she was my link to Mirek, and having her with us tonight was like having Mirek with us, a little. I had told my brothers about the man who had helped me in camp. They were grateful to that phantom savior, and curious to meet Novakova.

"We'll miss you at the wedding, Babicka."

"Nonsense, you'll have a good time. Who wants a hag like me around?"

"You're only forty-eight."

"Forty-nine, plus the war."

That was a joke we had made up together. I was twenty, plus the war.

I had turned twenty on March 23, while still in Mühldorf. I had not celebrated in any way, I had not even thought about the importance of that date, which during my teens had loomed like a significant landmark. Not until after the liberation, when the Americans had issued me my DP card, on which my birthdate was erroneously marked March 25. I had not even attempted to correct that mistake.

Twenty years old.

Back in Zhdenev I used to wonder what I would be like at twenty. I should have some experience and understanding of life. In Zhdenev, most women of twenty were already married and mothers of at least one child. I should know my strengths and weaknesses, I should have the necessary resolve to make the right choices and not be swept away by blind passions. In short, twenty was that lucid vantage point from which I could glimpse my future.

Now, I had reached that vantage point.

I didn't glimpse my future at all.

"Are all your brothers going to be there tonight?"

"Yes. Henju and Mechel are coming this afternoon from Budapest."

Henju and Mechel traveled to Budapest often. One of the

best black markets for cigarettes was there, and Henju and Mechel were in the cigarette black market business. They bought the sought-after brands of the day—Luckies and Chesterfields and Camels—from illicit wholesalers and sold them in the Russian-occupied territories. Without operators like my brothers, Prague and Budapest would only reek of *mahorka*, a Russian tobacco as foul as the dried corncob tassels smoked by the Ukrainian kids in our village.

"Well, shouldn't you be home cooking for the feast?"

"What feast—soup, one big goulash, latkes, and a salad?"

"No wedding cake?"

"We didn't have enough food coupons for a cake. But we'll buy some *pecivo* (pastries). And," I added to brighten the picture, "we'll go dancing after the dinner."

The cooking had all been done the day before. I had helped, but the bulk had been prepared by Leizer's fiancée, Ruchi, who was from Sinover, my father's home shtetl. Ruchi was petite, as petite as Novakova, with round features and brown eyes and a voice that sometimes sounded scared. Leizer had known her before the war—we went to Sinover in the summers to visit my paternal grandparents. I knew Ruchi, too. But I had never imagined that one day she would be my sister-in-law.

I had done the cleaning. Tying a babushka over my hair, I went after dust and stains like a fiend—but how easy it was to clean an apartment of only three rooms and a bathroom, even if six or seven people bunked down in it at all times. The hardest part had been scrubbing the stairs leading to our apartment, because a gang of Russians passing down the street the night before had urinated on them, singing and reeling drunkenly. So I sudsed and cleaned the stairs three times, letting them dry off in between. The third time, as I looked at my hands scrubbing, I glimpsed my mother's hands in mine. I saw them clearly. The texture of the skin, the bending of the fingers and the roundness of the knuckles. I remembered them well but didn't know that mine resembled hers in such detail. Instead of thinking "I'm going crazy," I was happy. I had her hands in my hands.

Now the stairs smelled of nothing but detergent and Prague air—I'd kept ajar all the windows to the building's inner courtyard. I was pleased with myself. We had fifteen guests and a rabbi, Rabbi Rappaport, who was of high standing in Prague's Jewish community; we didn't want them to walk up through a stench of piss.

The surviving Jews were marrying, marrying, marrying. Few married whom they had had in mind. Few had anyone in mind. They married who was left. They bumped into each other, looked each other over, paired up, and hurried to buy the *otdaci list* (marriage certificate), which cost ten crowns. Everyone could afford ten crowns, and everyone had to start over, *now.* So they married every day, without wedding rings, gifts from friends, dowries, printed invitations, or rabbis even—Leizer had lucked out. They didn't know whom they had by their side, in bed, in life. One essential mattered: they should both be Jews. If they had grown up the same way, if they knew the same things, they had a chance.

Too bad that Babicka could not come. And too bad that she had no news for me.

I got up. There were still some preparations to be made at home. I wondered if Leizer had managed to rent a huppah. Till this morning, he still hadn't found one.

Babicka told me that if the deal with that buyer went through, she might have to move at short notice. But she would drop me a line at my downtown address, Truhlarska 17.

My new home was so centrally placed that I could walk from it to Stare Mesto, the old town; to Republic Square, a hub of trade, business, and entertainment; and to the Masarik train station, where I had arrived in June, with Suri and Manci, from Germany.

Margit had stayed behind to take care of Tsilka, who had come down with typhus in the DP camp of Feldampfing. But Margit had also met a Hungarian, David, a former kapo who had that rare reputation of having been sweet. She was interested in David, and David was trying to start a business in Germany.

Until I left Germany, Gabi Petilon surrounded me with his affection, making sure, while we lived in the Greeks' home, that I got my share of the daily food, then, when we moved to the DP camp, visiting me every few days. His German was even more atrocious, if possible, but he cheerfully tried to teach me some Greek, brought me clothes pilfered from abandoned German homes, and kept asking me to go boating with him on the lake—rowboats lay on the lakeshore, abandoned just like the houses. Finally, I did once. He rowed us far from the shore, then stopped the boat, hung the oars in their cleats, and I thought, That's it. He'll try to force himself on me in the middle of the lake.

But Gabi had brought me here only to ask me a question, and it was the same question he had once asked me through the camp wire: "Nix svester?" (not sister)—by now, that word meant "wife" to him. I was afraid to respond, until I saw his expression—passionate but not possessive—and I realized that I did *not owe him*, not even in his mind. By giving him the hope that I might be his, I had held him up as much as Mirek had held me up. If he was alive now and could row strongly, like a true native of that Greece made of islands, it was thanks in part to me.

So I shook my head: no, no sister. We'd had our romance. Back there, through the wire. Always in the shadow of my obsessive yearning for Mirek, always lasting just seconds, while my times with Mirek were counted in minutes.

For the second time—the first time had been when we had been marched out of the burning camp—I experienced the most bizarre, most unwanted kind of nostalgia. Gabi was part of my youth, like my bunk bed in the barrack, like that hiding place in the ceiling where I kept Mirek's flower. Those gifts that did not seem to be gifts had been granted to me, and I could not, I would not, throw them out of my life—without them I'd be left with nothing.

So I kissed Gabi, just once, in the middle of the lake.

Then he rowed me back to the shore, sad and yet appeased.

When we had arrived under the smoky vaults of Prague's Masarik station, I still had no idea whether any kin of mine was alive. Apart from Mirek's tales, I didn't know the "golden city" or possess one useful address. But on the train platform I heard Yiddish being spoken by three soldiers in the uniforms of the Czech army, Yiddish that sounded Subcarpathian! The soldiers were here looking for relatives—all over Europe, in any train station, at any time, thousands of people looked for relatives. I approached one soldier, and he turned out to be from Sinover, Father's home village!

But my luck did not stop there. The soldier knew two cousins of mine from Sinover, Ludvig Berger and Hani Godinger—both had survived and were now in Prague. Hani, a girl one year older than I, lived on a street called Truhlarska, in an apartment owned by Ludvig. It was originally a German family's apartment, but when the Russians had entered the city and Prague's German minority had fled en masse, Ludvig had made himself master of the abandoned apartment, no questions asked. Ludvig was away that day; he'd just gone up to Ústí nad Labem, in the Sudeten. There, where the Sudeten Germans had once cried so shrilly for the dismemberment of Czechoslovakia, there were now thousands of German businesses and homes, deserted, waiting for takers. And the enterprising Ludvig had rushed to Ústí, to check them out.

There were no public phones in the station—among the Red Army's smaller acts of conquest was that of tearing off public phones to take them home as souvenirs. But a phone wouldn't have helped; Ludvig had no phone. The soldier told us to wait right there while he went to find Hani. After four hours of waiting, during which Suri, Manci, and I fought off the advances of a throng of Russians, and had *rochliki* (rolls) and chicory coffee at the station's cafeteria—free because we came from camp—the soldier did reappear with Hani. She looked exactly the way I knew her from our summer visits to Sinover: big-boned, ruddy-faced, and with thick glasses. Practically blind without them, she'd worn those glasses through camp, and God had decreed that they would not end up on a pile like the ones I had sorted out in Brejinka. Hani hugged me. I hugged Hani. Hani hugged Suri and Manci and was hugged back by them. Hani's glasses fogged up from tears, and she faltered. "Blanka, your b-brothers . . ."

I could not breathe.

She cleared her voice: "They're ah-live. All four. In Budapest."

We both cried so hard now that we shook in each other's arms. I made Hani's shoulder wet. Suri and Manci cried, too. That providential soldier, whose name I hadn't even asked, was dabbing his eyes with his handkerchief.

"Come home," said Hani. Then she corrected herself—"Come to the apartment. It's just two streets away."

Thousands of DPs on the go slept at best in *imkas* (Czech for YMCAs), but most often under the open sky. But Suri, Manci, and I spent our first night in the "golden city" in a blood relative's apartment.

. . .

Days later, under the same vaults dirtied by smoke, inhaling the same reek of coal doused with water, I welcomed my two older brothers, Leizer and Pepo. I soaked their shoulders, too. I could not believe how much they had changed—my eyes tried to fuse the adolescent faces I remembered with their current ones, and failed. Leizer looked like my father when he was young, a bittersweet resemblance. Pepo, always my favorite and confidant, was a man now. I had fantasized that if they came to Prague, we would live together, they working and I cooking and cleaning, recreating a piece of our home universe. But Leizer had brought Ruchi with him. And Pepo had brought a tall and sensual Hungarian whose name was Pearl, whom everyone called Piri. Piri had lost every soul she had grown up with. But she had found Pepo.

So. My life reestablished itself around my brothers and my visits to Novakova.

But as I departed today, Granny opened the door behind me and called me back.

I was almost at the bottom of the stairs. I climbed back to the apartment. When I stepped in again, she spoke hurriedly: "Dear girl, I didn't want to tell you this, but I think I have to. Now, what do you want most? That Mirek is alive, right?"

"Right," I squeaked. Her question had hit me like a punch in the stomach.

"He is alive. Someone I trust just met him in Frankfurt. Mirek is working for the Americans; he is working on the de-Nazification program." I felt the blood draining from my face. Why was Babicka giving me this information, what else did she have to tell me? "But he may not return to Czechoslovakia. My friend asked him: D'you have any messages to give to anyone in Prague? And he said no." I probably looked destroyed, because she clutched my hands with her small bony ones, whose grasp had so far been a conduit of hope. "Dear girl . . . Many new things can happen in a man's life. Love is strange. Maybe because you both were where you were, it burned so brightly there. But once outside . . . Please—you are young, smart, and pretty. God gave you back so much already."

I managed to say, "Can I speak with that man who saw Mirek?"

Babicka hesitated, but only a few seconds. "I can arrange for you to meet him. But you won't find out more than what I told you. This man was in Germany, with Mirek, and he decided to return. Mirek's not returning."

Not returning.

"I'm sorry . . . I don't know how he could keep someone like you waiting . . . and then not turn up . . ." I felt how my hope that he would return had become Novakova's, too, a romantic dream by proxy.

She came down the stairs with me and took my hands in hers again, on the sidewalk. "I'm so sorry that I had to tell you this on such a festive day."

TWENTY-NINE

I walked slouching to the streetcar station. This was the terminal, from which several lines departed for Prague. As I walked, I felt how much my sandals had thinned—I felt the bang of the cobblestones on my feet each time I took a step.

He was alive, that was the main thing.

The very words he had once told me: You are alive, that's the main thing.

What do you want? I argued with myself. He brought you back to life; then he protected you. He gave you hope and romance. He made you feel pretty, important, special, at a time when you looked awful, worse than awful, not even human. Do you realize how much he did for you? Now other men stare at you. You no longer need him, I tried to convince myself cynically, you're covered. Then, I felt so sad that I sank onto a dirty bench in the terminal and rummaged inside my purse, looking for something to stop my tears with.

I found nothing, I carried no handkerchief, no scarf. Just my comb and my DP card and a few crowns. So I hung my head and let the tears seep onto the top of my dress.

Then I wiped them off and glanced back toward the little street I had just left. In the distance, Babicka's apartment showed like a box of peeling plaster with a blank window in it. With the selfishness of youth, I had never wondered about her future. She was not even fifty. I had never asked her about her late husband—though I knew that she was widowed—or whether she took any interest in some new man. I had sipped her chicory and taken the hope from her hands, and never asked her: What were her plans? Did she need help? What did she expect from the rest of her life?

I had not even shared with her the one thing I'd learned about Mirek that she did not know. Maybe I wasn't really selfish, maybe I just thought it wasn't important for her. I had learned it on Charles Bridge. Where Mirek had told me to wait for him, by that crucifixion with Hebrew letters, on Tuesdays and Fridays.

"You know, that's the only crucifixion in the world with Hebrew words on it?" he had told me in camp.

"Really?" I had replied.

Mirek had nodded, proud about his native city.

I had made those Tuesday and Friday pilgrimages to the bridge for about three weeks; then I had stopped. There was always Novakova. And I felt ridiculous planting myself twice a week next to that crucifixion—a beautiful sculpture no doubt, but not my taste—and then staring, staring, right and left, left and right, craning my head until I got stiff-necked, jumping whenever a passing male had a body like Mirek's, or features like his, or moved with his gait, strong and full of bounce.

Enough. I could go crazy here. There was always Novakova.

Yet, that last time on the bridge . . .

It was a few minutes after noon. The echoes of all the church bells tolling midday had not quite died over the openness of the waters. The bridge, loaded with thirty-odd statues of saints, a Vatican built over a river, stood under a drizzling rain. And I stood at my guardpost, by the Jesus with Hebrew lettering around his face.

To pass the time, I watched the pairs of lovers. Charles Bridge was always rife with lovers; even in the rain they strolled and kissed under umbrellas. Then I gave up spying on the lovers. I glanced again at the Hebrew lettering around that Jesus. Then, without any premeditation: "*Prosim vas,*" if you please, I asked a woman who passed me carrying an empty shopping bag, "can you tell me what this says?"

I pointed to the Hebrew letters around the thorned forehead.

She looked at them, hesitated. "I don't know, *sleczno* (miss). Something religious, I guess . . ."

She moved on, swinging that limp bag.

A man approached. Middle-aged, with a big puffy mustache. He looked like a night watchman.

"*Prosim, pane . . .*"

Same question. Same look of ignorance from the mustachioed man toward the Hebrew letters.

"*Ne vim.*" I don't know. And he walked on.

I continued, hooking in a couple of people every five minutes. Anyone who came along except for those who looked Jewish—this one, too dark, that one, hair too curly, I let them pass. I looked for Slavic types: high cheekbones, stick-straight hair, round faces. *Prosim pane, pani, sleczno,* do you know what this means?

They looked at the gilded lettering as if they'd seen it many times. They were Praguers. Totally familiar with this statue. And yet . . .

Something holy, I think . . .

Could be from a psalm . . .

Maybe it means Jesus, in Jewish . . .

I don't know, I don't know, was the most common answer.

Here came someone who looked like an undertaker. Black pants, black jacket. Old, with a book under his arm. Maybe he would know.

"*Prosim pane,* this Jesus"—the man in black stopped, examined me, disturbed from some meditation—"is not like all the others." Some nerve, Chaia Binah Davidovich, how many

Jesuses have you ever examined? "It's got all this . . . Jewish stuff. You know what it means?"

"Why are you asking me?" the man in black countered dryly.

I shrugged. "Because you seem educated."

I looked at his Adam's apple, scrawny and hanging over a strange collar. White and closed round his neck like a choker. He looked me over. I felt that he had even noted the condition of my sandals, and I remembered that I definitely needed a new pair.

"What's your interest in this Jesus?"

I shrugged. "It's so different. I've seen so many others"— nerve again—"that are not . . . embellished with writing."

"It's different, all right."

"So, you know what it means?"

"Holy, holy, holy, Lord of the Hosts," he declaimed unhesitantly. "You go to church often?"

His unusual collar gave me the clue. "Are you a priest?"

He stood before me, not confirming, not denying. "I'm a minister," he acknowledged at last. "Protestant. And you're not a Christian. Are you in the Communist party?"

Those days, young Communist activists harassed clergymen in the streets. I rushed to reply, "Oh, no, no, and I didn't mean to make you uncomfortable. I'm Jewish, and I was curious." The minister's anxiety diminished; he gave me a look slightly tinged with scorn. I did not care, I pressed on: "Would most non-Jews know the meaning of this inscription?"

Every Praguer knows the meaning of it. So Mirek had told me.

"Oh, no, hardly any. Hebrew is not taught in schools. Church people know some Hebrew because they study it at the seminary, and, of course, Jews know Hebrew. I'm surprised you don't."

I felt so strangely at ease and friendly. "I'm from a little village; village girls don't get much education. So, would you say that if someone from Prague does know this inscription, he would be Jewish?"

"Very likely. But I don't understand—"

"Thank you," I said quickly.

The minister gave me a confused and not entirely reassured look, then walked off, a man perhaps as uncertain of his future as I was of mine. The campaign against the churches was in full swing, well orchestrated by the Russians. As for me, I felt like dancing in the rain. Why had that idea not occurred to me earlier, why?

Because I trusted Mirek. He had told me: Every Praguer knows the meaning of those letters.

I gave the bronze Jesus a conciliatory look. I had no reason to fear him anymore, and almost felt free to enjoy him as art . . . The thorned forehead glowed softly inside its Hebrew halo: Kadosh, kadosh, kadosh, Adonai Tz'vuot. Holy holy holy, Lord of the Hosts.

Mirek had lied to me about his faith.

To protect me, most probably.

We were, most likely, of the same faith.

Lord of the Hosts, help me.

I turned toward the Vitava's flow. Staring at the water because I could not face that tortured visage of bronze, which now seemed to evoke so much tragic and useless misunderstanding, I prayed: God, I want Mirek to be like me—but he is already like me, anyway he might be. . . . A Jew who forgot that we don't fast on Rosh Hashanah (the memory pierced to the surface but had no power to diminish this fresh revelation about him), or just a kind human, it's all the same, I've learned that much from death, I have. God, I deserve him . . .

I looked to my right, toward the busy Old Square, then left, toward the Hrad Castle, magnificent even on this morning without Mirek in it, magnificent forever. Then up, to the gray sky. What was left for me but to raise my face to the sky, and say: You know something, God? I find some of your jokes as cruel as your punishments.

THIRTY

*T*he rabbi was in his early thirties, a pale man with gold-rimmed glasses and a scraggly beard. I met him on the stairs as I was rushing out one more time, to buy the *pecivo*, which were supposed to have just arrived at the bakery on the corner.

"Do the Davidoviches live on the fourth floor?" he asked me.

I nodded. Yes, fourth floor.

My brother Leizer was very proud that he had gotten Rabbi Rappaport to officiate at the wedding—free, Leizer had stressed. The rabbi's eyes were very bloodshot, his voice tired, and he carried a thin narrow object some six feet long, wrapped in newspapers. Quaint city type, I thought. He spastically wound that object up the stairway's spiral, bumping it on the rail, then on a door.

I hurried to grab the other end of the object. "I'm one of the Davidoviches, rebbe, let me help you."

Through the newspapers, the long object felt like a bunch of wooden sticks.

"Shalom Aleichem. Thank you. Are you the bride?"

Up to that moment, I had held myself together quite well. I almost believed that I could forgive Mirek—he was, like me, like anyone else, a fallible human. But when Rabbi Rappaport asked me: "Are you the bride?" I felt so overwhelmed by bitterness that I snapped, No, I wasn't the bride, I was the bridegroom's sister. And what were these sticks, his fishing rods?

"They're the pillars of the huppah. Has someone upset you?"

I was about to blurt in his face: God has upset me.

But as they said in the shtetl, I swallowed my tongue, muttering instead: "No, I'm just a little tired . . . the pressures of the wedding . . . you know?"

"Where were you rushing?"

"To the store to buy pastries." I was not used to young rabbis, or to ones so friendly toward females.

"There is no more pleasing event for the Lord than a wedding. Try not to be upset when you come back."

"I'll try. Here it is, rebbe."

The door to the apartment was open. I pushed him and his huppah inside, then rushed down the stairs again.

God would have to do something pretty spectacular to pacify me after this last one. Now that I had admitted how unhappy I was, I felt like wailing to the sky: Hashem, why did you do this to me, why did you do it? El Melekh, lord of the universe, could you not allow one stupid girl to have a little luck? Couldn't you suffer Mirek to be alive, Jewish, and also mine? Have I not paid enough?

Upstairs, Leizer was tying his tie under the creaky stiff collar of a white shirt. Suri, who still lived in our apartment, had made starch like back home, from the juice of two grated potatoes mixed with water. He would wear a blue suit, which he had paid for in cigarette currency. We had all wanted to chip in for a white dress for Ruchi, but she had insisted on wearing a white blouse she had brought from Germany and a green skirt that looked great on her—and no one could tell what it was made from. Ruchi had told me: a U.S. army blanket that had saved her life one freezing night after the liberation. A good luck skirt, a good luck start in her new life.

The other women, Suri, Hani, Piri, Ruchi's sister Rita, tried to convince her to at least borrow a white dress—a wedding was a wedding. I snapped, Leave her alone, it's her wedding and her life.

They were stunned by my tone. There was tension in the apartment. The lack of privacy, which for three months we had found so comforting, felt stifling now.

Ludvig, in town for the occasion, wore a suit also, and acted important because he was the oldest of us: thirty-nine. He explained what opportunities he had located for all of us in Ústí nad Labem—a salami factory looking for a manager: Leizer would be perfect for it. A hardware store being sold for peanuts: excellent for Pepo and Piri; everyone needed everything these days, from kitchen knives to coffins.

So it had been agreed that Leizer and Ruchi and Pepo and Piri and Ludvig and Mazhenka (a quiet schoolteacher of twenty-eight whom he had just met and brought with him) would travel back to Ústí right after the wedding. Ruchi had whispered to me that she hoped she and Leizer would stay at a hotel in Ústí and have a little honeymoon. I told her to make the most of it. Mazhenka and Ludvig followed each other across the apartment. Twenty-eight and thirty-nine: that would have been a big age difference back home, sure to set all the tongues wagging. But not now, not here. We were happy for every soul left alive. Besides, what was their eleven-year difference compared to that of the pretty nineteen-year-old girl living two floors above us, who had married her father's older brother? I heard them come home late at night: he shuffling carefully over the broken steps, while the girl sauntered ahead. The few male survivors between forty and fifty were in demand; they were the toughest men, they learned the ropes fast, they squeezed money from rock—some were even rumored to have gold that they had buried before the war. Gold, not valueless *papir gelt*. How could those orphan girls reject them?

"You'll end up with one of those letches if you don't move faster," my brother Pepo teased me.

I quickened my steps toward the bakery on the corner.

• • •

I found a line: the fresh bread had just arrived.

Ahead of me, side by side, two nondescript men in their forties waited to buy bread. They sneaked glances at each other until one couldn't hold back anymore: *Du lebst?* You're alive? Amazed incredulousness lit the other man's face: *Yo, unt du?* Yes, and you?

They had known each other "before"—a term that needed no elaboration. Their arms shot out and around each other, stiffly, as they intoned together: *Geloibt sei Got.* God be praised. Then the talk wandered between the painful past and the uncertain present. You work? *Yo,* in the *papirosen gesheft*—selling cigarettes on the black market. Me, I'm in *tsikorye,* chicory coffee. But for you, I can get *echte,* the real stuff, anytime, you just tell me when you want. *Sheinem dank,* kind thanks, and same for my papirosen, when you want. Thanks, but I don't smoke. But maybe for your friends . . . Ah, yes. Maybe for my friends.

Reflective silence on both sides.

Then, the first one again: *Der tateh, die mameh? Nisht tsirik gekemmen?* Your mom, your dad? They didn't return? The cheerful reunion fell into mourning: *Zoln zich mien,* muttered the one who had asked the question. May they rest easy. Both nodded, a hybrid nod of an acknowledgment and a daven. Both were silent again, not mentioning their wives, their children, who had also not made it—all were mourned together within that silence; then the silence was broken again: *Nu, eintsik?* You're single now? The other answered with a powerless shrug: What else? *Ich oichet, ober . . .* Me, too, but . . . A brief pause. *Ober ich hob a meidel g'troffen, a git meidel.* But I met a girl, a nice girl. *Recht git?* Really nice? Vigorous nod, eyes misty though, with guilt. As if the wife he would have stayed faithful to was listening in. The man cleared his throat, pulled back his shoulders, breathed deeply, in, out. The present was here, the present was stronger than the past and its pain. So when's the *chasene?* the wedding? Soon as we gather enough coupons. You come? I come. Bring your coupons.

Why wasn't I fated to meet Mirek like that, randomly, in a bread line? *Du lebst? Yo, und du?* I didn't care about romance anymore. He might be injured, even missing parts of his body. Every day, I saw people with empty sleeves tucked in the pockets of their jackets, or hobbling on crutches. I squirmed at the thought, it rent my heart, but I still wanted him back, just enough of him. His eyes, his smile. His voice. If he did come back like that, would we still be together, would I have the needed strength? And, a horrible thought, what if he wasn't returning because he had been maimed, and he felt unworthy, ineligible, half a man? Stop, *stop.* Had that been the case, Babicka would have told me. Or maybe not. She was a kindhearted woman. She would surely have told me what hurt less.

I'll settle for him being whole, and not being mine. It's all right.

The two men ahead of me were exchanging addresses: I live on Narodni Trida, 38. You know where it is?

Of course I know. Where do you live?

On Soukenicka, 124. You know it?

Of course I know it.

Even if they didn't know it, they would pretend that they did. They would pretend that they knew everything, that was part of the daily battle with the unknown which was called life after survival. City addresses? City addresses were a benign riddle compared to the overwhelming enigma of why we were here again, after a promised and almost complete obliteration.

Had we had addresses in the shtetl? Not ones made of street names and numbers. We lived up the road, down the road, by the shul, by the midwife's, by the grocer's. Left of the Ukrainian marketplace. By the home of Itsik the tall, Itsik the short. Itsik the tall had a big home and a big oven where all the Jews gathered before Pesach to make matzo; the women rolled the dough, the men put the trays of matzo in the oven. Itsik the short had no big oven—he wasn't as popular. But those were not addresses. Those were the places forever carved in our minds where we had opened our eyes to the world, we had grown, we had realized that we were male or female, we had taken note of the seasons, rain, hail, sunshine, the passage of time. Who needed an address? We all knew each other, the shtetl's main street was part of our home, the human settlement was us.

While today, everything was alien or unfriendly or bizarre. And what was not was regarded with grave suspicion.

But we had city addresses. We had made it into civilization.

The two men paid for their bread and cleared my path to the cash register. Refined Prague pastries, two crowns each. Multiply by twenty guests: forty crowns.

I didn't have forty crowns. I'll buy ten pastries and cut them in two.

The smell of fresh bread gave me a headache. According to the tradition, only Leizer and Ruchi were supposed to fast before the wedding. But all of us had fasted, because all the pots were filled with the precooked feast. Oh, God. If I bought bread, I couldn't buy the sweets. A wedding without sweets?

THIRTY-ONE

I hurried back with the pastries.

I had just missed the arrival of my baby brothers, Henju and Mechel, whose sweaty temples indicated that they had raced from the train station on foot. Henju winked at me, and I winked back. We'd hug later.

Despite the presence of twenty people, it was quiet in the apartment, because that tired young rabbi was speaking so low, as if to himself: "I need four strong men"—he unveiled four sticks tied to the corners of two prayer shawls sewn together— "to prop up this huppah." Henju, Mechel, Pepo, and a friend of Pepo's from home, Benczi Mermelstein, who as a boy had saved Pepo from drowning in the mikva's water (of all places), stepped up to grab a stick each. The rabbi saw me setting the pastries on the table: "Here's the pretty sister of the bridegroom. Pretty and angry, and not telling why." I blushed; I thought I was covering it up perfectly.

"Did you bring a challah, too?" the rabbi asked, examining my pastries.

I started. No, I had not.

"I need to make a *berakhah* (blessing) over the wine, and one over the challah. How can I do that without a challah?"

I nodded dumbly. Yes, the blessing over the challah. Done after the newlyweds stepped out from under the huppah, and the whole party sat down to dinner. How could I have forgotten that blessing?

"Please, rebbe, she forgot," said my brother Leizer.

"Never mind then," said the rabbi. *"Barukh attah Adonai, elocheinu Melekh haolam,"* he intoned extremely rapidly, holding up a bottle of red wine, half full. Suri guessed what he needed and rushed with a wineglass. "Excellent." He filled the glass, handed Suri the bottle. Suri was nervous; her fingers almost slipped on the bottle. The rabbi noticed, his bloodshot eyes missing nothing. "Easy, I got another wedding after this one." He raised his voice a little: "The berakhah is the Jewish way by which man is brought face to face with God. Just the words 'Barukh attah' make us instantly aware of God's presence. Barukh attah," he repeated. "God is with us now. Let's try not to be angry at God right now, even if we have reason."

There was a silence in our little crowd. A silence so full that it hummed. Angry at God. But the rabbi had said it, not us.

"The sticks have to be held upright," he said. With his free hand, he corrected my brother Mechel's grip on the stick. Mechel swallowed, clutched that stick so firmly that all the other men had to clutch theirs, too, to keep the huppah stable.

"Who are the *shushvinim?*" asked the rabbi.

The shushvinim!

We looked at each other. In traditional ceremonies, there was a pair of shushvinim (subleaders) who would escort the bride up to the huppah. From the time of the tents in the desert, when bride and dowry had to be accompanied, lest they fall prey to robbery on the way to the bridegroom's territory, there had been shushvinim, who had protected the bridal march.

But usually, they were the parents of the bridegroom or of the bride. But here and now, there were no parents to act as shushvinim. So we had completely overlooked that point.

"We have alternative shushvinim?"

My cousin Ludvig took a breath, then stepped to where Mazhenka stood in the women's little crowd, and took her hand. "We're the shushvinim."

Mazhenka turned crimson—even the alternative shushvinim had to be a married couple. Was Ludvig taking a symbolic step? He placed her on the other side of the bride. For an instant, we all were still, all was quiet, and despite the humbleness of the huppah or of the food in the covered pots, we felt if not God, at least the memory of His earlier goodness, passing over all of us. We were still numerous enough to breed, which was the first law of our faith. We had a canopy. We had food for the body, and hope in our souls, even if it was painful.

Mazhenka remained crimson as she and Ludvig walked on each side of Ruchi. And the dining room's length of a few meters seemed to elongate, miraculously. The march to the canopy felt so slow that I and everyone else in the room had the time to think, repeatedly: This is really happening.

Leizer stood under the canopy, and his brown and wavy hair touched the joined talliths. His forehead and eyes, his formal demeanor were so much like my father's that I had to grit my teeth hard.

Then Ruchi stepped a little shakily inside the four sticks. As in biblical times, she was entering her man's tent, joining him forever.

The rabbi pronounced the Erusin, the ritual of betrothal, sipped from the glass of wine, then held it in front of the couple. Ruchi raised her hand, then looked terribly embarrassed when the rabbi signaled with his eyes: first the *husen*, then the *kale*. Leizer drank, then smiled at Ruchi and passed her the glass. She took a tiny swallow. Leizer pulled out of his pocket the small square box with the gold wedding band, plain, no gems, with which he was to "buy" his wife. The box got snagged in the folds of his pocket, but he yanked it free, careless of the lining, opened it, and put the ring on Ruchi's finger.

I found myself praying: May the price of that ring equal the price of what we all have paid to stand here now. Mom, Dad, look down with blessing and pride on your firstborn son, and on his bride. Look down with blessing, if not with pride, on

your unworthy daughter, too. I've just made a decision. Even
if I'm not fated to enter the huppah with the man of my
choice, even if I won't lie down with the man of my dreams
and yearnings, I will find another man. I will fulfill what you
taught me to fulfill.

The rabbi finished reading the marriage contract, the *ketu-
bah*, and, in accordance with the ancient custom, handed it to
the bride. With a pleasant low voice, he sang the Sheva
B'rachot, the seven blessings. Leizer, who knew the seven blessings by heart, rounded his lips silently, repeating the blessings.
Then he crushed a plain glass under his foot, in remembrance
of the Temple's destruction. The rabbi concluded: "Where
there's peace and harmony between husband and wife, there
the spirit of God abides."

Then he started to gather his huppah. Leizer asked him to
share our dinner but he declined; he had to go to another
wedding.

The ceremony was over, and it had lasted twenty minutes.

I congratulated my brother, hugging him and kissing him on
the right cheek, then left cheek, then right cheek. Then I
kissed Ruchi, who shook with emotion and whispered to me:
I want us to be sisters—more than sisters, she corrected herself,
for we had just become sisters. We'll be more than sisters, I
promised her.

I felt that I understood our new existence. There would be
no poise in our lives anymore, no sense of middle ground, even
as we relearned how to look, act, and speak with the same
calm and composure as everyone else. We would seem normal,
peaceful even. But inside, we would live ill at ease, always. We,
the inexplicably spared. Even in happiness, we would feel ill
at ease. We would feel too much, and too deeply. Whatever
we would have, it would be too much.

Chair legs screeched across the floor—starved and happy,
everyone hurried to sit at the table. Looking for a seat next to
one of my brothers, I saw that the rabbi was sailing his huppah

out, through the straits of cigarette cartons that my brothers had stacked in the apartment's hallway. Suri and I ran to help him.

Out on the landing, he turned to me: "Do you know the temple on Jerusalemska Street?" Having heard about it, I nodded. "Come to the temple sometime. It will help you."

Did my distress show on my face so clearly? I became angry, but reckoning that my anger would show, too, I suppressed it as best I could, and nodded. I would come. Sometime.

"God was surprised," he said. I said nothing. "He was caught unawares, both by the evil of the murderers and by the unpreparedness of the innocents."

"Have you been in camp, rebbe?"

"Yes," he said quickly. "And now I ask to be allowed to perform marriages and brisses. Your brother did not ask me to come here. I asked him."

"You look tired," I said, to say something.

"Guilt is tiring. Anger is, too."

Then, unexpectedly, he laughed: "Actually, I'm running around too much. Shalom aleichem. Don't help me, I think I can manage now."

He focused his gold-rimmed glasses on the stairs and descended, steering his itinerant huppah.

THIRTY-TWO

*G*et off, Blanka, get off," my brothers urged. They hugged me, stuck their heads out of the car window, checked the train station's clock, hugged me again. The train for Ústí nad Labem was due to leave in one minute. "Good-bye, and now get off." I kept hugging them back. "We'll only be gone a few days."

Ludvig had described Ústí in such attractive colors that finally everyone had decided to look into its opportunities, even my cousin Suri and Ruchi's sister Rita. Mechel and Henju hoped to be able to expand their cigarettes business there. In short, everyone was going to Ústí—everyone but me.

I had argued that someone had to stay and mind the apartment, which contained all we had.

My brothers had agreed, after cautioning me in detail about watching out for drunk Russians on leave, avoiding the once lovely parks by the river—now unpatrolled and full of desperate refugees—and double-locking the door at night. And if a thief tried to pick the lock, I was to scream out loud. Mr. Kahoun, a next-door neighbor who was also the building's manager, would hear me and run to my rescue.

There was a whistle. The train moved.

I jumped off and four pairs of brotherly eyes watched my landing on the platform. Safe and already waving my arms in farewell.

The train moved a little faster, and I ran on the platform, catching Leizer's hand, then Pepo's. Henju bent low to touch hands, too, but we only brushed fingers. Then Leizer yelled at me to stop running. I stood as the car and its window grew smaller, that knot of arms waving less and less clearly, until the train vanished in a hazy jumble of suburbs.

I thought of the empty apartment. Privacy already felt unsettling.

I headed for the exit.

I walked out of the station and proceeded south. One block, two blocks, three blocks. I was still in walking distance of my apartment.

I entered a street of abundantly ornate buildings in neoclassical and neo-Gothic style. Once they were the abodes of affluent burghers. Now they were occupied by working-class families who had split the refined interiors between them. Their noises, their linen spread across the artful old balconies, their bicycles chained inside old carriage gates announced the new Communist era. But I was not interested in the houses.

I followed the street called Jerusalemska until it joined with another street, perpendicular to it, called U Pujcovni: At the Usurers'. At this junction stood the Jubilee Synagogue, built at the turn of the century in Moorish style, with a three-arched entrance over which was written: THIS IS THE GATE OF THE LORD, THE JUST ONES ENTER THEREBY.

The Usurers. The street's name was ancient, showing that wealthy Jews had always lived outside the old ghetto. At the turn of the century, when the ghetto and its crummy old shuls had been torn down, the onetime usurers, now finance kings, had erected their stately new synagogue right near that symbol of progress, the train station. Here I stood now on my sore feet (I still needed new sandals badly) and fought the almost dizzying effect that the synagogue had on me. A kind of pull and repulsion at the same time.

Shall I go in? Shall I walk away?

I looked at the two street signs. The name of the Holy City connected with the power of money. Those Victorian Jews had been quite successful, if the city of Prague had allowed them to erect such a palace. The Jubilee Synagogue had been closed by the Germans. Recently, the Russians had allowed it to re-open, and now its interior was undergoing repairs. That was why the front entrance and the two auxiliary entrances were open, and I could step inside freely, my head not even covered.

Like a just one, I entered thereby.

Inside, old pews had been removed, new ones were already being set in their place.

I looked around, admiring what had not been damaged: the sustaining pillars, of veined marble, the women's gallery, rounding the nave like a huge suspended horseshoe, the fili-greed ironwork of the *bimah*. When silent, this place lent echo to the lightest footfalls. Just now, workers shouted in the rapid idiom of Prague as they raised scaffolding to replace the chan-deliers.

I took the stairs to the women's gallery. A shames overseeing the work, bearded, with his hat on, saw me but turned his attention back to the workers.

Up in the gallery, only a few of the old pews were left. I smelled mold, old mortar that had absorbed humidity, wood rot.

This was my first time in a synagogue since I had left Zhdenev.

The one I wanted was here.

But He would not tell me what He had in mind for me.

I waited, though I knew that He would not tell me.

Clang!—a scaffolding pipe snapped out of its joint, and a worker slipped and remained suspended from it by one hand. Below, the other workers ran madly—even the shames ran madly, losing his hat, all opening their arms under the dangling worker: "Jump, Jenda, jump!" Then there was a silence that wheezed with their anxious breathing. "Jump!" the shames urged. But Jenda gripped the pipe with both hands, arched himself back onto the leaning scaffolding, then uttered a whoop of relief that echoed under the vaults.

The shames picked up his hat. The men rushed to prop the scaffolding from falling.

I breathed in deeply and descended the stairs.

I exited into the street and walked away. I had time. No one waited for me at the apartment.

The afternoon and the evening stretched in front of me, empty.

Walking toward Stare Mesto, my feet hurt so much that I considered taking off my sandals: the bare sidewalk would be kinder to my soles. But after four months of freedom, I had regained enough decorum not to walk with my shoes in my hand on a city street. I saw a *kavarna* that advertised real coffee, not chicory. I'd stop there for a minute and rest.

There were hardly any customers. At the counter, I paid for a cup of real coffee, then carried it to a table by the window. It was Sunday. Prague's streets were pretty just to look at.

Through the window, I saw two American soldiers (by the agreement between the Allies, they had free access to Prague) walking with a girl between them. She held both men by the arm, and all three were laughing; had it not been for the shop's window, I could have heard their laughter.

Then my hand fell into the steaming cup, rattling it on its saucer. The coffee spilled and spread on the table.

I sucked on my scalded fingers, tasting the forgotten flavor of real coffee.

The Americans were crossing the street, toward the coffee shop and toward me, sitting by its window. The woman's arms curled affectionately around the men's arms, and one of the men was Mirek, whose other arm pointed, showing the girl something. The other American looked in the direction pointed by Mirek; he was short but wiry, tough-looking. All three, relaxed and confident, walked directly toward the coffee shop. A drip of sweat crept across my forehead—nothing seemed more painful to me, more embarrassing, than to see Mirek alive, and then have to greet him and his friends, if they walked in.

A bus drew up to the curb. Mirek and the other two broke into a trot, though not a hurried one, toward the bus, and Mirek motioned to the driver. Wait! Then, he embraced the other man.

So. He and his girl would disappear in the next few seconds.

I could have read the bus's route; it was printed on its side. But I chose to shut my eyes instead. I had not seen this. I had not seen Mirek, his girl, his buddy. I had made a pledge that I would get on with my life, and seeing him safe and sound did not help. How lucky I was that they hadn't entered the coffee shop. I peeked and saw the bus take off, a big indifferent red mass.

The other man in uniform stood on the sidewalk alone, his back to the coffee shop, waving good-bye.

But he was suddenly taller. He was Mirek, not the other man.

He did not turn around, but I had no doubt that it was him. Then he stood in profile, and I saw the determined line of his nose, and his lips, which looked fresh and healthy.

I could not think.

Mirek headed away, disappearing from the shop's window, and I felt that his steps were striding directly on my brain. I ran out of the coffee shop and saw him walking away, alone.

Only now did I notice that he carried a little brown object. A small suitcase. Then, expecting every second that he would turn into a stranger, or just melt into thin air, I plunged into pursuit.

THIRTY-THREE

*T*o keep up with him without being seen, I ran across the street (thank God for the thin Sunday traffic; I could have ended up under a car) until I was abreast of him on the opposite sidewalk. I spied on his expression again: he seemed thoughtful, almost downcast. But it was him, Mirek, alive and strapping and healthy, wearing a well-fitting American uniform. Taking him in, I paid no attention to the pedestrians coming my way, or to the waist-high city trash cans, of rusty iron. Somehow I didn't bump into anything.

He stopped.

I froze on my side.

He was looking at a peeling three-story building, with small square windows.

Then he went inside. I had lost him.

But I'd lost him once, to the war. I would not lose him again to a building.

I started to cross the street when the front door reopened: Mirek came out, gave the building a brief look, and off he was again, until the quadrangle of Republic Square opened in front of both of us. He waited for a light to change. I did the same on my side, and during that spell I realized that I had left my purse in the coffee shop. It contained five crowns, my displaced person's card, my comb. . . . To hell with them. I didn't need those few crowns. And I was sick of that DP card.

We both crossed Republic Square.

The closest street ahead was Na Porici; the next one to the left was my own street, Truhlarska. Mirek looked around, missing me because of a lamppost, then continued toward Truhlarska. He turned into it. He looked at a street number, then peered right and left, to cross the street.

And he saw me. I was three steps behind.

"Blanka!" he said, thunderstruck.

He turned, rushed to me, and stopped right before me.

"Blanka," he repeated, warmly, with longing. Then he dropped his suitcase on the sidewalk. I stood glumly, until I remembered that I could still speak; then I asked him the only thing I could ask him: "Are you here for me?"

We made eye contact, and I felt that old dizzying drowning sensation. Maybe he felt it, too, for he whispered, "For you. For you, Blanka."

My eyes had played no tricks on me. Mirek's lips were not cracked anymore, I could see that clearly because he was freshly shaved.

I took his hand. I squeezed it so hard that my own fingers ached, but I forgot the pain the second I felt it. I saw . . . all my worrying about him, my sleepless tossing in my barrack bunk, my fears after being liberated, even my uneasiness on that bridge loaded with saints: I saw it all in Mirek's eyes. Matched by his own worrying, by his own sleepless tossing. They made him look shy and guilty. I had never seen him look guilty before!

He cleared his throat, and I did the same. Then we spoke at the same time: "How did you know I was alive?" I asked, but he was already replying: "I called someone I knew from the underground. Arnost Lemberger, he's head of the OBZ now." The OBZ was the MGB's arm in Prague. "I phoned him from Frankfurt, gave him your name and asked him to check. He called me a week later, told me you were in Prague, and gave

me your address—he can get any address, you know, you had
to register with the police. . . ."

I nodded. My brothers, myself, anyone I knew had had to
register with the police. So wasn't it just like Mirek to find out
that I was fine, and then sit calmly in Frankfurt until the fancy
took him to show up?

Whatever feeling that angry thought caused, it must have
shown on my face, for Mirek looked worried, then asked with
excessive politeness, "Were you going home? Can I come with
you?"

I nodded.

He put his hand on my arm. I allowed the touch and saw
on his face that the words we had exchanged had no weight
whatsoever compared to the assuaging effect that our physical
contact had on him. I was alive, I was here, his palm reported
to the rest of him. He let out a deep breath, and even seemed
to regain some of that mocking air with which he had addressed me first, when our marching columns had met on the
road to the camp.

Then the mocking expression disappeared. He examined me
for what felt like a long time.

I stood face-to-face with him, amazed that I could be so
patient.

Mirek coughed and cleared his throat, but sounded choked
as he asked, "Blanka . . . You have someone—?"

It was not a question. It was a raw concern, low, strangled,
decisive.

I finally smiled. Mirek, Mirek. You couldn't get that information from Arnost, could you?

Oh, God. How I wished I could torture him now. How I
wished I could keep him in the dark. Not for long, certainly
not for five months. Just for a week or two. Maybe not even
that much. A few days? One day?

I could have done it. All I had to do was say, Sure, come

home with me. But you can only stay a few minutes. Someone's taking me out tonight, so I have to get myself ready.

"I live alone," I said. "I waited for you."

As I said it, I saw the blood draw out of his face, in a delayed reaction, making his lips look even softer. I read in his eyes how much he had feared that he would find me with someone else, for his next question was almost a squeak. "Really?"

I laughed and nodded—he was so lucky. Or I was so stupid.

He laughed, too, and stood on tiptoe, as if to gain a higher angle, to amass more of me in his field of vision, while he smiled incessantly. He let go of my arm and clutched my hand, yet he was worried that if he squeezed it too hard he might injure it; so he held it in an inexperienced delicate grip, then we made eye contact again and he blushed to the roots of his hair. He stared beyond me, across the street, and I felt the need to look away from him, too. We had never looked at each other for so long without panicking that we might be caught. Except for those times down in the quarry, when he was so beaten up that looking at him was sheer agony. And then that last time, in the effects room, inside Suri's little enclosure.

I remembered what I had felt then. He would vanish in a few minutes, and that was the last time I would see him.

Then he was gone, into the sun's radiance. Walking away from me into the flames of the unfinished war.

But he wouldn't vanish now. I wouldn't let him.

I remembered the bridge with saints and wanted to tell him what I had discovered about him. But I could not find my words, and what I had discovered did not matter, it did not matter at all. He could be anything, I could be anything, and it did not matter now, although it would at all other times. What mattered was that he was here, and I was here.

"D'you live over there?" he asked.

I lived at number seven, right across the street.

Mirek picked up his suitcase, then took my arm. As we

walked across the street, he squeezed my arm, gently. "I have so much to tell you. It's nice and warm, would you rather take a walk? We could go to Letna . . ."

"I'd love to walk, but my feet are too sore from these sandals."

He glanced at my sandals. They looked pitiful indeed.

"Then let's talk at your place." He eyed me furtively. My place. Had I told him the truth, was there really no other man there?

He was still not sure. I could still torture him if I wanted to. I did not have the heart. "My place is fine."

"Fine," he echoed me, and helped me step over the curb.

He walked me through the vaulted entrance, into the little inner courtyard lined with garbage cans and shaded by two dusty acacias. Here, I realized that we could not get into my apartment: the key was in my lost purse. I explained what had happened, and that Mr. Kahoun the manager had an extra key. But we would have to wait for the Kahouns to return; they played cards with some friends every Sunday afternoon. Or walk back to that café, where we might still find my purse.

"We'll talk here," Mirek decided. "On that bench."

There was a little bench between the two acacias. But it was broken.

And so, we sat down on the stairs. We could have walked along the Vitava's shore, or climbed to the castle, to have Prague's panorama at our feet, or even strolled on the bridge—oh, that intriguing bridge. Of all the beautiful places in a city like no other, we ended up on the stairs to my apartment, which I had so zealously scrubbed just days before.

My work had been rewarded.

We sat close to each other. Shoulder to shoulder, hip to hip. And Mirek clasped my hands in his.

Then he started talking.

Slowly, under his breath, he explained that he had never been great with words (fancy that!), but he could be silent or alone for long spells of time, and that was why he decided that he'd do very well in the underground. Before joining, he had warned his family to leave Czechoslovakia; maybe they had left and saved themselves, maybe they hadn't—he didn't know yet. In camp, for my own safety, he hadn't told me his real name: it was Karel Elias Friedman.

Karel Elias Friedman, I repeated silently, as if I had to memorize it, as if he would never tell me his real name again.

Karel aka Mirek had made the underground his faith, and his faith had been tested severely. The underground was split into fighting factions, which made it easier for the Russians to take it over. And the war became a war of deals. One of the Americans he had taken out of Mittergars when he escaped, Charles Womack, an intelligence lieutenant, has asked him in Frankfurt, after Mirek had helped identify the top brass of Dachau and Mühldorf: Which of these Germans could be useful to America, and what kind of deal did Mirek think would be fair to offer to them? "Fair," Mirek commented, "can you believe that?" Thus, some SS and army NCOs and Aufseherinnen were hanged, but many higher leaders, such as the ones who determined which workers were *T* and which weren't, went free. Eberle was not caught at all, despite an extensive manhunt. That expert on Jews, Eichmann, was caught, but his name was misspelled as *Eckman* by an unsuspecting U.S. corporal, and the bastard slipped through the net soon thereafter and vanished. Helped, not helped? It was too soon to tell.

So, Mirek concluded, this had been a strange war, whose heroes would often not be on parade, whose real victors would not be the warriors. He had not known that. He knew it now, as he sat next to me on the scrubbed steps. Neither of us had been part of the victory celebration. And we could not even protest, or grieve too long. The war's end had imprinted a different speed to life. If we really wanted to survive, we had to catch up.

"We'll catch up," I said. "We're alive, so let's not be bitter."

"I have a great reason not to be bitter. Do you want to marry me?"

He waited. I did not reply. He took a breath, gestured at the dark stairway. "Can you believe this? No one's coming out from anywhere, to shout at us, to hit us with a stick?"

I smiled. "Tell me your name again."

"Karel, like King Karel, the builder of the bridge." Then, a little impatiently: "Karel Friedman. I am . . ."

I cut him off. "Jewish, I know. I've known that for a while."

I needed to be quiet for an instant. I needed to be aware of what I was feeling.

So I took my hands out of Mirek's and pulled away—not far though, there were only a few inches left between me and the wall of the staircase. I leaned against the wall and stared at Mirek, expecting to notice some kind of transformation in him. He was finally all the things I wanted him to be—wouldn't that make him different?

But I saw no transformation, except that he watched me with some anxiety. He could not guess what was going on in my mind.

I was silently calling out to God, with one of those challenges that would, as usual, remain unanswered: So, God. You gave him to me, You gave him to me exactly the way I wanted him. Yet he is still the same as he was before. But suppose You had made him a Catholic, as I thought he was all those months in camp, and given me back my parents, or my sisters? Instead of one gift, another gift. How would I have felt now? But, had Mirek not been Jewish, how could I have explained him to my parents or my brothers, how could I have persuaded them to accept him? (All four of my brothers popped up in my mind, their dark shtetl eyes rounded with alarm—their sister in love with a *Gentile*, even the best of all Gentiles? Even the one who saved her from despair and madness, and maybe from death?)

I started to titter. Mirek blinked, perplexed, and I thought, What do you know about the complications of the Jewish mind? But . . . he was Jewish, I reminded myself. And yet he was so uncomplicated. The thought that my parents would have liked him precisely because he was so uncomplicated and reliable overpowered me. I started to cry.

He immediately pulled me into his arms. "Blanka. Stop—"

"I will," I moaned. "Give me just one minute."

What had been taken from me, no one could give me back, not even Mirek. And I should not expect that from him.

I made myself smile. "Can I still call you Mirek?"

And Mirek, happy to understand what had moved me to tears—women are so sentimental; this one here wanted to stay in love with that old him, so let her—gathered me in his arms tightly, tightly. He brought his lips closer, ready to kiss me, then suddenly pulled back and stood up.

A lumbering shadow filled the arched entryway as Mr. Kahoun the landlord walked toward the stairs, followed by his wife.

I stood up, too, and explained to the Kahouns how I had lost my key.

Mr. Kahoun examined Mirek (he was taking seriously my brothers' request that he watch over me), then looked undecidedly at his wife, a small woman with a crumpled face, whose face crumpled even more when she smiled. Mrs. Kahoun smiled. "Don't you have the master key, Pavlik?"

"Right here," said Mr. Kahoun. He started up the stairs with the three of us behind him, and when he came to my apartment, he pulled out his master key and unlocked the door. I led Mirek inside, shut the door on everything and everyone, so we could be together, he and I, not one soul more, then turned to him with my arms open: You see? I'm alone here.

He nodded, taking in the ramparts of cigarette cartons built along the walls.

I felt like asking: Remember how you taught me about cigarettes? But, as he did not say anything, I wondered if he already knew that they did not belong to me; his friend at the MGB might have told him about my brothers' business. Then I realized that there were thousands of couples in this city who discussed and negotiated all sorts of issues—but Mirek and I would be in agreement about so many topics of life without talking at all! Then I sat on my bed, which was set, due to lack of space, against the living room window, and took off my sandals. I lay down fully clothed, and Mirek did not know what to do. He took off his jacket, draped it carefully over the back of a chair. I moved to make room for him, and he lay next to me and took me in his arms. He kissed me slowly, inhaling my scent, touching my face with his hands, whispering: "Remember when we kissed in the rain? You told me"—he pointed at the narrow space between us—"freedom is here. That helped me so much."

I burst into tears again.

He scrambled to get out his handkerchief, pulling it clumsily, unfolding it like a flag. A handkerchief checkered in white and brown, just like the ones from back home. He tried to wipe my eyes, and I fought off his hands—what was the matter with him? He muttered that he couldn't see me crying. I dried my eyes with the back of my hand, I was all right, all right! I had just remembered again that night, the rain on my feet, the smell of that wet timber, the fear. . . .

As on that night, I buried my face against his chest and thought: I have no parents to ask for approval. I am the sole person who can say yes and no for me, and so it will be from now on. I will make my decisions, all my decisions. I and this man, if I choose him. But I had already chosen him. I had belonged to him, that night in the rain, and all the nights thereafter. And I could tell from the clumsy way he tried again to wipe my tears that I had been on his mind every single minute since he had met me, for a reason he did not understand and did not try to. I was the one.

He finally bundled up the handkerchief and stuffed it in his pocket. Was I all right? Really all right?

I was.

We were silent. We could hear an acacia leaf, like a green finger, scratching the windowpane.

He wanted to cheer me up, so he told me jokingly how hard I had made it for him in camp. He had to lie to me, and he didn't like lying. With the SS it was easy—they went by the book. He was a politiker, he lied; they believed it, they were so stupid—even now, I wriggled with pleasure hearing him abuse our defeated masters. "But with you, I always worried. Should I tell you this, not tell you that? Is this something you'd tell your cousins? I knew that if someone gave you up, you couldn't hold on, you or one of your cousins would crack." He laughed. "It was terrible. I worried about all five of you."

"But you felt better the last few months," I said, certain that he would miss my irony.

"Absolutely," he replied in earnest. "What's the matter?"

"Five months," I said. "I waited five months."

"Blanka . . ." Very uncomfortable—I relished his discomfort—he got up on one elbow, just like that night behind the wire. "I didn't know what to do . . . so what good would I have been to you? I wanted to see clearly into the future. I do now. We won't be able to live here; the Russians are going to clamp down, and we'd be fools to swap one camp for another. You want to go to America? I made a lot of American friends, but you know—" He hesitated, as if what he had to say might hurt me. "The Americans don't understand what happened here, at least not right now. They won the war, they liberated us, they don't want to hear complaints. So we'll have to behave . . . like we forgot about it, you know? We'll have to be strong."

"We were strong—"

"We'll have to be stronger than in camp. Much stronger."

I shrugged. So? What else was new, Karel Elias Friedman?

"Blanka?"

"Mirek?"

I knew it. He would always remain Mirek.

"You want to get married today?" He held me tight, as if to preempt a possible rejection. "A friend of mine, Franta, married yesterday in fifteen minutes, I was one of his witnesses. Did I ever mention Franta to you?"

I did not remember. But I said yes, I knew Franta, I'd just seen him get on that bus, with his brand-new Mrs. Franta. Who was so friendly to both of them, it was hard to tell who she belonged to.

Mirek distanced his face to scan mine. How long was I behind him in the street?

I said never mind. He had gone inside that gloomy yellow building. What was he doing in there?

He shrugged. "Just looking around. That building used to be the boys' trade school. Now it's a Russian supply store. I asked the Russians what happened to Bobasch, the principal. But they didn't know. He probably died, he was too old. Listen, I didn't tell you another thing. . . ." He gave me an embarrassed glance.

Here we go again, I thought to myself. But I managed to study him with a tolerant, even amused expression.

"I'm . . . not really from Prague. But I came to Prague at thirteen."

I laughed crazily. What? The big city boy was not a born city boy? That was serious. And where was he born?

"A place called Rachovo. It's way east of here, a little place with a railroad yard by it—"

"A shtetl?"

"Not really. Ten percent of the people were Jews. But it was so small, you couldn't call it a shtetl. . . ."

"What were your parents' names?" It suddenly felt so important that I know his parents' names.

He answered that his father's name was Yehuda Hersch. And his mother's name was Malka. My mother's name was Faiga, I told him. But my father was named Yehuda, too. Chaim Yehuda.

I took his head in my hands and kissed him on the lips, on his forehead, on the bridge of his nose, on his temples, on his chin. I kissed his whole face, even the dip in his upper lip. Shaved, it felt soft and babyish. I kissed him as if checking that not one piece of him was missing.

I felt dazed, incapable of thinking of anything except that I might not have been in that café a few hours before, and I would have not seen him out in the street.

But he was on his way to my apartment.

I would have found him here, waiting for me.

Afterword

While taping the testimonies of Blanka and Mirek Friedman, and of their contemporaries who witnessed their extraordinary love story, the issue of the "voice" of this book was not at the forefront of my mind. During stage one of my work, which resulted in over seventy hours of taping, I was overwhelmed by the reminiscences of my heroes and felt that, in capturing them, I was holding on to history as if on to an untamed beast. The fact that two individuals, so young and unprotected, had fallen in love at such a time and in such circumstances, perplexed me. I told myself that the instinct for love is the strongest in any human being, and therefore has to be fulfilled no matter when and how—yet my heroes' love for each other, even though impulsive and passionate, was not pure instinct, for love is never just that. In the camp, Blanka and Mirek enacted the whole range of love's manifestations—kindness, courtesy, possessiveness, exaggeration, miscommunication, wrath, and forgiveness—even though they did it for just a few minutes at a time. After each instance together, they were separated. They met again days later, weeks later. They gave each other tiny material gifts, or the gift of that special word or special glance, that "something" which we all reserve for the stranger destined to become our mate. Their interactions, even if they lasted just minutes, figured enormously in their subconscious, for they remembered them fifty years later, faultlessly.

Love in itself is a feeling of great desperation. Until it is fulfilled and stabilized into a relationship with a future, we all suffer from love. We agonize about it, and we are desperate that it may not happen, or not continue. But it is also re-demptive, and able to restore any individual's dignity and hope. To write about love is a challenge; to write about love in those unique circumstances could have been totally intimidating. But, there were my in-laws, talking with contained emotion, there was the tape recorder turning, myself taking notes, asking questions—a hypnotic process during which Blanka's, Mirek's, and my own voice seemed to blend. They were from Eastern Europe. I, too, was born in Eastern Europe. They spoke about life reduced to its essential elements, and I'd experienced such a life in the country I fled from, captive Romania. I knew the cadences of their speech. I could often guess the terms they would use. To me, my own voice sounded identical to theirs.

After the taping was over, I went to stage two: as thorough a research of the historical background as I could undertake. During its course, I was counseled and helped by historians of repute, whom I mention in the closing acknowledgments. I traveled to Prague, to Munich, and to eastern Czechoslovakia on the border of my native Romania. I traveled, with my wife, to Dachau. There, outraged by how sanitized the place looked—freshly reconstructed barracks made the old death pit seem like a former summer camp—my wife wrote, with a marker pen I happened to find in my pocket, "Jews forever!" on a barrack's wall. In short, I delved into my in-laws' past. I read studies and documents about the Nazi state, I investigated the "survivor psychology" studies conducted in the United States and Israel. As that research was added to the tapes, the book started to emerge. The particulars of the war, of the Czech underground, of shtetl life before the war, of Jewish cul-ture and the misunderstandings of it by Christians (and some misunderstandings of Christians by Jews), plus a certain need to reflect about the moral universe in which my heroes met—all these wider dimensions demanded their place in the book, for the simple reason that without them, a reader of today could not understand a love story that occurred in 1944 and 1945, in a work camp in crumbling Nazi Germany, or the frantic adjustment to life after the liberation.

One might envision *The Oasis* as a *Gone With the Wind* set in the forties in Europe. Its own civil war was specifically the one between the Nazis and the Jews; between the technological Nazi state and partisans like Mirek, who found his emotional anchor in a lost, terrified, yet morally unwavering virgin deportee like Blanka. When my heroes (Mirek was twenty-four, Blanka twenty) came out of the war, they had nothing except their own bafflement at being alive; they ignored or had forgotten the ways of a normal world. And yet they knew about the one value that mattered: humanity versus inhumanity. I felt the same way when I defected from my own concentration camp: Communism. I knew. About humanity versus inhumanity, I knew all too well.

This brings me to stage three of the process of writing this book. Was it difficult to harmonize their voices with my own, and then to blend all three into a common voice? I cannot answer with a mere yes or no. This book was exhausting to write, for on an emotional level it demanded my full participation. I could not slip away from my true life characters, I could not take the stance of the omniscient author. I had to be *them*; my characters, at all times, hoping that empathy and patience would be my best guide.

This book is a testimony and a true story. Yet in any testimony, the writer is essential, and I had known that long before, when I read Primo Levi's *Se questo è un uomo*, more widely known as *Survival in Auschwitz*, then Elie Wiesel's *Night*, then the big sagas about survival written by nonsurvivors, notably *Sophie's Choice* and *Schindler's List*. The quality of all those books was *the voice*: a stream of emotional directness beyond fiction, yet somehow raising the standard of literature. I did not find that voice by using a particular literary technique. I just followed the plot which the tapes had revealed to me, reacting to it as if I were inside the characters. And I kept hoping that, at the deepest level, this story spoke for all of us.

When I finished the book, I handed it to my in-laws to read. Dear readers, few of you have witnessed this incredible scene: to watch Holocaust survivors read about themselves. There was an incredible tightening of my in-laws faces, a razor-sharp vigilance in their eyes, as they read, slowly. There was an awesome finality in the way they turned a page, settling it face down on top of the ones already read, before moving on to the next. I lingered for hours, waiting for some early reaction, but that early reaction did not come. Several times, I almost panicked. What did that silent, patient perusal indicate? Did they recognize themselves *at all?*

I kept waiting, invisible—my in-laws kept reading, my in-laws remained lost in my pages, facing the people they had been back then. My father-in-law read, moving his lips, repeating words to himself. My mother-in-law stopped now and then, and wiped her eyes with the heel of her palm.

The reading lasted into the evening.

The next day, the book was on the kitchen table, in a heap of dog-eared pages. I asked what they thought of it. My father-in-law nodded, then said, for both of them: Yes.

The voice could be heard. They had heard it.

Therefore, if I am to claim my own merit, it is the merit of having faced that storm of emotions without defenses, without turning away, without cluttering it with too many of my own thoughts. This book is a testimony, yet its chronicler is important, because he is the one who takes us back into history. A history we may feel we already know. But to reset our moral compass, we need to revisit it.

Acknowledgments

Ironically, one of the most challenging parts of this book is the ending—the acknowledgments, which are usually so predictable and routine. I am supposed to confine my sincere thanks to a few lines, but my thanks are connected with feelings I have had for over fifteen years. Ever since I met the protagonists, whose daughter I married.

The experience of marrying into a survivor family, absorbing emotions and interractions that are so special, deserves its own book. Here and now, I will say the minimum: Blanka and Mirek's story is true, and as a chronicler, I hope that I did it justice. I wrote it not for its thrill as literature, but for its haunting truth about the human soul.

For this book's historic documentation, I thank first and foremost Dr. Radu Ioanid, associate director of the International Programs Division of the U.S. Holocaust Memorial Museum. Radu prepared for me an ample file about camp Mühldorf (also known as Dachau 3b); it included testimonials of survivors, eyewitness accounts by soldiers of the 99th U.S. infantry division, which liberated Mühldorf, documents of the Todt Organization, minutes of the trials of the SS camp brass. Those data corroborated Mirek's and Blanka's testimony with icy accuracy.

Two other experts checked on the accuracy of my research. One is Dr. Michael Berenbaum, former president of the Shoah Foundation and author of seminal studies on the Holocaust, the other is the legendary scholar professor Raul Hilberg—both showed enough trust in this book to interrupt important work of their own and have meetings or long-distance phone conferences with me, repeatedly. I will not add here a (long) list of works consulted, because I want the reader to understand that this book, above all, came from the lips of the survivors themselves. Thus, I want to thank the direct witnesses who agreed to be interviewed by me, including Mirek's and Blanka's relatives: the late Chaim Friedman (Mirek's brother), and his wife, Lisa: Blanka's brother Leizer and his wife, Ruchi: brother Pepo and his wife, Piri; and the late Henju Davis and his wife, Magda: Blanka's cousin Chani Godinger Fixler. Among friends and countrymen: sisters Hilda Wasserman and Eta Moss (Eta met her future husband in Mühldorf; he was one of the Greek musicians), Benet and Steven Mermelstein, Blanka's childhood friends; my wife, Iris, and her brother Yon Friedman; Frances Simon, Faiga Weiss, and Brana Zoldan, deported to Auschwitz at the same time with Blanka, and Brana's husband, Sam. Finally, a belated homage to the late Oliver Lustig, Romanian survivor who published two books about his Auschwitz experience—the editor of those books, back in Bucharest, was my father.

I also want to thank some friends who read the manuscript and whose supportive reaction was invaluable during the stormy months of writing; for although I waited on edge for Blanka and Mirek to read batches of pages and approve or disapprove of the way I had re-created their younger selves, I kept wondering if this book would satisfy a contemporary audience. The indications that it would do so came from, in approximate chronological order: Marlene Hier (who also helped appraise the accuracy of the religious and rabbinical research), Hy Ash, Ellen Benson, Michael Elias, Moe Shore, Dennis and Sandra Dembs, Judy and Doron Ben-Yehezkel, Karl Epstein, Lloyd Evans, Alissa Roston, Stasia Kopeikin, Jeffrey Davis (who is also Iris's cousin), Anton Mueller (who was my editor on *The Return*), Lili Bosse, Dr. Patrick Bezdek, Sherry Hirschfeld, and Virginia Maas. My agent, Ellen Levine, gave me invaluable advice about how to shape the epic structure of this book, warning me not to do what was almost impossible not to do: get lost in the wealth of testimony and research. Thank you, Ellen. And I was truly lucky that my editor, Alicia Brooks, and George Witte, editor-in-chief at St. Martin's Press, discovered this book.

Finally, my parents-in-law: Blanka and Mirek, who never cease to surprise and inspire me. Mirek, a role model whose strength of character I honor, and Blanka, who in many ways is my twin soul. I thank you both publicly, something which I hope you can accept.

I thank my wife, Iris, who, out of the complex sense of protectiveness of children of survivors, initially did not want me to write this book, but eventually made me feel that I was destined to write it as much as we were destined for each other.

I also want to thank my parents, Radu Popescu and Nelly Cutava—all the way back in space and time, in Communist Romania, they taught me lack of prejudice.

I thank them all, again.

—Petru Popescu

About the Author

Petru Popescu is an author of novels, nonfiction, and film scripts. He defected from Ceausescu's Romania in the late seventies and has been writing in English ever since. His *Amazon Beaming* and *Almost Adam* were international bestsellers, while his personal memoir *The Return* received high critical acclaim. He wrote and directed the feature film *Death of an Angel*, co-produced by the Sundance Institute and released by 20th Century-Fox, and wrote the scripts for *The Last Wave* (UA), *Obsessive Love* (CBS), and *Nobody's Children* (USA Pictures).

The author is married to Mirek and Blanka's daughter, Iris. They have two children, Adam and Chloe.